The Acts of the Apostles

1 Corinthians & Galatians

A Study

Rewarding Learning

Colourpoint
Educational

Juliana Gilbride

First Edition
Second Impression

© Juliana Gilbride and Colourpoint Books
   2008

Designed by: Colourpoint Books, Newtownards
Printed by: GPS Colour Graphics Ltd, Belfast

ISBN: 978 1 904242 91 8

Except where otherwise stated, the Scripture quotations contained herein are from The New International Version.

Cover picture: iStockphoto.com

Colourpoint Books
Colourpoint House
Jubilee Business Park
21 Jubilee Road
Newtownards
County Down
Northern Ireland
BT23 4YH
Tel: 028 9182 6339
Fax: 028 9182 1900
E-mail: info@colourpoint.co.uk
Web-site: www.colourpoint.co.uk

The author
Juliana Gilbride

Juliana Gilbride, B.Ed (Hons), M.Ed, is the Principal Examiner for AS Religious Studies (Acts of the Apostles) for CCEA.

She has fifteen years experience of teaching 'A' level Religious Studies. She lives with her family, Martin, Tom and Kate in Shercock, County Cavan.

In memory of
Pierce Gilbride

Contents

Author Preface

This text has been written specifically to assist teachers and students to meet the requirements of CCEA's GCE Religious Studies AS and A2 courses on the Acts of the Apostles, 1 Corinthians and Galatians. The first section of the book covers the AS course (An Introduction to the Acts of the Apostles) and the A2 course (A Study of Acts, Galatians and 1 Corinthians). At the end of each chapter there is a list of 'Learning Intentions' to enable students to assess their understanding of what they have learnt. Particular attention is also paid to CCEA's requirement to explore 'other aspects of human experience', with various suggestions made throughout the text.

Every effort has been made to acknowledge sources, opinions and points of view in the footnotes at the end of each chapter. I am indebted to the excellent variety of material available on Acts, 1 Corinthians and Galatians, in both written form and on the World Wide Web. The book represents a collation of the work of renowned biblical and theological scholars such as Bruce, Fitzmyer, Marshall, Constable, Hewitt and Guy, to name but a few.

Thanks are due to a number of people who kindly lent commentaries and books to me: Philip Barnes (King's College, London), Debbie Francis (Rainey Endowed, Magherafelt), Sonia Wilson (Bangor Academy and Sixth Form College), Derek Irvine (Lurgan College), Dominic Kealey (Our Lady and St Patrick's College, Belfast), Paula McCullough (Methodist College, Belfast), Sean McIlroy (Sacred Heart College, Newry), Sister Bríghid Vallely, and the staff at Armagh Library. I would also like to thank Donna Finlay (CCEA) and Colourpoint Books for giving me the opportunity to write this textbook. In particular I would like to thank Sheila Johnston (publisher) and the editors at Colourpoint for their professionalism and thoroughness: Julie Trouton, Michael Collins and not least, Una McCann. I would also like to thank Anne Hughes (Our Lady and St Patrick's College, Belfast) for listening to me for hours on the phone as I read sections of the book to her when seeking reassurance.

Special thanks go to my husband Martin for his patience in coping with an untidy house while the writing progressed; and to my children, Tom and Kate, who became very used to the phrase 'Mummy's working'. I look forward to spending some quality time with them and it is to them that I dedicate this book.

A note for students on footnotes

The text is the result of a study of a number of commentaries and books by biblical scholars. As such, a number of footnotes are referenced at the end of each chapter. The footnotes themselves provide you with the opportunity to see where quotations and viewpoints originate from. It may be a useful exercise for you to become used to referring to the footnotes in order to build up a bank of scholarly viewpoints. Evidence of scholarly opinion is a particular requirement of the A2 examination.

Juliana Gilbride, June 2008

Chapter

Background to Acts

INTRODUCTION

THE BOOK OF 'The Acts of the Apostles' is an attempt to set out the early history of Christianity in an orderly way. It is regarded by most scholars as a sequel to Luke's Gospel, which tells the story of the life and work of Jesus. Acts continues the story, describing how Christianity spread rapidly until it reached Rome, the centre of the ancient world. Packer[1] points out that the title, 'The Acts of the Apostles' is strange for a book that says nothing at all about the majority of the apostles. It focuses mainly on Peter and Paul, giving some insight on the contribution to the spread of Christianity of individuals like Stephen and Philip. Lake and Lake[2] comment that the value of Acts "is that it affords us a unique series of glimpses into the beginnings of Christianity. It is not a complete or a perfectly connected story, but our whole knowledge of the founding of the Greek-speaking church depends on it."

Christianity began in Galilee in Palestine in the first century AD following the death and resurrection of Jesus. The first followers of Jesus, who were all Jews, began a movement or sect within Judaism with Christ as the central figure. The word 'sect' as we know it, implies separation. However the Greek translation means 'choice' and before AD70 (the Fall of Jerusalem) there was a great variety of parties within Judaism, who laid stress on particular aspects of their religion,[3] which Jews could choose to follow. The only condition was an insistence on loyalty to the belief in one God (monotheism) and to the Jewish way of life.

The movement was called 'the sect of the Nazarenes' (Acts 24:5; 24:14; 28:22). While we would assume that the term 'nazarene' derives from Nazareth, Jesus' home town, most other Jews in the first century would have taken it to mean 'observant people' or people who observe a certain way of life,[4] as the word is derived from a root which means 'to observe'.

Almost immediately one of the other Jewish parties, the Sadducees, were antagonistic towards the Nazarenes. The Sadducees strongly opposed the belief in the resurrection and unsuccessful attempts were made to suppress the movement in its early days. However, it was too popular and even priests and members of the Sanhedrin (Jewish Council) were drawn to it. Most members of the party of the Pharisees could find little fault with the Nazarenes and regarded them as pious Jews who observed the Law. While the belief that Jesus was the Messiah would have been looked upon as absurd, the fact that it was based on Jesus' resurrection would have been viewed as 'a sign of grace'.[5]

The sect of the Nazarenes appealed mainly to the ordinary people because of its simple message of forgiveness. Acts tells us that from Galilee the movement reached Jerusalem and flourished. Many converts were made when the apostles preached that Jesus was the long awaited Messiah who was crucified, rose again and ascended into heaven. The movement spread through Judea and Samaria, and following the death of Stephen (Acts 6–8; 11.19) it extended to Syrian Antioch. Initially the movement consisted of Jews alone but gradually Greek-speaking Jews and Gentiles were accepted.

As a result the sect of the Nazarenes came to see itself as a new religion, separate from Judaism, although the term 'Christianity' was not used until after New Testament times.

Jerusalem evolved as the centre of the Jewish branch of the movement while Antioch became the centre for Gentile Christians. From Antioch, Christianity spread through predominantly Gentile cities in Asia Minor and Greece until its eventual arrival in Rome.

THE STRUCTURE OF ACTS

The book of Acts covers a vast amount of information giving us a chronological record of events in the church in the first century. However, in places it is fragmentary, for example, sometimes one verse will cover many miles (Ch 18:22) or sometimes no detail is given of a visit (Ch 19:1), while other events are described in great detail (Ch 15). It is difficult, therefore, to analyse the way the book has been structured by the author. Different theories have emerged, which as you will see later, are linked to the purpose of the book.

Theories on the structure of Acts

1. The structure of Acts can be viewed in three parts, based on the pattern of Jesus'

command in Acts 1:8, which involved the gospel spreading to:

.....Jerusalem (Ch 1–7)

.....Judea and Samaria (Ch 8–12)

.....Rome, the centre of the world (Ch 13–28)

2. Another possible division of Acts is into two parts, explained by the parallel between the ministry of Peter and that of Paul:

......Peter (centred in Jerusalem) Ch 1–12

......Paul (centred in Antioch) Ch 13–28

Guy[6] explains that Chapters 1–12 deal with the Church in Palestine and Syria – how it spread from Jerusalem to Samaria, Joppa, Caesarea, Damascus and Antioch, with Peter as one of the main characters. Chapters 13–28 tell of the Church in the Gentile world, with Paul as the leading character. Luke "relates the journeys to Cyprus and Asia Minor, to Macedonia and Greece, and how Paul was arrested in Jerusalem, held prisoner at Caesarea and eventually taken to Rome."[7] An outline of the parallels between the ministries of Peter and Paul is set out below:

Peter's Ministry	Paul's Ministry
Missionary to Jews	Missionary to Gentiles
Jerusalem	Antioch and Gentile world
Speech at Pentecost (Ch 2)	Speech at Pisidian Antioch (Ch 13)
Healing of Lame Man (Ch 3)	Healing of Lame man (Ch 14)
Judgement of Ananias and Sapphira (Ch 5)	Judgement of Elymas (Ch 13)
Escape from jail in Jerusalem (Ch 12)	Escape from jail in Phillipi (Ch 16)
Raising of Dorcas from the dead (Ch 9)	Raising of Eutychus from the dead (Ch 20)

This division of Acts acknowledges the importance of the work of bringing the gospel to the Jews (by Peter) and the Gentiles (by Paul). However, it does not take into account material in Acts that has nothing to do with Peter or Paul.

3. Parallels have also been made between the structure of Luke's Gospel and Acts, which of course is based on the theory that Luke was the author of both. Smith[8] points out that:

• both acknowledge the importance of Jerusalem;

• both are arranged in the form of journeys;

- both end with accounts of trials;
- in both there is the pattern of rejection of Jesus and his teaching by the religious authorities.

4. Short summaries which occur at intervals throughout the book are another feature of the book of Acts:

Summary Reference	Events
Ch 2:42–47	The lifestyle of the believers
Ch 4:32f	The use of possessions
Ch 5:12	Signs attributed to the apostles
Ch 9:31; 16:5	Progress up to that point
Ch 5:42; 15:35	Teaching and preaching
Ch 6:7, 12:24; 19:20	Expansion of the Church as the Word of God

5. A special feature of Acts is the 'we' passages which indicate that the author was present at the events. This has led some to regard the structure of Acts as influenced by Luke's travel diary.

6. Finally there are certain similar phrases used in Acts based around the term 'The Word of God' which may influence the structure of the book. These phrases comment on further expansion of the Church:

Reference	Phrases	Expansion of Church
Ch 6:7	The Word of God increased	After the appointment of 'The Seven' to support the apostles
Ch 12:24	The Word of God grew and multiplied	After Antioch has become an important centre for mission, and when the Church at Jerusalem is experiencing problems
Ch 19:20	The Word of the Lord grew and prevailed mightily	After the success of Paul's missionary journeys

Outline of the Book of Acts

Main Events	Detail	Reference	AS or A2
The beginning of the Church	Prologue	Ch 1:1–2	AS
	Jesus' initiation of the Church's mission	Ch 1:3–11	
	The Pentecost Event	Ch 2:1–13	
	The first preaching of the Gospel (Pentecost Speech)	Ch 2:14–42	
	First Summary of the life of the early Church	Ch 2:43–47	
The Church and the Jewish Authorities	The Healing of the Lame Man and Peter's Explanation	Ch 3:1–26	AS
	The arrest of Peter and John	Ch 4:1–22	
	Prayer for Boldness	Ch 4:23–31	
	Second summary of the life of the early Church	Ch 4:32–37	
	Ananias and Sapphira	Ch 5:1–11	
	Growth of the Church	Ch 5:12–16	
	Second arrest of apostles	Ch 5:17–42	
The Church starts to grow	The Appointment of the Seven	Ch 6:1–7	AS
	Stephen's speech and martyrdom	Ch 6:8–8:1	
	The evangelising activity of Philip	Ch 8:4–25 & Ch 8:26–40	
	Paul's conversion	Ch 9:1–19a	
	Paul begins to preach	Ch 9:19b–31	
The start of the Gentile mission	Peter's miracles	Ch 9:32–43	AS
	The conversion of Cornelius	Ch 10:1–11:18	
	The Church at Antioch	Ch 11:19–30	
	The imprisonment and escape of Peter	Ch 12:1–25	
The First Missionary Journey	Cyprus, Pisidian Antioch, Iconium, Lystra	Ch 13:1–14:28	AS/A2

The Council of Jerusalem		Ch 15:1–35	A2
The Second Missionary Journey	Derbe, Lystra, Macedonia, Thessalonica, Berea, Athens, Corinth	Ch 15:36–18:22	AS/A2
The Third Missionary Journey	Caesarea, Antioch, Ephesus, Miletus	Ch 18:23–21:17	AS/A2
Paul's Arrest and Imprisonment	Paul in Jerusalem	Ch 21:15–23:22	A2
	Paul in Caesarea	Ch 23:23–26:32	
	Journey to and stay in Rome	Ch 27:1–28:31	

WHEN WAS ACTS WRITTEN?

The dating of the book of Acts is not a foregone conclusion. Three dates have been suggested by scholars, which differ by almost as much as forty years. There is an early date, around AD63; an intermediate date, around AD75; and a late date, around AD98.

Early Date – around AD63

There are several factors which contribute towards the argument for an early date:

1. Abrupt ending of Acts

The book of Acts finishes rather suddenly with an account of Paul reaching Rome and being held under house arrest for two years (Acts 28:30). Luke does not record the death of Paul which happened during the reign of the emperor Nero (AD54–68), probably around AD65. Therefore it can be argued that Acts must have been written before Paul's death because otherwise Luke would have recorded it.

However, it is not clear whether Luke finishes his account with Paul alive and well in Rome because events had caught up with the time of writing or because he had taken the story as far as he wanted it to go. Marshall[9] believes that Luke's purpose in writing Acts was to show how the gospel reached Rome, rather than tell Paul's life story; therefore the question of when Paul's death took place remains open. Streeter even suggests that Acts might be renamed 'The Road to Rome'.[10] Guthrie[11] points out that some scholars believe that Luke knew of Paul's death, and agrees with Marshall that it was no part of his purpose to close with this because it would draw too much attention towards Paul and away from the progress of the gospel. Another possibility is that Luke planned to write a third volume to tell the rest of the story, including the death of Paul.[12] Although, if this was the case then surely a better breaking-off point should have been possible between the end of Acts and the start of the 'third volume', similar to the smoothness of the break between Luke and Acts.

Guy[13] believes that "it is more probable that Luke ended the Acts in this way in order to emphasise that even in the imperial city Paul was allowed to teach and receive visitors, showing that the Roman authorities were tolerant towards him and his message even when he was a prisoner". Hanson[14] even suggests that Luke omitted to mention Paul's death because everyone already knew about it.

Bruce comments[15] that the fact that Paul's death is not mentioned in Acts is not a decisive argument for the dating of the book. It may even be that the outcome of Paul's trial is not mentioned because Luke himself died before he could finish writing the book.[16] But Bruce[17] believes that Luke probably finished his book exactly as he intended to do.

2. Positive attitude towards Romans

Another point supporting the early date concerns the positive attitude that Acts reveals towards the Romans. It can be argued that Acts must have been written before the atrocities of the Emperor Nero's persecution of the Christians (AD64). Harnack[18] points out that "the generally optimistic and hopeful atmosphere of Acts would have been impossible any time after the Neronian persecution". When we look at Revelation 17:1–6, for example, we see Rome portrayed as "the scarlet woman drunk with the blood of saints and martyrs", a very different picture to that reflected in the book of Acts.

3. Dominant issues in Acts

Acts focuses on issues which were dominant in the Church before AD70, for example, the admission of Gentiles into the Church, Jewish-Gentile relations within the Church, and arguments over food laws. After Jerusalem was destroyed in AD70 such matters became less important as the church became predominantly Gentile. This observation supports an early date.

4. Theological outlook of Acts

The theological outlook of Acts reflects primitive or very early Christianity. Primitive titles are used, for example, to describe Jesus ('Christ', 'Son of Man', 'Servant of God'); and Luke uses the term 'disciples' to describe Christians, which is not a feature of Paul's letters.

5. Paul's letters

Paul wrote thirteen letters to the Churches he founded and yet Acts does not offer any knowledge of their existence. It is possible that Paul's letters were not collated and issued until the end of the first century. It may even have been the heroic picture of Paul in Acts that led to the collection of his letters in the first place.[19]

One great difficulty with the early date is raised by Guy,[20] who points out that Luke used Mark's gospel when writing his own gospel. The probable date for Mark is AD65–70, shortly after the death of Paul, which means that Acts must have been written after that time. This will be discussed further in the next section on an 'intermediate date'.

Intermediate Date – around AD75

Given that Luke wrote a gospel as well as Acts, it is useful to consider the dates of both pieces of work together to get a more accurate picture.

Most scholars agree that Luke based his gospel on Mark's gospel, which is usually dated after AD70 – the year Jerusalem fell to the Romans. They base their argument on the fact that Luke seems to see in this event the fulfilment of a prophecy made in Mark Ch 13. These scholars tend to be in agreement that such a prediction could not have been written before the event took place. If Mark's gospel was written after AD70 it would have to have been in general circulation before Luke could use it. Therefore it has been suggested that Luke wrote his gospel around AD72 followed by Acts around AD75.

In the gospels of Matthew, Mark and Luke the fall of Jerusalem is foretold:

Matthew 24:15f

"So when you see standing in the holy place 'the abomination that causes desolation' spoken of through the prophet Daniel …".

Mark 13:14

'When you see 'the abomination that causes desolation' standing where it does not belong – let the reader understand – then let those who are in Judea flee to the mountains".

Luke 21:20f

"But when you see Jerusalem being surrounded by armies, you will know that its desolation is near".

In Matthew and Mark there is a prophecy, based on a saying in Daniel. However, this is not the case in Luke. Instead there appears to be a description of an historical event which has already taken place. Matthew and Mark's version tends to hint at some desolate sacrilege whereas Luke speaks plainly of surrounding armies. The argument is that Matthew and Mark wrote before the event happened whereas Luke wrote after it. Therefore Luke's gospel, and subsequently Acts, must have been written after AD70.

However, this then raises the question of why Luke did not mention an event as important as the fall of Jerusalem (AD70), or have anything to say about the martyrdom of James in AD62 or the martyrdom of Peter and Paul. Guthrie[21] suggests that the destiny of Jerusalem would perhaps not have appeared as tragic to the Christian church as it would to the Jewish people. This may be why Luke did not mention the event. However, du Plessis[22] argues that Jewish Christians in Jerusalem could not have been unaffected by the fall. He regards the failure of Luke to mention it as a reason to doubt whether the events had yet happened.

Another point, which we have already touched on, concerns the attitude of the Romans towards Christianity in Acts. Would the favourable attitude presented in Acts be realistic after Nero's persecution in AD64, when many Christians were tortured and put to death?

Finally, if Luke wrote around AD75, why did he not use Paul's letters? Guy[23] points out that Paul's letters would not have been collected together by that time and circulated extensively. So they would not have been available to Luke, especially if he was writing in Rome, for most of the letters had been sent to churches in Asia Minor or Greece and were probably collected at Ephesus.

A Late Date – around AD98

Some scholars believe that in writing Acts, Luke has carefully considered all aspects of his story to present it in a meaningful way, rather than simply recording a mere chronicle of events. Marshall[24] comments that "it is arguable that a writer cannot do this successfully unless he stands at some distance from the events so that he can see them in perspective". This gives some support to the argument for a late date, although there are other significant points to consider:

1. In the writing of Acts, Luke used the work of a Jewish historian, Josephus of Alexandria. This work, 'Antiquities of the Jews', was published in AD96. Therefore it is argued that Acts was probably written shortly after this, around AD98. However, it should also be noted that by AD98 Paul's letters would have been well circulated and at Luke's disposal. If Luke was prepared to use the work of a Jewish historian then he would definitely have used the work of Paul, the man who dominates much of the story of Acts.

2. Another factor against the suggestion of a late date is that Acts does not reflect the interests and outlook of the church at that time. There is no mention, for example, of the sacraments, the development of the three-fold ministry or apostolic succession – issues which were of utmost importance to the church in the second century. Moreover, there is no mention in Acts of the deaths of James (AD62) and Peter, who was martyred in Nero's persecution.

3. Finally, it is important to take into consideration Luke's own life-span, which is difficult to estimate. Guthrie[25] argues that "it would certainly not be impossible for Luke to have written Acts any time up to about AD85 but it could hardly have been much later."

Conclusion

The question of when exactly Acts was written remains unanswered. Acts gives no information of events in Paul's life after his two years in Rome, and yet at the same time the book gives the impression that the author is looking back on events with a sense of reflection. Bruce[26] believes that the writing of Luke-Acts took place over an extended period of time and that the story was brought to an end at a significant point, that being '"he completion of the process of bringing the gospel to Rome."

 TASKS

a) **Explain the reasons for the various proposed dates for the book of Acts.**

Your answer should include some of the following:
- Internal and external evidence for the dating of the Acts of the Apostles – early (c AD63), middle (c AD75) and late (c AD98) dating options explored
- The views of modern scholarship regarding dating

b) **Explore the claim that the relationship between Paul and the author of Acts is central to the dating of Acts. Justify your answer. (This question should be answered after completion of Chapter 1)**

An exploration of the claim may include, for example:
- Information on the authorship of Acts and implications regarding the dating of the text
- The link between the writer of Acts and Paul's travelling companion 'Luke'
- Controversy regarding the travel diary/ 'we' passages

WHO WROTE THE BOOK OF ACTS?

It is generally accepted that Luke's Gospel and Acts were written by the same man, but neither the Gospel nor Acts actually claims this to be Luke. Tradition names the author as Luke, "the beloved physician" (Col 4:14) and a co-worker of Paul (Philemon 1:24 and 2 Tim 4:11), although his name is in fact only mentioned three times in the New Testament. Barclay feels that it is obvious that Luke was a doctor because he instinctively uses medical words.[27] However, Banks highlights the view of Cadbury that the language used does not require a medical author since it is found also in the language of non-medical authors.[28]

We can also work out from Colossians 4:11 that Luke was a Gentile. The verse concludes with a list of greetings from Jews and a new list begins in verse 12. The natural conclusion is that this is a list of Gentiles. Luke is mentioned in this list, and if we accept that he is the author of Acts, then the fact remains that he is the only Gentile author in the New Testament. Banks[29] also points to Acts 1:19 where the author refers to "their language" when speaking of the Aramaic of the residents of Jerusalem. The quality of the author's Greek, the general lack of Semitic (Jewish) words and the universalism found in Luke-Acts also imply that he is a Gentile.[30]

There are two types of evidence to support the argument that Luke is the author of both pieces of work. The first type of evidence we will look at is 'external' evidence, meaning that it is found 'apart from' or outside Luke's Gospel and Acts. The second type of evidence is 'internal' evidence, so called because we look inside the Gospel and Acts for clues to the authorship.

External Evidence

1. Packer[31] points out that as early as the end of the second century AD the tradition of the church held that Luke wrote Acts. Irenaeus was an early Christian writer who lived in the second century. He held that Acts was written by Luke and he was supported by other early Christian writers, ie Clement of Alexandria (AD150–215) and Tertullian (AD160–225).

2. In the early days of Christianity the New Testament did not exist in the form that we have it today. Rather it developed over a long period of time, with some books being rejected from the final 'Canon of Scripture' which closed in the fourth century. However, some earlier evidence of a compilation of New Testament books exists. Around AD170 a list of New Testament books was collected known as 'the Muratorian Fragment'. The Acts of all the Apostles is one of the books included on this list, naming Luke as the author.

3. Another piece of evidence is found in a preface to the third Gospel, written at about the same time, called 'the anti-Marcionite prologue'. In it Luke is named as the author of Acts as well as of the Gospel.

Internal Evidence

1. Luke's Gospel and Acts can be looked upon as a two-volume work. Acts continues the story at the point where the Gospel finishes. Freed points to Acts 1:1 which indicates that Luke intended the second volume to complement the first.[32] This argument is further supported by Guy[33] who comments that, "The end of the Gospel overlaps with the beginning of Acts" and Barrett,[34] who adds "the end of the story of Jesus is the church; and the story of Jesus is the beginning of the church". Furthermore, both Luke's Gospel and Acts were addressed to the same man, Theophilus.

2. Acts is written mainly in the third person pronoun (He did this; they went to), a style which suggests that the author was not present at the events which he is recording. However, there are four passages in Acts (16:10–17; 20:5–15; 21:1–18; 27:1–28:16) where the pronoun changes from the third person to the first person (I did this; We went to). These are referred to as the 'we' passages because it is obvious that the author was present at these events. These passages can be described as eye-witness accounts and were written like a travel diary record. "In these passages we find more exact notes of place and times than in other parts of the book. The natural conclusion is that the writer was himself present at these points".[35]

3. Freed[36] also points out that "common vocabulary, similarities in literary style, and some of the same religious beliefs also support the views of common authorship." Longenecker[37] agrees, adding that "stylistically and structurally, the Gospel of Luke and the Acts of the Apostles are so closely related that they have to be assigned to the same author."

 TASK

Rather than trying to work out who the author was, work backwards and use the method of elimination. In other words, who could the author not have been? For example, if you were writing a diary account of a day spent with friends it might read as follows:

> Tom, Kate, Amy and I drove down to the beach yesterday. It was a really hot day and we ran into Jon and Sam at the café so we all went for coffee and had a right laugh.

Who wrote this account about the day at the beach?

Well we know it wasn't Tom, Kate, Amy, Jon or Sam because they are mentioned. It must have been someone else.

In Paul's letters he mentions nine travelling companions: Aristarchus, Crescens, Demas, Justus, Luke, Mark, Timothy, Titus and Trophimus.[38] The author of Acts has to be one of them. Using the 'we' passages from Acts (see below) work out who the author could not have been by matching the names of Paul's travelling companions from these passages to those mentioned in his letters:

'We' passage	Paul's companions
Ch 16:10–17	
Ch 20:4–15	Sopater, Aristarchus, Secundus, Gaius, Tychicus, Trophimus and Timothy
Ch 21:1–18	Philip, Mnason, James
Ch 27:1–28:16	

Who does this leave as a possible author?

• *Crescens, Demas, Justus, Luke, Mark or Titus*

From Acts and the letters we know that Mark was no longer a travelling companion (Acts 15:36–41) and Demas had deserted him (2 Timothy 4:10). This reduces the possible list to the following:

• *Crescens, Justus, Luke or Titus*

Crescens and Justus had very little contact with Paul so they can be dismissed which leaves us with:

• *Luke or Titus*

Titus is not mentioned in Acts or in any Church traditions and so we are left with:

• *Luke*

Luke was not an original eyewitness or disciple of Jesus. He was a professional who researched his information and compiled his document under the inspiration of the Holy Spirit. In Colossians 4:14 Luke is described as "the beloved physician and friend" of Paul. He was with Paul during his imprisonment in Rome (Philemon 1:23–24), which is also a period covered by the last 'we' passage. Lewis[39] argues that the author was one who reached Rome with Paul and did not leave him.

Conclusion

Gasque[40] concludes that if Luke did not write the third Gospel and Acts, it is difficult to explain how the tradition connecting his name with these documents ever arose, since he is otherwise an insignificant figure in the early Church. Lewis[41] agrees, adding that "tradition can be quite unreliable, but in this instance, where authorship is ascribed to a comparatively unimportant person in the early church, it carries more weight since the tendency is always to attach works of such religious value to great names."

Although the external evidence unanimously identifies Luke as the author of Acts, the internal evidence is inconclusive.[42] However, throughout this book for the sake of convenience the author will be referred to as Luke.

 TASKS

a) **Explain the main arguments surrounding the identity of the author of the Acts of the Apostles.**

Your answer should include some of the following:
- Internal evidence such as the preface to Acts and Luke, the 'we' passages, language style, Gentile interest
- External evidence such as tradition, Irenaeus, Muratorian Fragment
- The silence of Acts in relation to authorship
- The presentation of Paul in Acts and his Letters
- The views of modern scholarship

b) **Comment on the claim that the 'we' passages support the evidence that Luke was the author of this book.**

An exploration of the claim should include some of the following:
- Familiarity with the 'we' passages within Acts.
- Significance of the 'we' passages regarding the authorship of this text.
- The issue of whether these passages are eye-witness accounts, extracts from a diary (Lukan or otherwise) or merely serve as a literary device employed by the author of Acts.
- You may wish to challenge the view that these passages serve any value in attributing to the authorship of the text.

THE SOURCES OF ACTS

The value of an historical work depends upon the quality of the sources used to write it. The more reliable the sources used in writing, the more valuable the end result should be. Therefore, in determining the origin and reliability of the sources used by Luke, we are really asking 'where exactly did he get his information from?'

However, this is not as straightforward as it sounds. Hanson[43] points out that "it is very difficult indeed to reconstruct, or even tentatively to identify, Luke's sources for the book of Acts." Johnson[44] agrees, pointing out that unlike his Gospel, "Luke apparently had no overall guide for his extended narrative". Lewis[45] feels "when we come to Acts we are helpless, so scholars are still speculating and disagreeing about Luke's sources." However, it is certain that Luke relied on various sources which can be divided into two main types:

Primary Sources – Luke's own experiences of events

Secondary Sources – The experience of others passed on to Luke

Acts 1–15 (secondary source material)

As well as having direct experience of some of the events, the author of the 'we' passages would have met significant people who could give him valuable insight into other events for which he was not present. Hunter[46] argues that this could have been through the three great centres of early Christianity: Jerusalem, Caesarea and Antioch. For example, it appears that the author of Acts was at one time a companion of Paul (Acts 16:10). "Beyond a doubt Luke's friendship with Paul would bring him into touch with all the great men of all the Churches and all their records and stories would be at his disposal".[47] As Paul's travelling companion, Luke would have had immediate access to the information recorded in 9:1–31; 11:25–30; 12:25; 17; 28–31. Guthrie[48] also points out that it is known from Colossians 4:10–14 that Luke was with Mark and could certainly have obtained useful information from him regarding the early growth of the Church. Stott[49] agrees, adding that Mark may have kept a written account. Acts 12:12 refers to a prayer meeting in the house of Mark's mother, so it is reasonable to assume that this home was a regular meeting place for Christians. Mark would certainly have been familiar with much, if not all of the events preceding the Council of Jerusalem.[50] Therefore, as one who knew Mark and was a travelling companion with Paul, Luke was certainly in a position to write a reliable account of the growth of the early Church.

Acts 16–28 (containing some primary source material and secondary source material)

Johnson[51] points out that in this section "the information available to Luke seems to have been both more substantial and reliable". There are a number of passages written in the first person (I, we) which are known as the 'we' passages. The implication is that Luke was present at some of the events that he has recorded. Such access to first-hand evidence would mean that the 'we' passages are very valuable as sources.

TASK

Using this information and the references in the table below, record knowledge of the events that Luke may have received from each of the men he met.

Who the author met	Information given	Reference
Paul		Ch 9 Ch13–14 Ch 16–28
Philip (close companion of Stephen)		Ch 6:1–7 Ch 6:8–7:60 Ch 8
James		Ch 21:18 Ch 15
Mark (close companion of Peter)	Mark's house appears to have been used as a sort of headquarters in the early Church.	Col 4:10 Ch 12:12 1 Peter 5:13 Ch 1–5 Ch 9:32–12:19

Some scholars argue that the author of Acts was not the author of the 'we' passages. This means that the author perhaps directly used someone else's diary in his work, which was one of several sources that he had gathered.

Other Sources

1. Aramaic documents

It has been suggested that among the various sources gathered by Luke were certain 'Aramaic' documents. In the first century, Aramaic was the native language of the Jews in Palestine, for example, Jesus and the disciples would have spoken in Aramaic. It has been pointed out by scholars[52] that the Greek of the early chapters of Acts is not as good as the Greek of later chapters. Since Luke could clearly write in good Greek then perhaps the early chapters of Acts were a source used by Luke which was a translation of an Aramaic document into Greek. Torrey[53] was quite certain that Luke used an Aramaic source, which underlies the whole of the first fifteen chapters, and has given an Aramaic flavour to the whole book.

Other scholars disagree, however, arguing that the basic Greek used in the early chapters of Acts are due to either Luke's desire to copy the style of the Old Testament writers or to Luke's use of the 'Septuagint', which is a Greek translation of the Hebrew Bible.[54]

2. Church records

Some of the more important churches, such as Jerusalem, Caesarea and Antioch, may have kept records of events as they occurred in their areas. Luke may have used these in his writing of Acts.

Problems in identifying sources

It is clear that any attempt to identify the sources used by Luke in writing Acts is reduced to guesswork. The following is a summary of the main problems in identifying sources for Acts:

- Acts is the only record of a history of the early church that has been written, which means there is nothing to compare it with.

- Luke's style of writing is so consistent throughout the book that it is impossible to see where he might be using a different source. Dillon[55] aptly describes this as "the author's consistently strong hand in rewriting his sources".

- While Luke may have gathered information from eyewitnesses, "such information was most likely available to him in anecdotal rather than in ordered form."[56]

- Haenchen[57] believes it is "highly unlikely that there were in existence written collections of the Apostles sayings or accounts of what they had done." The first Christians thought that Jesus was going to return (Second Coming) within a matter of years. Therefore as a result, the churches probably did not keep any records.

- Paul's letters were not a source in the writing of Acts. The difference between the 'Paul of Acts' and the 'Paul of his letters' are such to suggest that Luke had no knowledge of Paul's letters. This will be further explored at A2 level.

This chapter has highlighted the information available in an attempt to determine the sources of Acts. Clearly it is no easy task. However, as Johnson[58] argues, to question the possibility of identifying sources, is not to deny that Luke actually used sources.

TASKS

a) Describe the main sources that may have been used by the author of the book of Acts.

   Your answer should include knowledge and understanding of some of the following:
   - Travel diary ('we' passages)
   - Eye-witness reports (Paul, Philip, Peter)
   - Paul's letters
   - Antioch and Jerusalem church reports
   - Council of Jerusalem report
   - Greek Old Testament
   - Aramaic documents

b) Explore the view that the 'we' passages are not the most important of Luke's sources. Justify your answer. (You may want to discuss this as a class before attempting an answer.)

   An exploration of the claim may include some of the following:
   - The importance/significance of the 'we' passages and the theories surrounding them
   - A consideration of the other sources available to Luke
   - An evaluation and explanation of which you think are more reliable as a source

THE PURPOSE OF ACTS

In determining the purpose of Acts (ie why it was written), Marshall[59] comments that we are dealing with the second part of a two-volume work. Luke tells the story of Jesus (in his Gospel) and the story of the beginning of the Church (in Acts), which together form the basis of the Christian Church. Bruce[60] points out that the two parts, for all their stylistic differences, make up an integral whole, with one coherent purpose .

> *"Many have undertaken to draw up an account of the things that have been fulfilled among us, just as they were handed down to us by those who from the first were eyewitnesses and servants of the word. Therefore, since I myself have carefully investigated everything from the beginning, it seemed good also to me to write an orderly account for you, most excellent Theophilus, so that you may know the certainty of the things you have been taught."* (Luke 1:1–4)

The strong link between the two books is further highlighted by Neil[61] who points out that, "It is thus not without significance that he tells the story of the Ascension twice; once at the end of his Gospel and again at the beginning of Acts". However, the question of why Luke wrote this companion to his Gospel, and what the two-volume work was meant to achieve, is one that has produced a variety of responses.

Acts as a history book

Marshall[62] comments that most people approach Acts as "the history book of the early church". As a piece of history it traces the ascension of Jesus, the story of the beginning and spread of Christianity from Jerusalem, through Asia Minor, Macedonia, and Greece until the arrival of the Gospel in Rome, the centre of the world at that time. Stott[63] adds that Luke was well qualified to write such a history, for "he was an educated doctor, a travelling companion of Paul, and had resided in Palestine for at least two years."

As well as being an historian, it has been suggested that Luke was writing more as a preacher and as such he was selective. The history Luke presents is not simply a chronological record of everything that happened from one day to the next. He is forced to be selective of events due to the broad range of his subject so it is written in such a way as to highlight significant moments and events. Furthermore, as an ancient writer, Luke would have written on a papyrus roll, which would have only been about thirty feet long, just enough to hold Acts as we know it. Such circumstances would also have been factors in his reasons for being selective. Guthrie[64] agrees, adding that "Luke intended his work to be regarded as historical, but not in the sense of a dry chronicle of events." There is much we would like to know, of which Luke is silent. Guthrie wonders if this is due to Luke's desire to write about Paul as soon as possible.

On the other hand, there are those who argue that the Church never suspected it would have a history.[65] After all, most early Christians believed that Jesus' return (parousia) would be in their own lifetime. What would be the point of writing anything down if the world was going to end? Dibelius[66] had earlier made this point, commenting that "to write down the history of the oldest community, to give an account of its difficulties and conflicts, to describe its spread to Rome and to tell how the way was prepared for the reception of the Gentile, and of the obdurate refusal on the part of the Jews – all this could not have seemed an obviously necessary undertaking to those Christians who were waiting for the end of the world, and who had neither inclination nor ability for literary work."

A Work of Literature

Luke uses impressive language and a certain style which suggests that Acts was written to attract an educated audience. The style used by Luke is that of the Greek Old Testament (the Septuagint), which may be an indication that he regarded the history he was recording as sacred.[67] It is probable that Luke believed he was recording events that were the fulfilment of Old Testament prophecies and that his purpose was to convince the educated in society of the validity of Christianity. Bruce[68] argues that "at any time in this period a work which gave an intelligent history of the rise and progress of Christianity, and at the same time gave a reasoned reply to popular calumnies against it, was sure of a reception among the intelligent reading public – or rather listening public – of Rome, of whom Theophilus was probably a representative."

Haenchen[69] sees Acts as an edifying piece of literature, in which the author uses literary means to make the events memorable to his readers. Hunter[70] describes Luke as "a literary artist" commenting that Acts "abounds in memorable narratives" such as:

- Stephen's martyrdom   6–7
- Paul and Barnabas at Lystra   14
- Paul and Silas in prison at Philippi   16
- The riot in the theatre at Ephesus   19
- Paul's defence before Agrippa   26
- The storm and shipwreck on the journey to Rome   27

To Promote Universalism

However, others believe that Luke was writing to a wider audience, ie rich and poor; educated and uneducated; Jew and Gentile. Scholars point to the roll call of countries in Acts 2:9–11 as a sign that the gospel was for everyone. As previously mentioned, both Luke's Gospel and Acts are dedicated to Theophilus (Luke 1:1; Acts 1:1), which is a Gentile name. It can be argued therefore, that its purpose was to show that the gospel was for Gentiles as well as for Jews. This idea is known as 'universalism' because it shows that Christianity is for everyone. Hewitt[71] supports this view, pointing out that in Acts Christianity gradually embraces Gentiles, as Stephen, Philip, Peter and finally Paul include them in its baptism.

Some scholars[72] believe Luke's main purpose was to describe the breaking down of the barriers between Jew and Gentile as the church moved outwards in the power of the Spirit from Jerusalem to Rome. Lewis[73] argues that Luke writes with an eye on Rome as the destination of the gospel which is his concern in both his books. In his gospel he tells how Jesus brought the Good News to the Jews. In Acts he tells how the gospel travelled from Jews to Gentiles, and from Jerusalem to Rome.

Lewis[74] comments that "Luke is not out to write a biography of Paul in Acts, any more than he was out to write a biography of Jesus in his Gospel."

The Gospel of the Spirit

Some scholars believe that for Luke it was important to acknowledge the divine activity behind the events in the early church, and therefore his work places great emphasis on the work of the Holy Spirit. Bruce[75] comments that "Luke wishes to make it clear that the progress of this faith was no mere product of human planning; it was directed by divine agency." Scott[76] agrees, arguing that this progress happened 'through the energy of the Spirit'. Guthrie[77] therefore points out that "it is not inappropriate that this book has been called the Acts of the Holy Spirit" (see Chapter 5 of this book).

However, Williman[78] argues that "it would be a mistake to infer that Acts features the Holy Spirit the way that the Gospel features Jesus", commenting that there are great portions of Acts where the Spirit is not mentioned or only mentioned in passing. For example, the Holy Spirit is mentioned most often in the first half of Acts and there are eleven chapters where He is not mentioned at all.

An Apology

Many scholars see in Acts an apologetic purpose. Banks[79] explains that the term 'apology' comes from the Greek 'apologia' meaning 'defence'. So an apology may be a speech or piece of writing that defends Christianity against attack. When the Christian Church began, opposition came from the Jews only and Christians were left well alone by the Romans. The Romans initially regarded Christianity as a branch of Judaism, which allowed it to have the status of '*religio licita*' (legal religion). Judaism was tolerated by the Romans because, as Banks[80] explains, "it was an ancient and national religion which Rome had the good sense not to confront." However, once the Roman authorities realised that the Christians were different from the Jews they no longer extended the same freedom to the Church and persecution was inevitable.

Acts can be regarded as an apologetic work in two ways: firstly, defending Christianity against Jewish attack; and secondly, against Roman attack.

1. An apology to the Jews

Luke stresses the close connections between Christianity and Judaism which may be an attempt to convince Jewish readers of the validity of Christianity. Some examples of this include:

Reference	Example
2:17–21; 2:25–28; 2:30; 2:34–35; 3:22–23; 4:11 (some examples among many)	Appeal to Old Testament prophecy (Jewish Scriptures)

Reference	Example
16:3 23:6 18:18; 21:17–26 15	Christian observance of Jewish ceremonial requirements: • Timothy circumcised • Paul's claim to be a Pharisee • Paul's vow • James' insistence on relationship between Judaism and Christian procedures at Council of Jerusalem

2. An apology to the Romans

Acts can be perceived even more as an apologetic work in its presentation of the relationship between the Christians and the Roman authorities. Guy[81] comments that in Acts the Romans were either favourably inclined towards Christianity, adopting a lenient attitude, or "exhibited the official attitude of cold indifference" towards it. Perhaps Luke presented the Romans in this light in an attempt to establish Christianity, like Judaism, as one of the accepted religions in the Roman Empire. Bruce[82] comments that in general there was a widespread suspicion that Christianity was, "a subversive movement, a menace to imperial law and order' and Luke himself wrote that 'people everywhere are talking against this sect".[83] Stott[84] states that Luke produced evidence to show that Christianity was harmless, innocent and lawful and he argues that Luke was deeply concerned about the attitude of the Roman authorities towards Christianity, going out of his way to show how the Romans were impartial in relation to Christians.[85] Hunter[86] agrees and regards this as deliberate on the part of Luke who is eager to vindicate Christianity in the eyes of his Gentile readers, to convince them that it was no threat to the '*pax Romana*' (peace), as its enemies were insinuating. It is significant to note that almost a quarter of the book is taken up with Paul's trials, through which Luke is "at pains to present Paul as a loyal and law-abiding Jew."[87]

The following table gives examples from Acts of the attitude of the Romans towards Christianity:

Reference	Example
Acts 10	The conversion of the Roman centurion, Cornelius
Acts 13	Sergius Paulus is presented as being very favourable towards the Gospel message.
Acts 16	In Philippi the magistrates apologised to Paul.
Acts 18	Gallio had no interest in the religious concerns that formed the basis of the Jewish charges against Paul.

Acts 19	At Ephesus the city secretary was very reasonable, declaring Paul and his friends to be innocent; the Asiarchs were friendly to Paul.
Acts 26	Agrippa and Festus agreed that Paul could have been released if he had not made an appeal to the Emperor.

Williman[88] adds some doubt to the theory that Acts was an apology to the Romans, pointing out that much of it "would be unintelligible to pagan Romans". It is hard to imagine that a Roman official like Felix would take the time to read Acts just to learn about Christianity.

A Defence for Paul's Trial

This is based on the idea that Paul's trial is in progress and Luke is preparing a detailed account of the background and nature of Christianity for Theophilus, a high-ranking Roman official who may have influence over the outcome of the trial.[89] However, some scholars[90] consider it far-fetched, if not absurd, that a book such as Acts would have the power to dispel the suspicions of someone like Emperor Nero. Also, Lewis[91] argues that much of Acts is concerned with Jesus' continuing deeds through his Holy Spirit which suggests that Luke "is addressing a wider public than just Theophilus".

A Theological Purpose

It has been suggested that Luke had theological concerns at the forefront of his mind in writing the Book of Acts. Williams[92] for example, comments that Acts revealed the triumph of Christianity in a hostile world. Therefore the spread of Christianity from Jerusalem to Rome can be argued to have theological significance.

Marshall[93] insists that Luke is both historian and theologian, and that as a theologian he was concerned that his message about Jesus and the early church should be based upon reliable history. Hunter[94] agrees, commenting that "Luke may also claim to be a theologian in his own right, and no mere historian." His is a theology of salvation, with Jesus as Saviour, the exalted Lord, in whose name the forgiveness of sins is offered to men. This salvation is for Gentiles as well as Jews; and it is the apostles' task to confirm it, build up the church and carry the gospel to the ends of the earth.

To mend the split between the followers of Peter and Paul

Acts can be regarded as an attempt to minimise the split between the followers of Peter and Paul. Baur[95] came up with a theory that the early church was split into two camps: those who supported original Jewish Christianity represented by Peter; and those who supported Gentile Christianity, represented by Paul. He argued that Acts was an attempt to deny the hostility between Peter and Paul. Stott[96] points out that most scholars think Baur took this theory too far. Stott regards Luke as "a peacemaker in the church" who wanted to show that the apostles Peter, James and Paul were in fundamental agreement about the gospel. He adds that "the reconciliation between the leading apostles was real, not fictitious".

However, from reading Acts it is obvious that the real split was between James and Paul, with Peter caught up in the middle of it. Further insight into this can be gleaned from reading the following: Acts 11:1–18; Acts 21:17–26 and Galatians 2:11–14. According to Paul, it was James who intimidated Peter about associating with the uncircumcised.

Conclusion

While many suggestions have been put forward for the purpose of Acts, it is important to keep in mind Luke's own statement of the purpose of his writing, that is "to confirm the Christian message by providing a reliable account of its beginnings".[97] All other purposes should take second place.

 TASKS

a) **Explain the various reasons suggested for the purpose of Acts.**

Your answer should include knowledge and understanding of some of the following:
- A range of purposes: apologetic, missionary, evangelical, historical etc.

b) **Explore in particular the claim that the author of Acts has a special interest in the acceptance of Gentiles into the Church. Justify your answer.**

An exploration of the claim should include:
- Identification of the needs of Luke's audience and the context in which Luke wrote
- Specific textual examples concerning the acceptance of Gentiles into the church
- Identification of other interests shared by Luke, for example, concern for the poor and oppressed

c) **Comment on the claim that the purpose of Acts was to give an account of the growth of the Church. Justify your answer.**

Your answer should include an exploration of the following examples:
- A defence of the claim showing the progress from Jerusalem to Rome

- Other purposes: a continuation of Luke, for Theophilus, legal defence, apologetic, a defence of Christianity before Rome, a second volume

d) **Explore the claim that it was important for Luke that the Gospel message reached Rome.**

An exploration of the claim should include some of the following:
- A defence of the claim showing the progress throughout the book from Jerusalem to Rome with examples from the text
- Comment on Acts 1:8 as a theme for the book
- Paul's determination to reach Rome
- Comment on the ending of the book

THE CHARACTERISTICS OF ACTS

The characteristics of Acts are the main features which are prominent in the book. If we approach Acts thematically it may be easier to distinguish certain characteristics that dominate its pages, for example 'Universalism', 'Role of the Holy Spirit' or 'Theology'. The main characteristics are described below, although some will be explored in more detail later in this book.

The Place of Acts in the New Testament

It is significant that in the canonical order (ie the chronological order of the books in the New Testament), Acts has been placed between the gospels and the letters. Hunter[98] comments that it "is the link which holds together the Gospels and the rest of the New Testament" and it certainly connects the accounts of Jesus with the apostolic correspondence that follows. In many ways, the letters are not fully understood until they are read alongside the book of Acts. Acts reveals the main trends in the development of Christianity, making a vital contribution to an understanding of the relationship between the teaching of Jesus and the apostolic doctrine.[99]

Universalism

The fact that Christianity is for everyone and not just the Jews is a major theme in Acts. For example, in Ch 15, there is an account of a debate at the Council of Jerusalem concerning the terms through which Gentiles could be admitted into the membership of the church. Many Gentiles, who knew little of Jewish traditions, accepted the gospel message and were baptised. However, Jewish Christians were alarmed because they felt that all new members should be circumcised and instructed in the Law of Moses. The decision made at the Council, that Gentiles need not be circumcised to become Christians, broke huge barriers and led to a greater spread of the faith.

Role of the Divine control and guidance

The events which occur in the life of the church in Acts are seen to be brought about by the will and power of God, and as such are a fulfilment of Old Testament Scripture.[100] The following table gives some examples of this:

Reference	Fulfilment of Prophecy
2:17–21	the outpouring of the Holy Spirit
13:47	the mission to the Gentiles
15:16–18	the acceptance of the Gentiles into the church
28:25–27	the refusal of the Jews to accept the gospel

Such events, as listed in the table, would not have been possible without God's power, which is primarily seen through the work and influence of the Holy Spirit. Luke describes the continuing work of Christ in the Church through the power of the Spirit. Guthrie[100a] comments that God is seen to be as active in the early Christian community through the Spirit's power as he had been in the life of Jesus (13:2; 15:28; 16:6). Marshall[100b] agrees; however he points out that while sometimes the Spirit directed the church what to do, at other times angels spoke to Christian missionaries (5:18–20; 8:26; 27:23) or messages were mediated by prophets (11:28; 20:11f), and on one occasion the Lord himself appeared to his servants (18:9; 23:11). The work of the Holy Spirit in Acts is explored in a later chapter.

Primitive Church Life and Worship

Acts does not give a detailed account of early church worship, but we do find a general impression of church life. Christians are seen to be spiritual and moral individuals. The church was united, as reflected by a communal lifestyle, regardless of significant differences of opinion. There is an obvious element of joyfulness among these early believers, although there were problems which Luke did not shy away from reporting. For example, the story of Ananias and Sapphira shows a moral lapse which was not tolerated.

Theology

Drane[101] regards much of the theology in Acts as having a far less sophisticated character than the theology either of Paul or of the church later in the first century. One of the places where it is possible to detect a form of primitive theology is in the many speeches recorded in Acts. For example, the titles ascribed to Jesus in the speeches in Acts are a valuable guide to the early development of Christology (the study of the person of Christ).

 TASK

Look at the following references from Acts and complete the table, listing the primitive terms used to describe Jesus, the Christians and the church:

Terms	Reference in Acts	Equivalent in Acts
Jesus	Acts 2:36; 3:20; 4:27	The Messiah/Christ
	Acts 3:13, 26; 4:25–30	The Servant of God
	Acts 2:36	Lord
		Prince of Life
		Saviour
		The Righteous One
	Acts 7:36	The Son of Man
Christians	Acts 6:1–7; 9:25–26	Disciples
The Church	Acts 9:2; 19:9, 23; 24:14, 22	The Way

Marshall[102] is another scholar who regards Luke's writings as having theological significance. He argues that Luke brings out this significance in the way that he tells the story of the church. This view is supported by Fernando[103] who highlights some evidence from the text of Acts to stress Luke's concern with theology. For example, the results of the ministry in Derbe during the First Missionary Journey produced "a large number of disciples" (14:21) and yet there is only a single sentence about Paul's work there. On the other hand, the ministry in Athens produced only "a few" converts (17:34) but takes up nineteen verses. The argument is that Luke selected material because of the value it had in promoting theology that was important to him.

Kerygma (Early Christian Preaching)

Although Acts is not intended to be a theological or doctrinal book, it does provide insight into the elements of early Christian preaching, which Dodd[104] has called 'kerygma'. Marshall[105] points out that the main message proclaimed in Acts "is expounded in a series of public addresses scattered throughout the book." The content of this message contains essential truths about Jesus. An outline is provided below:

The 'Kerygma of the Early Church'	References in Acts
• Old Testament prophecies have been fulfilled with the coming of Jesus the Messiah	2:30; 3:19, 24; 10:43; 26:6–7
• God anointed Jesus as Messiah at his baptism	10:38
• After his baptism, Jesus began his ministry in Galilee	10:37
• Jesus' ministry is characterised by good deeds and miracles through the power of God	2:22; 10:38
• Jesus the Messiah was crucified according to God's purpose	2:23; 3:13–15, 18; 4:11; 10:39; 26:23
• He was raised from the dead and appeared to his disciples	2:24, 31–32; 3:15, 26; 10:40–41; 17:31; 26:23
• He was exalted to the right hand of God and given the name Lord	2:25–28, 33–36; 3:13; 10:36
• He gave the Holy Spirit to begin the new Christian community	1:8; 2:14–18, 38–39; 10:44–47
• He will come again to judge	3:20–21; 10:42; 17:31
• Everyone who hears the message of salvation should repent and be baptised	2:21, 38; 3:19; 10:43, 47–48; 17:30

Focus on Peter and Paul

One of the most striking features about Acts is that it has so much to say about the work of Peter and Paul and yet says so little about the work of the other apostles. Nothing is said, for example, about the Christian mission in Alexandria, the second city of the Roman Empire, inhabited by as many as a million Jews.[106] Luke chooses not to record every expansion of the Church but is instead selective, and as a result Acts is dominated by Peter and Paul.

In chapters 1–12 Peter is the main focus as the narrative moves from Jerusalem to Antioch. He takes the lead before and after the dramatic events at Pentecost. It is Peter who commands the lame man at the Temple gate to walk in Jesus' name; and twice, he defends the Church before the Sanhedrin. Peter is not afraid of confrontation and condemns Ananias and Sapphira for lying to God; and confronts Simon the Sorcerer in Samaria. And such is Peter's presence that his very shadow heals the sick.

Then from chapter 13 to the end, the missionary activity of Paul becomes the main focus of attention. He is introduced dramatically as an enemy of the faith at Stephen's death in Ch 7, which stands in great contrast to his conversion in Ch 9. Scholars have pointed out that several of the features of Peter's ministry are repeated (refer to table in 'Structure' section). Both men heal cripples. Both heal people by strange means. Both encounter sorcerers. Both are miraculously released from prison. Perhaps these parallels are drawn to suggest that Paul was just as much an apostle as Peter. The narrative at the end of Acts (chapter 20 onwards) centres almost totally on Paul and shows him moving inevitably towards Rome, but with courageous determination.

 TASKS

a) Describe the main characteristics of the book of Acts.

Your answer should include knowledge and understanding of some of the suggested characteristics of Acts, for example:
- Emphasis on the geographical spread of the gospel
- The message of the gospel
- Emphasis on the Holy Spirit
- The Jewish response to the Gospel/Gentile inclusion
- Focus on Peter and Paul
- Relations with Roman authorities

b) Explore the claim that the main characteristic is a record of the early Christian message (Kergyma)

Exploration may include some of the following points:
- The recognition that the kergyma is one of the focuses in the book of Acts, with examples from speeches studied at AS level
- Arguments concerning the importance of other characteristics, eg Role of Holy Spirit
- Personal evaluation on which characteristic stands out

THE HISTORICAL RELIABILITY OF ACTS

Introduction

The book of Acts has faced some severe criticism regarding its historical accuracy and reliability. For example, the Tubingen School[107] regarded Acts as a piece of propaganda literature, written in the early second century and as such was considered unreliable as an historical document. They argued that Acts was written mainly for the edification of the church, and its author was a theologian who manipulated the historical facts to suit his purpose, even inventing material when it suited him.[108]

It has been suggested that historians in ancient times were tempted to write from their own biased agenda and therefore should not be trusted to give an accurate historical account.[109] However, the most reliable ancient writers were careful to accurately present the facts in the same way as practised by modern historians.[110] McCann[111] believes that Luke deserves to be placed among these ancient historians and only differs from today's historians because he does not present every historical detail but is deliberately selective, choosing to concentrate on events relevant to the growth of the Church. At times it may seem that Luke got his facts mixed up, especially where he is relating events which happened long before he himself came to the scene, but to suggest that Luke made up history to suit his theological purpose is to question his trustworthiness and integrity.

Perhaps a compromise can be reached by regarding Luke as both an historian and a theologian; in other words, a man who composed his book on the basis of real history but who used the historical facts to preach the gospel of salvation through Christ.[112]

The Original Purpose of Luke's work

Although we have already looked at the purpose of Acts, it might be useful to consider Luke's original purpose for writing his gospel (Luke 1:1–4). As pointed out by Fernando: "the prologue of the Gospel of Luke, which applies to Acts as well, indicates that Luke intended to write an account that was historically accurate (Luke 1:1–4)".[113] Therefore, it is generally agreed amongst scholars that Luke's intention to be accurate extended to Acts as well as his gospel.[114]

Relationship between Acts and Paul's Letters

Scholars, such as Haenchen,[115] who question the historical reliability of the book of Acts, point to the discrepancies between the account of the Council of Jerusalem in Acts 15 and the writing of Paul in Galatians 2. While Luke provides a simple account of the Council in Acts 15, difficulties arise when Luke's account is compared with what appears to be the same event in Galatians.[116] For example, in Galatians Paul is speaking about his second visit to Jerusalem after his conversion, but in Acts Luke says that it was his third visit. Another difference is that the conference in Galatians is held in private, whereas the meeting in Acts 15 is held publicly, before the Jerusalem Church. Bruce[117] argues that the differences arise because the authors are in fact speaking about two entirely different events. Wainwright[118] supports Bruce in these differences and feels that Galatians 2:1–10 has actually more in common with Acts 11:27–30, than with Acts 15.

However, if we put the differences between the above texts to one side, it is possible to consider other examples in Acts which support the idea that Luke was an accurate historian:

- Luke gives correct details regarding Paul. Paul reveals that he was trained as a Pharisee (Phil 3:5; Gal 1:14) and Luke tells us that Paul was trained under Gamaliel, one of the most important Pharisees of the day (22:3).

- In Paul's own letters he claims to belong to the tribe of Benjamin (Rom 11:1; Phil 3:5), and Luke tells us that Paul's name was 'Saul' (7:58), which is the name of the most distinguished member of the tribe of Benjamin.

- Paul mentions that he persecuted Christians (Gal. 1:13) and Luke comments that Paul had put Christians to death (Acts 8:1).[119]

Archaeological Evidence

The reliability of Acts is supported by Luke's attention to detail, which Bruce[120] argues proves to be accurate in the field of archaeology. Hunter[121] agrees and points to Ramsay's archaeological digging in Asia Minor at the beginning of the 20th century, where a study of inscriptions showed how accurate Luke actually was regarding certain terminology. Bruce[122] regards Acts as "a masterpiece of historical accuracy" because Luke shows himself to be correct every time. McCann[123] provides evidence of this accuracy through a discussion of details of titles, groups of officials, names, descriptions of customs and practices, and other historical events. Each of these will be explored in turn:

1. Titles

McCann[124] explains how titles used in Acts to describe various authorities have proven to be correct. Luke always uses the right word to describe Roman administrators, and sometimes uses words that would only be familiar to people living in certain cities.[125] For example, McDowell[126] points out that some scholars assume that Luke's use of the term 'politarchs', which was a title for civil authorities in Thessalonica (17:6), was inaccurate since the word was not known to exist in classical literature. However, recent discoveries have shown Luke to be perfectly accurate in his use of this word, since around nineteen inscriptions were discovered which use the title, five of which are used in specific reference to Thessalonica.[127]

The title 'chief man' is also an accurate description used by Luke to describe the Roman governor, Publius, of Malta, which was the island where Paul was shipwrecked (28:7, studied at A2). Bruce[128] comments that this official title has been archaeologically verified by the discovery of two Maltese inscriptions, one in Greek and the other in Latin.

Drane[129] provides further evidence of Luke's precision. In Acts 13:7–8 and 18:12, Sergius Paulus and Gallio are correctly designated 'proconsuls'; Philippi is accurately described as a Roman colony, ruled by 'praetors'. This unusual word has been discovered on inscriptions, showing that it was a colloquial term used in Philippi itself (Acts 16:12, 20–22). Guy[130] comments that such evidence proves the writer of Acts to be trustworthy. Hunter[131] agrees, adding that Luke "never wittingly played fast and loose with his historical facts".

2. Names

Acts refers to individuals by name and is correct in describing their positions in society: Achaia was a Senatorial province from 27BC to AD15, and then from AD44 onwards.[132] In Acts 18:12–16 the proconsul of Achaia, Gallio, is named, which is supported by a letter written by the Emperor Claudius where he indicated that Gallio must have become Proconsul of Achaia in AD51.[133] It is significant to note that Luke, like Claudius, accurately calls Gallio 'proconsul of Achaia' and not 'of Greece', which was a departure from Luke's usual custom of calling countries by their general title.

3. Events

McCann[134] describes how Luke is also accurate in describing events in the world at that time. Luke mentions Agabus' prophecy of a great famine extending throughout the world, being fulfilled in the days of Claudius Caesar (11:27–30). This has proven to be an historically correct reference when compared with other ancient writings. The historian Suetonius spoke of frequent famines during the reign of Claudius (AD41–54), Eusebius mentioned famine in Greece, and Tacitus made reference to two famines in Rome at this particular time.[135]

4. Geography

Luke is seen to be correct in his knowledge of geographical locations.[136] Cadbury offers the following examples from Acts:
- Perga in Pamphylia (13:13)
- Phillipi, a city of the first rank in that district of Macedonia, and a Roman colony (16:12)
- Fair Havens in Crete, "not far from the town of Lasea" (27:8)
- Phoenix, a Cretan harbour exposed south-west and north-west (27:12)

5. Religious customs and practices

Acts has also claimed to be reliable concerning common religious practices and ideas in the Roman world. Luke describes the popular longing for a "way of salvation" (26:17, 30) which often manifested itself in polytheism and mystery religions. For example, at Lystra (14:11) and Malta (28:6) he highlights the belief that the gods sometimes descended to earth and in Ephesus he speaks of the worshippers of Artemis, venerated by "all Asia" (19:27).

Similarly, in Athens, Luke's main character, Paul, makes reference to the intellectual curiosity and 'religiosity' of the Athenians (Acts 17:22), which has been backed up by other ancient writers.[137] Luke goes on to describe (Acts 17:23) an idol that bore the inscription "to an unknown god". Pauanias, who visited Athens in AD150, also mentions in his book 'Description of Greece' that there were "altars of the gods named unknown."[138]

Luke also provides information on the influence of sorcery in New Testament times. He describes the influence of sorcerers at Samaria (8:9ff) and at Cyprus (13:6ff); the sorcerers with their magical parchments (14:19) and the strolling exorcists who tried the names of any gods or spirits which might prove useful (14:13).[139]

6. Trade

Archaeology has shown Acts to be accurate in its references to trade. In Acts 16:11–15 Luke records how Paul and his companions speak with some local women at Philippi, including Lydia who is described as "a purple merchant from the city of Thyatira". Thyatira was a city in the ancient kingdom of 'Lydia', a place that was popular for the manufacturing of purple dyes extracted from the juice of the madder root.[140] In support of this, there is evidence to show that the trading in purple dye was common in Philippi at this time.[141]

Conclusion

Luke had of course his limitations and it is important not to expect modern standards of historical accuracy, based on critical research, to be found in Acts. His outlook was that of the first century and his purpose in writing Acts would have had a degree of influence upon his writing. It is true that his information is lacking in places and some of the historical references are doubtful. For example, Guy[142] is one among many scholars who points out that Luke's treatment of Paul differs from the Paul found in Paul's letters. When we compare his narrative with references in Paul's letters, we see there are many gaps, which may contradict the generally positive evaluation of Luke's trustworthiness as an historian. (The topic of Paul of Acts compared to Paul of his letters will be dealt with at A2.)

However, on the whole, the book of Acts may be relied upon as an accurate history of Christianity in its first half-century. Luke, as an eyewitness and travelling companion of Paul, was openly committed to providing an accurate and trustworthy historical account of early Christianity. McCann[143] concludes that it was his ability to do this that led to Ramsay's conclusion that "Luke is a historian of the first rank [who] should be placed along with the very greatest of historians."[144]

 TASKS

a) Explore the claim that the author of Acts attempted to write a true history of the beginnings of the Christian Church Justify your answer.

Your answer should include an evaluation of some of the following:

- The purpose(s) of the text – Acts as an historical and/or an apologetic/theological text
- The detailed establishment of the church, its early growth and development
- The significance of the 'we' passages
- Luke's honest description of strengths and weaknesses
- Evidence of Luke's reliability beyond the New Testament

b) Explore the view that the author of Acts skilfully tells the story of the early church and its growth. Justify your answer.

Your answer should explore some of the following:

- Luke's writing skill, structure, accuracy, dramatic story telling, clear message, reliability
- Luke's ability to describe early Christian faith (speeches), dependence on the Holy Spirit, miracles, Christian practices and lifestyle
- The expansion of the gospel from Jerusalem to Rome, Acts 1:8
- Other interests that Luke may have had

 TASK

Research/Revision – Powerpoint Presentation

In groups of three or four choose one of the topics from this chapter as a revision topic. Using the information from this book, and from other scholars (refer to footnotes for suitable references), present the main arguments in a PowerPoint Presentation to the rest of your class.

Include an evaluation of some scholars' opinions.

Conclude your presentation with a thought provoking question for the class to consider, which might inspire a lively debate.

LEARNING INTENTIONS CHECKLIST/ TARGET SETTING

By the end of this unit I will be able to:	Yes	No	To be achieved
• analyse the suggested dates for the writing of Acts			
• select relevant information to choose the most plausible argument for the purpose of Acts			
• apply the process of elimination to work out the most plausible author of Acts			
• apply the theory of primary and secondary sources to work out from where Luke may have got his information			
• explain at least three ways suggested for the structure of Acts			
• evaluate the effectiveness of scholars' opinions in reaching a conclusion			
• be able to identify the main themes or characteristics of the Book of Acts			
• analyse the extent to which Luke can be described as a reliable historian, ie identify his strengths and shortcomings			
• participate in a PowerPoint presentation on one of the topics in the Background to Acts			
• evaluate the effectiveness of scholars' opinions in reaching a conclusion			

Endnotes

1 Packer, JW, 1966, *The Cambridge Bible Commentary, The Acts of the Apostles*, London: Cambridge University Press, p2

2 Lake, K. and S., *An Introduction to the New Testament*, [SI] Christophers, 1938, p67

3 Guy, HA, *The Church in the New Testament*, London: Macmillan Education, 1969, p6

4 Bruce, FF, *The Spreading Flame*, Exeter: The Paternoster Press, 1958, p70

5 *ibid*, p72

6 Guy, *op cit*, p9

7 *ibid*, p9

8 Smith, M, *Acts*, London: Edward Arnold, 1988, educational pack

9 Marshall, IH, *Tyndale New Testament Commentaries, Acts*, Leicester: IVP, 1980, p47

10 Streeter, BH, *The Four Gospels: A study of origins treating of the manuscript, tradition, sources, authorship and date*, [S.I.] Macmillan, 1924, p532

11 Guthrie, D, *New Testament Introduction*, Apollos, Leicester: IVP, 1961, p357

12 *ibid*, p358

13 Guy, *op cit*, p18

14 Hanson, RPC, *NTS 12*, pp211–230

15 Bruce, FF, *The New International Commentary on the New Testament: The Book of Acts, Revised*, Michigan: William B. Eermans Publishing Company Grand Rapids, 1988, p11

16 Lietzmann, H, *The Founding of the Church Universal*, London: E.T., 1950, p78

17 Bruce, *op cit*, p11

18 Harnack, A, *The Date of Acts and the Synoptic Gospels*, Eng. Tr. RJ Wilkinson, [S.I.] Williams & N, 1911, cited in Barclay, W, *The Acts of the Apostles, The Daily Study Bible*, Edinburgh: the Saint Andrew Press, 1955

19 Barclay, W, *The Acts of the Apostles, The Daily Study Bible*, Edinburgh: The Saint Andrew Press, 1955, p246

20 Guy, *opt cit*, p18

21 Guthrie, *op cit*, p356

22 Du Plessis, I J, *Guide to the New Testament IV*, (ed. AB du Toit) 203

23 Guy, *opt cit*, p19

24 Marshall, *op cit*, p47

25 Guthrie, *op cit*, p362

26 Bruce, *op cit*, p13

27 Barclay, W, *The Acts of the Apostles, The Daily Study Bible*, Edinburgh: The Saint Andrew Press, 1955, XIV

28 Banks, R, *The Gospel of Luke, Introduction and Theology*, Newtownards: Colourpoint, 2006, p14

29 *ibid*, p12

30 *ibid*, p12

31 Packer, *op cit*, p2

32 Freed, ED, *The Apostle Paul and his Letters*, London, Oakville: Equinox, 2005, p14

33 Guy, *op cit*, p13

34 Barrett, KC, *Luke the Historian in Recent Study*, London: Epworth P, 1961, p57ff

35 Guy, *op cit*, p14

36 Freed, *op cit*, p14

[37] Longenecker, RN, *Expositors' Bible Commentary, volume 9*, London: Grand Rapids, Mich: Zondervan Publishing House, Hodder & Stoughton, 1995, p238

[38] Hewitt, FS, *Genesis of the Christian Church*, London: Edward Arnold, 1964, p22

[39] Lewis, ER, *The Acts of the Apostles and the Letters of St. Paul*, London: James Clarke & Co. Limited, 1960, p20

[40] Gasque,WW, *Luke*, ISBE, p179

[41] Lewis, *op cit*, p20

[42] Banks, *op cit*, p14

[43] Hanson, RPC, *The Acts (New Clarendon Bible)*, Oxford: Clarendon Press, 1967, p48, p50

[44] Johnson, LT, *The Acts of the Apostles*, Harrington DJ, Ed, Sacra Pagina, Collegeville, Min: Liturgical Press 1992, p3

[45] Lewis, *op cit*, p18

[46] Hunter, AM, *Introducing the New Testament, Revised Edition*, London: SCM Press Ltd, 1945, p74

[47] Barclay, W, *The Acts of the Apostles, The Daily Bible Study*, Edinburgh: The Saint Andrew Press, 1953, 1955, pxix

[48] Guthrie, *op cit*, p389

[49] Stott, JRW, *The Message of Acts*, BST, Leicester, IVP, 1990, p22

[50] Guthrie, *op cit*, p389

[51] Johnson, *op cit*, p4

[52] Torrey, CC, *The Composition and Date of Acts*, HTS 1, Cambridge, MA: Harvard University Press, 1916

[53] cited in Lewis, *op cit*, p19

[54] Marshall, *op cit*, p18

[55] Dillon, RJ, *Acts of the Apostles, The New Jerome Biblical Commentary*, ed. by Brown, RE, Fitzmyer, JA, & Murphy, RE, London: Chapman, 1990, p724

[56] Johnson, *op cit*, p4

[57] cited in Hanson, *op cit*, p50

[58] Johnson, *op cit*, p4

[59] Marshall, *op cit*, pp18–19

[60] Bruce, *op cit*, p6

[61] Neil, W, *The Acts of the Apostles*, London: Oliphants, 1973

[62] Marshall, *op cit*,

[63] Stott, *op cit*, p23

[64] Guthrie, *op cit*, p349

[65] Fuller, RH, *A Critical Introduction to the New Testament*, London: Duckworth, 1966, p123

[66] Dibelius, M, *Studies in the Acts of the Apostles*, Eng. Tr., London: SCM, 1956, p103

[67] Marshall, *op cit*, p18

[68] Bruce, *op cit*, p11

[69] Haenchen, E, *The Acts of the Apostles*, KEK, Eng tr, Oxford: Basil Blackwell, 1971, cited in Guthrie, *op cit*, p353

[70] Hunter, *op cit*, p79

[71] Hewitt, *op cit*, p20

[72] Hunter, *op cit*, p77

[73] Lewis, *op cit*, p16

[74] *ibid*, p20

[75] Bruce, *op cit*, p13

[76] Scott, EF, *The Literature of the New Testament*, New York: Columbia University Press, 1932, p95

[77] Guthrie, *op cit*, p350

[78] Williman, WH, *Interpretation: Acts*, Westminster: John Know Press, 1988, pp8–9

[79] Banks, R, *The Early Church, The Christian Church to 325AD*, Newtownards: Colourpoint, 2003, p105

[80] *ibid*, p73

[81] Guy, *op cit*, p12

[82] Bruce, *op cit*, p8

[83] Acts 28:22

[84] Stott, *op cit*, p26

[85] *ibid*, p26

[86] Hunter, *op cit*, p74

[87] Bruce, *op cit*, p10

[88] Williman, *op cit*, p9

[89] Williams, CSC, 'The Acts of the Apostles' *Black's New Testament Commentaries*, London: Adam & Charles Black 1975, p15f

[90] Barrett, CK, *Luke the Historian in Recent Study*, London: Epworth Press, 1961, cited in Guthrie, *op cit*, p350

[91] Lewis, *op cit*, p15

[92] Williams, *op cit*, pp24–33

[93] Marshall, *op cit*, pp18–19

[94] Hunter, *op cit*, p78

[95] Gasque, WW's translation of Baur, FC, *A History of the Criticism of the Acts of the Apostles*, Mohr, Tubingen/Eerdmans, 1975, p326

[96] Stott, *op cit*, p28

[97] Banks, *op cit*, p25

[98] Hunter, *op cit*, p80

[99] Guthrie, *op cit*, p351

[100] Marshall, *op cit*, p24

[100a] Guthrie, *op cit*,

[100b] Marshall, *op cit*, p24

[101] Drane, J, *Introducing the New Testament*, Oxford: Lion Publishing, 1986, p240

[102] Marshall, *op cit*, p23

[103] Fernando, A, *The NIV Application Commentary to contemporary life*, Michigan: Zonervan, Grand Rapids, 1998, p23

[104] Dodd, CH, *New Testament Studies*, Manchester: Manchester University Press, 1953, The Apostolic Preaching and its Developments, 1944, p7ff

[105] Marshall, *op cit*, p25

[106] Irvine, D, *Acts*, Farmington Fellowship, www.farmingfellowship.co.uk

[107] Munck, J, *The Anchor Bible, The Acts of the Apostles*, New York: Doubleday & Co., Inc., 1986, vol. 31, LV. Cited in McCann, V, Spotlight Ministries, 2003, p2

[108] Hunter, *op cit*, p77

[109] Carson, DA, Moo, DJ, and Morris, L, *An Introduction to the New Testament*, Leicester: Apollos, 1992, p207

110 Carson, Morris and Moo give the examples of Polybius, Lucian and Thucydides as ancient historians who were concerned to present facts as accurately as possible and who disapproved of exaggeration.

111 McCann, V, 'The Historical Reliability of the Acts of the Apostles', Spotlight Ministries, 2003, www.spotlightministries.co.uk, last accessed 22.01.08

112 Hunter, *op cit*, p77

113 Fernando, *op cit*, p23

114 Stott, *op cit*, p.22

115 Haenchen, *The Acts of the Apostles*, Oxford: Basil Blackwell, 1971, 462–468. Haenchen clearly favours Paul's letter "as the only real record we possess", over Luke's version in Acts which he claims does not possess historical value.

116 Bruce, *op cit*, p282ff

117 Bruce, *ibid*, p282

118 Wainwright, W, *A Guide to the New Testament*, England: Epworth Press, 1965, p175

119 Powell, MA, *What Are They Saying About Acts?* New York: Paulist Press, 1991, p89

120 Bruce, FF, *New Bible Commentary*, 3rd ed. Leicester: IVP, 1989

121 Hunter, *op cit*, p.78.

122 Bruce, *op cit*, p970

123 McCann, *op cit*

124 McCann, *op cit*

125 Drane, *op cit*, p240

126 McDowell, J, *Christianity: A Ready Defence*, San Bernardino: Here's Life Publishers Inc., 1991, p111

127 *ibid*, p111

128 Bruce, FF, *New Bible Commentary*, 3rd ed. Leicester: IVP, 1989, 499

129 Drane, *op cit*, p240

130 Guy, *op cit*, p9

131 Hunter, *op cit*, p78.

132 Bruce, FF, *Are the New Testament Documents Reliable?*, Leicester: IVP, 1943, p82

133 Unger, MF, *Archaeology and the New Testament*, Michigan: Grand Rapids, Zondervan, 1982, p245

134 McCann, *op cit*

135 Thompson, JA, *The Bible and Archaeology*, Grand Rapids, Exeter: The Paternoster Press, 1962

136 Cadbury, HJ, *The Making of Luke – Acts*, London: SPCK, 1924, cited in Hunter, *op cit*, p78

137 Thompson, *op cit*, p389

138 Unger, *op cit*, 238

139 McCann, *op cit*

140 Bruce, *op cit*, p311

141 *ibid*, p311

142 *op cit*, p11

143 McCann, *op cit*

144 Ramsay, W, *The Bearing of Recent Discovery on the Trustworthiness of the New Testament*, 1915, 81, p222

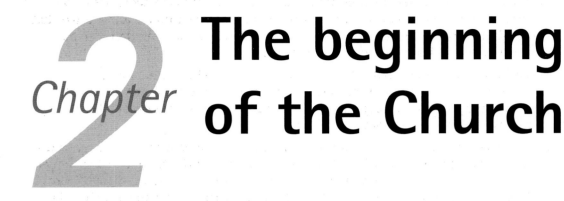

The beginning
of the Church

Chapter **2**

JESUS' INITIATION OF THE CHURCH'S MISSION (CH 1:1–11)

IN THIS CHAPTER, JESUS himself makes significant preparations prior to the founding of the church, which begins with Pentecost as described in Acts Ch 2. The detail described by Luke in Acts Ch 1 reinforces the importance of the events that lay ahead.

Jesus' initiation of the Church's mission is important because it sets the scene for the rest of the story in the book of Acts. Within this section vital 'behind the scenes' work takes place as preparation for both the Day of Pentecost and the events which follow in the growth of the church. Chapter 1 of Acts deals with two matters: Jesus' contact with his apostles prior to his ascension; and the choosing of Matthias to fill the vacancy among the 'Twelve', caused by Judas' betrayal and death. (The latter will be dealt with in the next chapter.)

Prologue (Ch 1:1–3)

As mentioned in the last chapter, there is much speculation among scholars concerning the identity of 'Theophilus'. Bruce[1] comments that it has been suggested that he was not an individual as the name 'Theophilus' means 'dear to God' and could refer to the Christian reader in general. However, most scholars feel that use of "most excellent Theophilus" indicates that Luke was probably addressing one man, who was someone of high rank. Hewitt[2] mentions that Theophilus was the secret Christian name of Flavius Clemens, cousin and heir of the Emperor Domitian. It is known that his wife admired the Christian faith and that he himself was an enquirer. Flavius Clemens was put to death by Domitian in AD96.

Bruce,[3] however, argues that it "is quite probable that Theophilus was a representative member of the intelligent middle-class public at Rome whom Luke wished to win over to a less prejudiced and more favourable opinion of Christianity than that which was current among them".

It is implied that Acts was to be an account of all that Jesus would continue to do and teach through the power of the Holy Spirit. The use of the term 'apostles' refers to the twelve men Jesus had chosen earlier in his ministry (excluding Judas). They would be the ones entrusted with the task of founding the Christian Church (v 2). Luke directs our attention to how they were given "decisive proof"[4] that Jesus was alive. Over forty days between the resurrection and ascension he appeared on various occasions to the apostles "in a manner which could leave no doubt in their minds that he was really alive again, risen from the dead".[5]

Jesus not only appeared to them, but he spoke about the Kingdom of God; Dodd[6] explains that the Kingdom of God "is conceived as coming in the events of the life, death and resurrection of Jesus, and to proclaim these facts, in their proper setting, is to preach the gospel of the Kingdom of God". Jesus also ate with his apostles, which highlights that he was not a spirit but a human that could be touched. Bruce[7] adds that Jesus would have no personal need of food, but would have taken it to convince the apostles that he was really with them and was not a 'phantom'. Marshall[8] comments that it may even have been communion that he shared with them. Stott[9] concludes that such experience of the risen Lord was an indispensable qualification of an apostle, which explains why Paul and James could be one.

Commission (Ch 1:4–8)

Jesus instructed the apostles to stay in Jerusalem until the Father (God) fulfilled his promise of giving the Holy Spirit to them. Bruce[10] comments that this promise was foreshadowed by the ministry of John the Baptist (Luke 3:16). John baptised with water but "the new baptism is to be something more than water, it is to be baptism into a source of power".[11]

The Jewish belief was that the promised Messiah would build up God's Kingdom here on earth. Hewitt[12] comments that even the disciples, who had received instruction on the true nature of the Kingdom of God, at the last moment, still clung to their Jewish beliefs and evidently hoped to see the kingdom of God realised in the restoration of Israel's national independence.[13] Their question in verse 6 concerning the time of the restoration of the kingdom suggests that they still regarded the Messiah's work as unfinished. Jesus did not directly say 'no' but rather he directed their attention to the task which lay ahead; they were commissioned to proclaim the good news of God's grace in Christ[14] and act as witnesses to Christ from Jerusalem to the end of the earth.[15] The dates and times are irrelevant as they are the Father's business not theirs.[16] Bruce[17] comments that "Instead of the political power which had once been the object of their ambitions, a power far greater and nobler would be theirs. When the Holy Spirit came upon them, Jesus assured them, they would be vested with heavenly power ...".

The Ascension (Ch 1:9–11)

In Luke's Gospel the impression is given that the Ascension took place on the same day as the resurrection. In Acts, however, Luke states that the Ascension took place forty days after the resurrection. Hewitt[18] comments that this tradition of forty days when Jesus appeared to the disciples on various occasions in places as far apart as Galilee and Emmaus, is regarded as more valid. Bruce[19] comments that during the forty day period Jesus was not 'earth-bound', meaning that he was trapped on the earth. Rather, he believes that Jesus paid visits to the disciples from "that eternal order to which his 'body of glory' now belonged".

Marshall[20] comments that Luke alone describes the ascension of Jesus as a visible event. In answering the question regarding what the disciples actually saw, Hewitt[21] admits that it is impossible to know. He argues that with our concept of the universe it is difficult to imagine Jesus 'going up' to heaven. Our understanding of heaven is that it is not a geographical location 'up there', but rather 'it is a condition of the Spirit'. Barclay[22] points out the importance of the ascension as there would have been something quite wrong if the resurrection appearances had just slowly faded out. Guy[23] suggests the possibility that the idea of a bodily ascension was introduced and the whole scene constructed by Luke to express a fitting conclusion to Jesus' human life and his work on earth. Marshall,[24] however, argues that the fact of the ascension is firmly attested elsewhere (1 Tim. 3:16; 1 Pet. 3:21f) and he adds that it is best not to interpret the story over-literally. Rather, it is wise to concentrate on the symbolism of 'ascension' which expresses the way in which the physical presence of Jesus left this world, to be replaced by his spiritual presence.

The two white-robed men who appear are angelic messengers. In asking the disciples why they are staring into the sky, the angels are really prompting them to get a move on; they have a command to follow and having witnessed the ascension they now have the assurance that as it was possible for Jesus to ascend into heaven, "so he would return in the same way."[25] This is called the Second Coming of Christ, or the 'Parousia', and is fundamental to the belief of the Christian Church. Bruce[26] argues that from Luke's perspective, the Parousia would not happen immediately. Stott[27] agrees, pointing out that much of the early church's life and thought was influenced by the mistaken belief that Jesus would return in the near future. The apostles' immediate duty was straightforward: they had to wait in Jerusalem until they received the Holy Spirit. So they returned to the city.

 TASK

Class Discussion: Did the ascension really happen? What do you think? Organise into two groups, one 'For' and the other 'Against'.

 TASK

Comment on the claim that the events that took place prior to Pentecost were significant in preparing the disciples for the coming of the Holy Spirit.

Your answer may include some of the following:
- How the disciples were given decisive proof that Jesus was alive
- Jesus spoke to them about the Kingdom of God
- The anticipation of the coming of the Holy Spirit and the significance of the promised baptism compared to John's baptism
- How the disciples witnessed the ascension and the significance of this event
- The significance of replacing Judas in keeping the number of apostles as twelve. (This will be looked at in the next chapter)

THE FIRST PREACHING OF THE GOSPEL

Pentecost Event (Ch 2:1–13)

Pentecost, the Jewish festival which celebrated the wheat harvest, means 'fiftieth', so called because it fell fifty days after Passover. (Another name for Pentecost is the 'Feast of Weeks'.) The Passover was celebrated in the middle of April, with Pentecost falling in June, a time when travelling conditions were at their best. As a result there was a very international crowd in Jerusalem at the time of Pentecost. The law stated that on the Day of Pentecost no one should work (Leviticus 23:21; Numbers 28:26) so there would naturally be more people out and about than usual.

The disciples were sitting together when suddenly the room was filled with what seemed "like wind". Bruce[28] comments that the wind was held to symbolise the Spirit of God which had come upon the disciples in power. John the Baptist had spoken of how one greater than he would carry out a baptism with wind and fire (Luke 3:16–17). In the Old Testament fire represented the divine presence (Exodus 3:2–5). Similarly, fire played a part on this occasion with what appeared to be tongues of fire resting on the head of each of the disciples. Marshall[29] comments that "with these outward signs came the Holy Spirit as an inward, invisible reality". The possible connection between the "tongues of fire" and the "other tongues" that the disciples began to utter has been pointed out by some scholars.[30]

Glossolalia

Glossolalia comes from the Greek term *'glossa'*, or 'tongue', used in the New Testament and refers to 'speaking in tongues'. This means a 'language miracle' where a person is able to speak under the inspiration of the Holy Spirit and in divine ecstasy utters words over which he has no control or understanding.

There is considerable debate over the nature of glossolalia in the New Testament. The difficulty lies in how to compare Acts Ch 2 with 1 Corinthians Ch 14, which seem to describe two different things. It appears that the tongues of Acts Ch 2 are understood by the foreign visitors (2:5f) while the tongues of 1 Corinthians Ch 14 cannot be understood without the spiritual gift of interpretation (1 Cor 12:10, 28–30; 14:2–19), implying that tongues are unintelligible speech. It was uttered in a speech that no one could understand until someone with the spiritual gift of interpretation explained what had been said.

Acts 2

Hewitt[31] points out that there are three possibilities for what is meant by speaking in tongues on the Day of Pentecost:

1. A literal interpretation where the disciples were blessed with the ability of speaking in foreign languages without the effort of having to learn them. However in this case an accusation of drunkenness would have been unlikely.

2. The use of common languages – Barclay[32] and Guy[33] point out that to speak in foreign languages at Pentecost was unnecessary. The crowd was made up of Jews, proselytes and god-fearers (ie Gentiles who had accepted the Jewish religion and way of life). Only two languages, Greek and Aramaic, would be necessary for a crowd like that to understand what was being said. Hewitt, however, adds that simple Galileans such as the disciples, would hardly have had the opportunity to travel outside their province and would not be likely to speak Greek. Therefore it is argued that 'other languages' in fact really meant 'languages other than Hebrew'.

3. The use of ecstatic speech or 'glossolalia' (see definition above). Guy[34] argues that glossolalia does sometimes include foreign words, which the speaker has heard and forgotten but which come from the unconscious under the stress of excitement. Some of those present may have thought that the speech of the disciples, unintelligible to them, was in someone else's language.

1 Corinthians 12–14

1 Corinthians 12–14 gives no impression that tongues can be translated through a natural knowledge of the language. They can only be understood spiritually through the spiritual gift of interpretation (1 Cor. 12:10). Bruce[35] comments that it was a spiritual gift that was highly valued in the Corinthian church.

Chapter 14 deals with the issue of tongues in the context of a potentially chaotic worship service. Many of the Corinthians favoured public expressions of tongues and ecstatic behaviour, which was bound to provoke confusion and ridicule from visitors not aware of spiritual matters (14:23). "Paul acknowledges that the Corinthian glossolalia is a genuine gift of the Holy Spirit, but deprecates the undue importance which some members of the church at Corinth attach to it".[36] He responds by favouring the intelligible forms of inspired speech such as prophecy for the public worship service (14:2–4; 17–18; 21–24). The unintelligible forms of inspired speech, such as tongues, are directed to God alone and serve to edify the individual speaking. Paul allows tongues to be expressed in public but only if accompanied by a spiritual interpretation, the responsibility of which is laid on the shoulders of the speaker (14:14–27). The chief purpose in public worship is to serve the edification of the church (14:26).

The primary function of tongues for Paul in 1 Corinthians 14 seems to be for private prayer, while prophecy is for the public (14:18–19). In other words, tongues are for self-edification before God as one gives thanks to God "with the spirit" (14:3, 14–15, 18).

How can these two descriptions of speaking tongues be reconciled?

1. Some explain the difference by pointing out the international nature of the audience of Acts Ch 2 compared to the provincial nature of the congregation in Corinth. The difference in audience between the two texts could explain why the tongues were understood naturally in Acts Ch 2, while they required a spiritual interpretation in 1 Corinthians Ch 12–14 (12:10).

2. Acts 2:6 states that each "one" heard "them", possibly implying that each person in the audience heard Jesus' followers speak in his or her language. Were the tongues of Pentecost unintelligible glossolalia that were accompanied by a miracle of hearing in which each person heard the Christians speak in his or her particular language (v 6, 8, 11)? Stott[37] objects to this pointing to evidence from v 4, they "began to speak in other tongues as the Spirit enabled them".

3. Different outlook between Luke and Paul: Luke seems to allow for tongues to have a public sign value that is not prominent in Paul. For Luke, tongues were a sign of the universal reach of the Spirit's witness. In Acts 2, the God of Israel is revealed in the languages of the nations – the sacred language is heard in the Gentile tongues of the nations. Similarly, the explicit reference to tongues at the

Gentile reception of the Spirit is not without significance (10:46). Luke's point is clear: the Spirit has been poured out upon all flesh in a way that mends divisions and brings about unity.

 TASKS

a) Discuss the following statement with reference to the role of speaking in tongues on the Day of Pentecost.

"What happened on that occasion was that the multitude of pilgrims heard the Christians praising God in ecstatic utterances; and were amazed to observe that many of the words which they uttered were not Jewish or Greek words at all, but belonged to the local languages of Egypt, Asia Minor and Italy"

(Loyd, P, 'The Holy Spirit in Acts', London, 1952, cited in Bruce, FF, 'The Book of the Acts', Michigan, Grands Rapids, 1988, p52, footnote)

You may find it helpful to refer to some of the following texts prior to discussion:
- 'The Book of Acts', FF Bruce, 1988, pp51–54
- 'Acts', H Marshall, 1980, pp69–70
- 'Introducing the New Testament', J Drane, pp222; 320

b) Discuss the following statement with reference to the role of speaking in tongues in the church today.

"Every new beginning in thought or life is inevitably accompanied by a disturbance. There is the struggle with the old, and the re-adjustment to the new environment. So the coming of the Spirit is followed by irregular and abnormal phenomena. Like Jordan, the full and plenteous flood of the Spirit 'overflows all its banks' (Joshua 3:15). At first the old worn-out vessels of humanity cannot contain it; and there is a flood of strange and novel spiritual experiences. But when it has worn for itself a deep channel in the church, when the laws of the new spiritual life are learnt and understood, then some of the irregular phenomena disappear, others become normal, and what was thought to be miraculous is found to be a natural endowment of human life."

(Rackham, RB, 'The Acts of the Apostles', London, 1901)

You may find it helpful to research (use internet) some of the following aspects of human experience prior to discussion:
- The 1859 Revival
- The Azusa Street Revival in Los Angeles, 1906
- The Toronto Blessing, 1994
- Argentina Revival, 1992–1995

Peter's Proclamation (Ch 2:14–36)

Joel's prophecy (Ch 2:14–21)

Whatever the ecstatic utterances were, they achieved the purpose of drawing a crowd, which Peter took advantage of in giving his first speech. He begins with a denial of the charge of drunkenness: it is only nine o' clock in the morning, much too early for them to have been able to drink in excess. Hewitt[38] (p45) also points out that the Law did not allow a Jew to eat or drink before the first hour of prayer (9 am). The men were not full of wine, but of the Holy Spirit, as had been prophesied by the prophet Joel.

Peter continues commenting that with the Spirit's coming the last days have come. Stott[39] argues that the age of the Spirit stretches between the two comings of Christ. God's Spirit will be poured out on all flesh, "irrespective of their outward status, and people would prophesy, through 'visions, dreams and by word of mouth'".[40] This can be considered as a "long day of opportunity, during which the gospel of salvation will be preached throughout the world".[41]

On first reading verses 19–20, it may seem difficult to understand. Stott[42] suggests the possibility that these predictions are upheavals of nature which began on Good Friday. On that day the sun darkened during the early afternoon and the paschal full moon may well have risen blood-red in the sky as a result of the darkening of the sun.[43] The prophecy concludes with a promise that whoever appeals to the Lord for help will be saved, which Christians regard as an appeal for salvation in the name of Jesus.

The resurrection of Jesus proclaimed (Ch 2:22–28)

Bruce[44] comments that Peter now takes up his main theme, which is the proclamation of Jesus as Lord and Messiah. He directs his speech to the "men of Israel," that is, the Jews. He immediately focuses on Jesus who had been marked out by God to them through the various miracles and signs which God had performed publicly through him.[45] Instead of treating Jesus as a man of God, the Jews put him to death by crucifixion. "Lawless men" refers to the Romans who carried out the death sentence but it is the Jews who are considered to be responsible. Bruce[46] adds that at this point Peter is addressing the people of Jerusalem, and not the visitors. However, all this was part of God's plan that the Messiah should suffer. Marshall[47] comments that "here we have the paradox of divine predestination and human free will in its strongest form".

TASK

Find out the meaning of 'paradox' and 'predestination' and explain the meaning of Marshall's comment in your own words.

Jesus' sentence and death were reversed by God's intervention in raising him from the dead. God raised him because it was not possible for death to hold him. Bertram[48] comments that "the abyss can no longer hold the Redeemer than a pregnant woman can hold the child in her body". To confirm his claim, Peter now uses an Old Testament prophecy, Psalm 16:8–11, which is regarded as a statement by David about the Messiah (v 25–28). Peter argues that the words of this prophecy cannot refer to David, for he did not rise from the dead. Therefore the passage must be referring to Jesus, David's descendant. Jesus is therefore the expected Messiah.

Jesus: Lord and Messiah (Ch 2:29–36)

David knew that God had promised that one of his descendants would sit on his throne (see Ps 132:11). Peter therefore claims that what was prophesied has been fulfilled in Jesus: the Messiah had risen from the dead. Having established that Jesus, as the Messiah, must rise from the dead, Peter can now go on to give the explanation of the pouring out of the Spirit[49]: that Jesus received the Holy Spirit from the Father and had now poured that Spirit out on his followers.

Call to Repentance (Ch 2:37–41)

Peter's preaching was successful in stirring the consciences of his listeners. If Jesus was the Messiah then the guilt they were feeling over their treatment of him was vast. In panic, it seems, they asked what they should do. Peter told them to repent and be baptised in Jesus' name. Stott[50] describes this as humiliating for them. Firstly, because Jews regarded baptism as necessary only for Gentile converts who wished to become proselytes; and secondly because they would be submitting to baptism in the name of the very person they had previously rejected. It would certainly be a public token of their genuine repentance and faith.

In return, they would not only receive forgiveness of sins but also the gift of the Holy Spirit – the gift which had been bestowed on the apostles themselves only a few hours before.[51] This promise was for them and the generations that followed; for those far off such as the dispersion Jews; for everyone called by God. "Through the apostolic witness Jesus thus acquired more followers in one day than in the whole of his public ministry."[52]

Packer[53] comments that there is no doubt that (similarly to some of the other speeches in Acts) this speech is one of Luke's compositions. Although like others, it is not his invention.

Summary of Peter's Speech at Pentecost:

- Charge of drunkenness denied – the apostles are full of the Holy Spirit; prophesied by Joel.
- Jesus was killed by the Jews.
- Jesus was raised from the dead. The resurrection of one of David's descendants was foretold in Ps 16:8–11 and Ps 89:4.
- Jesus is the descendant to which the prophecy applies.
- Jesus is ascended into heaven and given the promise of the Holy Spirit.
- Jesus has now poured out the Holy Spirit. The gift of tongues is evidence of this.
- Ps.110 speaks of the reign of a Messiah – Jesus is shown to be that Messiah.
- The challenge is to repent of sin and accept Jesus.

 TASK

"It would be a mistake to link the words 'for the forgiveness of sins' with the command 'be baptised' to the exclusion of the prior command to repent." (Bruce, FF, The Book of the Acts, Michigan, Grands Rapids, 1988, p70).

a) What does this statement mean? Rewrite it in your own words.

b) Do you agree or disagree with this statement? Justify your answer, using relevant information from other aspects of human experience, such as different Christian denominations in your answer.

(Refer to 'The Christian Church', Nelson, J, and Gilbride, J, Newtownards, Colourpoint, 2001).

OTHER ASPECTS OF HUMAN EXPERIENCE

Part of the questions in Section B of the AS examination paper requires an exploration of the ways in which the taught course can relate to other aspects of human experience. These aspects which are listed on the specification include: social; political; environmental; business; scientific; and artistic issues. Candidates may explore connections to alternative religions, spiritual and moral teachings, values, beliefs and practices. The connections which candidates make can have either/or both historical and contemporary contexts.

By definition it is not possible or indeed desirable to provide a prescriptive, exhaustive 'list' of other aspects of human experience to which the taught course can be applied. By its very nature this element of the exam is 'open' to whatever meaningful connections candidates can themselves make. The information below is intended merely to provide stimulus for further ideas or discussion on how some aspects of the taught course might be applied to some other aspects of experience.

How to Prepare for the Human Experience Element of the AS Examination

- Keep in mind that the connections you make should move beyond the taught course while still relating to content studied.
- They should give you an opportunity for exploration, discussion, and critical analysis, rather than being limited to simple comparative statements.
- Keep up to date with current affairs. Read newspapers and Church publications for the latest on current events, as well as on issues which are being debated within the Church and religious groups.
- Use the internet. It is a good idea to keep a file of resources and ideas you can use later.
- Take time at the end of every chapter to think about what you could do. Discuss with other members of your class.

Discuss how you might develop these connections to other aspects of human experience. Can you add to them?

- Large scale evangelical meetings where people are asked to step to the front to 'be saved'
- The Pentecostal movement compared to a more formal and structured church setting
- Famous Christian revivals
- The controversy surrounding the validity of speaking in tongues today
- The emergence of the house church movement in persecuted countries

Sample ideas on relating 'Pentecost' to other aspects of human experience:

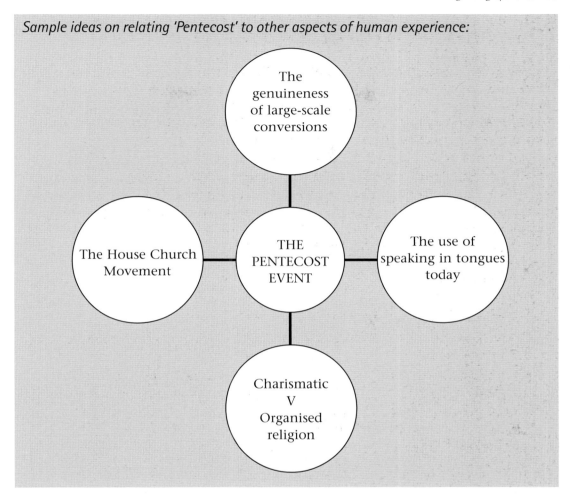

The First Christian Church (Ch 2:42–47)

As mentioned in 'The Structure of Acts' one of Luke's characteristics is to separate his story using short summary paragraphs. Lewis[54] points out that the second chapter in Acts ends with a fine summary of life in the early church. Christian worship was beginning to take shape with five main aspects: teaching, fellowship, the breaking of bread, prayers and sharing possessions.

1. Guy[55] comments that the "apostles' teaching" refers to the teaching which they had received from Jesus and to information about him. Considering that Jesus spent so much time teaching the crowds and his inner circle of followers, it is not surprising that teaching played such an important part.[56]

2. 'Fellowship' or *koinonia* is a term used for the believers meeting together. The

main meaning behind it is sharing company with each other but spiritual intimacy may also be implied.

3. The 'breaking of bread' seems to refer to a common meal which the believers observed in their own homes. These meals may have developed into the Agape (or 'love feast') and only later were they integrated with the Last Supper to become the Lord's Supper (see 1 Cor 11:20–21). Others disagree, arguing that the breaking of bread included both the Lord's Supper and fellowship meals at this early stage.[57]

4. 'Prayers' probably mean the Jewish hours of prayer and attendance at services in the Temple. Bruce[58] comments that while the community's prayers would follow Jewish models, the content would be enriched because of the Christ-event. However, there would also be times when they prayed on their own (1:24; 4:24; 12:12).

5. Drane[59] comments that the believers sold their possessions and pooled the proceeds so they could live as a true community of Jesus' followers. Within the community there was a spirit of rejoicing and goodwill.[60] Finally, the evangelistic activity of the church continued daily,[61] with their numbers being constantly increased.

 TASK

Another aspect of human experience that is similar to the description given here is that of the Qumran community, an unorthodox Jewish sect, who moved to live in the wilderness to establish their own monastic commune to the west of the Dead Sea. Their buildings have been unearthed by archaeologists and their documents, the famous 'Dead Sea Scrolls' were discovered in caves nearby. Like the early Christians they gave up their individual possessions and had a common meal (although there were clear difference between the two groups as well).

Are there any religious communities associated with Christianity today who would remind you of the Qumran community? Explore the lifestyle and vision of such groups and report back to your class.

 **TASKS**

a) **Give an account of the coming of the Holy Spirit at Pentecost.**

   Your answer could include some of the following:
   - Establishing the context: Pentecost, Jerusalem
   - Outline of the events in the upper room
   - The events in the street and the allegations of the crowd
   - Peter's speech (kergyma, Joel, the Psalms)
   - The response of the crowd and the significance of the events
   - Explanation of points of interest or debate

b) **Comment on the claim that the author of Acts has confused "speaking in tongues" with speaking in foreign languages.**

   Your answer could include a discussion of some of the following:
   - Suggested possibilities of what was meant by speaking in tongues on the Day of Pentecost
   - Comparison of Acts 2 with 1 Corinthians 12–14
   - Personal opinion supported by reasonable evidence from the New Testament

c) **Discuss the view that if the Pentecost event had not taken place the Church as we know it would not exist today. (This question requires knowledge of other aspects of human experience.)**

   Your discussion may include some of the following:
   - How the Holy Spirit changed the disciples
   - The immediate significance of the event for the life of the early church
   - The gift of the Holy Spirit in enabling the disciples to carry out Acts 1:8; the witness of the believers as a result
   - The growth of the church from the Day of Pentecost until Paul took the gospel to Rome
   - The expansion of Christianity in the first four centuries until Constantine made it the official religion of the Empire
   - Why Christianity appealed to all members of society and continues to do so today (You may find 'The Early Church: The Christian Church to 325AD' by Raymond Banks, 2003, Colourpoint, useful as a guide for further study)

LEARNING INTENTIONS CHECKLIST/ TARGET SETTING

By the end of this unit I will be able to:	Yes	No	To be achieved
• understand how the beginning of Acts is connected to the end of Luke's Gospel			
• be able to explain the importance for the apostles of the forty days between the resurrection and the ascension.			
• know Jesus' commission to the apostles			
• be able to explain why some people feel an actual physical ascension of Jesus is vital			
• be able to give a definition of the term 'parousia'			
• be able to explain why the disciples were waiting in Jerusalem			
• be able to explain why Pentecost is a Jewish festival as well as a Christian festival			
• understand the significance of 'wind' and 'fire' on the day of Pentecost			
• know the arguments surrounding "speaking in tongues" on the day of Pentecost			
• be able to summarise the main points of Peter's speech on the day of Pentecost			
• know how some of these events are relevant for today or for other aspects of human experience			

Endnotes

[1] Bruce, *op cit*, p29

[2] Hewitt, *op cit*, p30

[3] Bruce, *op cit*, p29

[4] Stott, *op cit*, p35

[5] Bruce, *op cit*, p31

[6] Dodd, CH, *The Apostolic Preaching and its Development*, London, 1936, pp46–47

[7] Bruce, *op cit*, p34

[8] Marshall, IH, *The Gospel of Luke*, Exeter: Paternoster Press, 1978, pp124–126

[9] Stott, *op cit*, p35

[10] Bruce, *op cit*, p35

[11] Hewitt, *op cit*, p29

[12] Hewitt, *ibid*, p34

[13] Bruce, *op cit*, p35

[14] *ibid*, p36

[15] Marshall, *op cit*, p59

[16] Packer, *op cit*, p22

[17] Bruce, *op cit*, p36

[18] Hewitt, *op cit*, p29

[19] Bruce, *op cit*, p37

[20] Marshall, *op cit*, p59

[21] Hewitt, *op cit*, p29

[22] Barclay, W, *The Acts of the Apostles*, Edinburgh The Saint Andrew Press, 1953, 1955, p6

[23] Guy, *op cit*, p21

[24] Marshall, *op cit*, p60

[25] Marshall, *op cit*, p62

[26] Bruce, *op cit*, p39

[27] Stott, *op cit*, p35

[28] Bruce, *op cit*, p50

[29] Marshall, *op cit*, p69

[30] Bruce, *op cit*, p51

[31] Hewitt, *op cit*, p41

[32] Barclay, *op cit*, p15

[33] Guy, *op cit*, p24

[34] *ibid*, p24

[35] Bruce, *op cit*, p52

[36] *ibid*, p52

[37] Stott, *op cit*, p67

[38] Hewitt, *op cit*, p45

[39] Stott, *op cit*, p73

[40] Bruce, *op cit*, p61

[41] Stott, *op cit*, p75

[42] *ibid*, p74

[43] Bruce, *op cit*, p62

[44] *ibid*, p63

[45] Marshall, *op cit*, p74

[46] Bruce, *op cit*, p64

[47] Marshall, *op cit*, p75

[48] Bertram, G, *TDNT*, 9, p673

[49] Marshall, *op cit*, p78

[50] Stott, *op cit*, p78

[51] Bruce, *op cit*, p69

[52] *ibid*, p73

[53] Packer, *op cit*, p30

[54] Lewis, *op cit*, p27

[55] Guy, *op cit*, p27

[56] Fernando, *op cit*, p120

[57] *ibid*, p123

[58] Bruce, *op cit*, p73

[59] Drane, *op cit*, p222

[60] Bruce, *op cit*, p74

[61] Marshall, *op cit*, p86

The growth and expansion of the Church

Chapter **3**

PETER AS LEADER, MIRACLE WORKER, EVANGELIST AND DISCIPLINARIAN

Key passages:
1:12–26; 3:1–26; 4:1–5:42; 9:32–43; 10:1–48; 11:1–30; 12:1–20

Introduction

PETER WAS ONE OF Jesus' main apostles. In Matthew 16:17–19, following Peter's declaration that Jesus was the Messiah, we learn how Jesus praised Peter and stated that he was the rock on which Christ's church would be built. Jesus seemed to be saying that Peter was the foundation of his church.[1] Throughout this chapter we will learn of various incidents where Peter can be described as acting in the role of leader, as suggested by Jesus himself. The focus of this section is to consider Peter's role as miracle worker, evangelist and disciplinarian. There may be situations where he acts in more than one role at a time. For example, in the healing of the lame man we observe Peter as both miracle worker and evangelist because following the healing Peter takes the opportunity to preach the gospel.

Examples of the role of Peter as leader, miracle worker, evangelist and disciplinarian					
Leadership	1:12–26 His role in replacing Judas	5:17–28 Reaction to persecution	11:1–18 Report to Jerusalem Church		
Miracles	3:1–10 Healing of the lame man	5:12–16 Many Healed	9:32–43 Aeneas and Dorcas healed	12:1–20 Peter's escape from prison	
Evangelism	3:11–26 Speech in Solomon's Colonnade	4:1–22 Opposition to evangelism	5:29–41 Speech to Sanhedrin	9:35 & 42 Effects of healing of Aeneas and Dorcas	10:1–48 Cornelius conversion
Discipline	4:32–5:11 Ananias and Sapphira	8:4–25 Simon the Sorcerer			

Peter as Leader

His role in replacing Judas (Ch 1:12–26)

Luke explains how the next ten days were spent before Pentecost: continuous praise in the Temple and continuous prayer in the home.[2] It is interesting to note that in addition to the eleven apostles, "the women" are mentioned. Presumably these women are the same referred to as supporting Jesus and the apostles in Luke 8:2–3: Mary Magdalene, Joanna and Susanna. Particular mention is also made of Mary, the mother of Jesus.

Peter takes the lead immediately, making his first speech, which sets the tone for subsequent speeches, namely that the recent events were part of God's plan of salvation of the world through Christ. He begins by claiming that in the case of Judas, it was necessary for the Scriptures to be fulfilled. Lewis[3] comments that we can see the profound insight of Peter in so reading the Scriptures of the Old Testament. With reference to Judas he quotes Psalm 69:25[4] and Psalm 109:8.[5]

"Both the defection of Judas and the necessity of replacing him are viewed here as subjects of Old Testament prophecy."[6] Judas had been one of the twelve with a share in Jesus' ministry; so his share would now have to be delegated to someone else.

These were the qualifications of an apostle:

1. He had to be someone who had been with the twelve disciples from the time of John's baptism up until Jesus was taken up into heaven.
2. He had to be a man who was a witness of Jesus' resurrection.

Two possible candidates were put forward, Joseph Barsabbas and Matthias. Luke highlights the importance of prayer before an important event.[7] Bruce[8] comments that it may well be that there was nothing to choose between the two. Casting lots therefore (which was interestingly a respectable method among the Jews) was a fair way to decide. Marshall[9] points out however, that 'the real choice was left to the Lord, since apostleship is not a humanly ordained office.'

With the lots cast, Matthias was selected as the man to replace Judas.[10] The stage is now set for Pentecost.[11] The apostles have received their commission, witnessed the ascension and replaced the apostle Judas. Only one thing is missing – the Holy Spirit.

What is a miracle?

From Wikipedia, the free encyclopedia:

"The word miracle, comes from the old Latin word miraculum meaning 'something wonderful'. It describes divine intervention by God in the world by which the ordinary course of nature is overruled, suspended, or changed. Although many religious texts and people confirm witnessing or prophesying various events which they refer to as 'miraculous', it is disputed whether miracles are scientifically confirmed. People in different faiths have varying different definitions of the word 'miracle'. In everyday usage, 'miracle' may also refer to any statistically unlikely but beneficial event, (such as the survival of a natural disaster) or even to anything which is regarded as 'wonderful regardless of its likelihood, such as birth.'"

What is an evangelist?

The word evangelist comes from the Greek language and is used in the canonical titles of the four Gospels, written by Matthew, Mark, Luke, and John (also known as the Four Evangelists). An evangelist is a Christian who shares his faith with others and in today's society evangelism is often associated with preaching, missionary work or American religious TV shows.

Peter as miracle worker and evangelist

The Healing of the Lame Man (Ch 3:1–10)

Dillon[12] comments that this first miracle story in Acts has a clear connection with Acts 2:43, which speaks of the various wonders and signs carried out by the disciples. It is noticeable that by acting "in the name of Jesus" Peter is able to perform similar miracles to those performed by Jesus in the gospels. Marshall[12a] regards this as an example of the continuity between the ministry of Jesus and the witness of the church

The story begins with the description of a man being carried by his friends to be set down at the entrance to the Temple. Many scholars suggest that this was probably the Nicanor Gate which separated the court of women and the court of Gentiles.[13] As people would have been on their way to worship, this was an ideal place to beg, particularly as the giving of alms was an exceptionally meritorious act in the Jewish religion (Marshall[13a]).

Luke begins by referring to the apostle John (presumably the son of Zebedee) as accompanying Peter. However, John plays no active role in the story. He remains the silent partner which is similar to the other occasion where his name appears (8:14–17). It has been suggested that Luke referred to two apostles witnessing together for legal purposes.[14] He was following the biblical pattern that two witnesses are needed to establish a matter (Numbers 35:30; Deuteronomy 17:6; 19:15; Matthew 18:15f; 1 Timothy 5:19).

 OTHER ASPECTS OF HUMAN EXPERIENCE

Team Ministry

This incident shows a good example of the team ministry of Peter in his evangelism. He was clearly following the example of Jesus who sent the twelve apostles and seventy disciples "two by two" (Mark 6:7; Luke 10:1). Peter and John later went out as a team again (8:14) and when Peter visited Cornelius, he took six brothers with him (10:23; 11:12).

a) What examples are there in team ministry today?

b) Putting aside the negative attitudes associated with people 'going around doors' to try to convert others, can you see any value in the notion of team ministry?

It is evident that the apostles were continuing to follow Jewish forms of worship. In so doing, they remained part of Jewish national life, providing an ideal opportunity to challenge people with the gospel message. The beggar began to ask for money from the people entering the Temple, including Peter and John. As they passed, Peter spoke to the beggar, building up his hopes that he was about to receive some money. However, Peter's reply of "I have no silver or gold" was quickly followed by the suggestion that he could give him something much more worthwhile. That something was healing in the name of Jesus. The man, who had been lame from birth, became very active, not only walking, but leaping for joy. To emphasise how dramatic this healing was, Luke goes into great detail of both the beggar's condition and his activity after being healed. First, the man's feet and ankles became strong (3:7); then he jumped to his feet and began to walk (3:8); next, he ran into the temple, walking and jumping, as well as praising God (3:8–9). Harnack[15] suggests that "that which the physician observes during the months of the ordinary gradual cure of a lame man is here compressed into a moment". Clearly it seems the power of Jesus has been passed on to his apostles.

Such was the man's appreciation that he immediately joined the apostles as they entered the Temple to praise God for what he had done. He had begged for so many years at the same spot at the entrance to the Temple that he was recognised by many inside. They had no doubt about the reality of his cure.[15a]

 DISCUSSION

Barclay believes that this incident brings us face to face with the question of miracles in the apostolic times compared to today.[16]

Have miracles really stopped today? Barclay suggests that a doctor or surgeon can now do things which in the apostolic times would have been regarded as miracles. In other words, God does not do things for people that they are perfectly capable of doing for themselves.[17]

a) What do you think?

b) Is it possible to be impressed by spectacular events like miracles, without responding to what they stand for: the power and grace of God?

 OTHER ASPECTS OF HUMAN EXPERIENCE

Beggars

The following articles are examples of how to explore 'other aspects of human experience'. They are concerned with a call to ban begging on the streets of Glasgow and Belfast.

Call to ban begging: Glasgow Council leader calls for change in law on begging[18]
News, 5 January 2005, The Journal of the Law Society of Scotland

Charles Gordon, leader of Glasgow Council, is calling for a ban on begging on the streets of Scotland. It is reported in today's Herald that Mr Gordon believes the law should be changed to allow councils to take tougher action against beggars – particularly those who act aggressively.

He wants to follow England's lead where several cities have used antisocial behaviour orders to banish persistent beggars. Last year Aberdeen tried to introduce a by-law to do the same but this looks likely to be overruled by the Scottish Executive. At present it is not a criminal offence to ask strangers for money.

Belfast: Call made over begging children

Action must be taken to protect children who are being used to beg for money in Belfast, the children's commissioner has said. Patricia Lewsley said she had been "shocked" by continuing reports of children begging at the behest of what appears to be organised gangs.

"Reports over the past number of days are extremely disturbing," she said. She said there was "an urgent need for agencies to act together to protect these children".

"When there are reports of babies being held by begging adults and children working selling flowers late at night it is a matter of extreme urgency that action is taken," she said.

Ms Lewsley urged anyone seeing a child being used to beg to contact either social services or the PSNI immediately.

In a statement the police said that using, procuring or encouraging a child to beg was an offence and would urge members of the public to report any incidents of concern.

The PSNI statement added that illegal begging was becoming an increasing problem in the city centre and officers were trying to deal with it. "As police have received reports of people of Eastern European origin involved in begging they have obtained the services of interpreters to assist them in dealing with the problem," the statement said. "Firstly by education – as there are cases when prosecution does not solve the problem. Then secondly by enforcement."[19]

Now answer the following question:

a) With reference to other aspects of human experience, comment on the claim that we have much to learn from Peter's attitude to the lame beggar at the Temple.

Peter's Speech in Solomon's Colonnade (Ch 3:11–26)

The healed man kept close to Peter and John as something like a stampede of people ran towards them, amazed at what had happened. Peter seized the opportunity to explain the gospel to them, directing their attention towards Jesus, the power behind the miracle. The apostles never regarded themselves as the sources of power but only as the channels of power.[20]

Many features of this speech are similar to the speech at Pentecost. However, Tannehill[20a] feels they are complimentary rather than repetitive. "The most remarkable feature of Peter's second sermon, as of his first, is its Christ-centredness. He directed the crowd's attention away from both the healed cripple and the apostles to the Christ".[21] The speech thus gives additional teaching about the person of Jesus, describing him as God's servant, the Holy and Righteous One, the Author of life and the prophet like Moses. It can be summarised as follows:

- The miracle had happened due to the power of God; the same God who had revealed himself to Abraham, Isaac and Jacob. In other words, the God that they, the Jews, worshipped.
- This same God had glorified his *servant* Jesus.
- They, the Jews, had denied Jesus, "*the Holy and Righteous One*", before Pilate and instead they had asked for Barabbas, a murderer to be released. Dillon[22] comments that no distinction is made between participants in Jesus' execution and any others.
- They had killed Jesus, "*the Author of Life*" and God had raised him from the dead.
- It was through faith in Jesus' name that the lame man had been healed. Hewitt[23] comments that in using the 'name' of Jesus, Peter was following a tradition. A name personified the character and nature of a person. To speak Jesus' name was to call upon the power and authority of Jesus to perform the miracle.

Packer comments that the list of titles (see previous italics) given to Jesus impresses upon the crowd the messianic nature of his mission.

Marshall[24] comments that Peter now moves into the specifically evangelistic part of the speech:

- What the Jews and their leaders had done was due to ignorance. Bruce[25] comments that "They did not realise that Jesus of Nazareth was their divinely sent Saviour." Peter was not interested in bringing an accusation against the Jews for their crime. Instead, he hoped they would act on the message of salvation which God had given them. This implies that their action could be forgiven.
- However, in reality, the Jews' action of killing Jesus had in fact fulfilled God's

plan, foretold by the prophets, that Christ should suffer.

- The Jews now have the opportunity to repent and be forgiven of their sins.
- Jesus was the Jews' Messiah and he would return at the parousia, although this would not happen immediately.
- Moses had spoken of a prophet that God would send (Deut 18:15–19; Lev 23:29), a second Moses was the general consensus among the Jews. Peter here assumes that Jesus is this prophet.
- All of the Old Testament prophets, from Samuel onwards, had been concerned about the end times, which were the events that were occurring.
- These promises made by the prophets were made for the Jews.
- Jesus had been raised to bless the audience by turning them away from their sin.

 TASK

Give an account of the healing of the lame man as described in the early chapters of Acts.

- First miracle story in Acts
- Links to Ch 2:43
- Continuity of Jesus' mission
- Background to the lame man
- Significance of where it happened in terms of being witnessed
- Healing in the name of Jesus
- Peter's lack of prejudice against a beggar
- Peter's speech

Opposition to Peter's evangelism (Ch 4:1–22)

This is one of the times when one of the followers is filled with the Holy Spirit (v 8) in order to be equipped for a special challenge. See also 4:31; 7:55, 13:9.

Marshall[26] comments that the witness of the first Christians brought them into conflict with the Jewish leaders. These leaders, from the party of the Sadducees, would have been responsible for public order in the Temple. They tried to keep on friendly terms with the Romans to keep their own wealth and power. They knew that while the Roman government was very tolerant regarding Judaism, it was merciless if there was any public disorder.[27]

As Sadducees, they would reject the belief in the resurrection. So they not only saw the apostles "as agitators but as heretics".[28] They arrested Peter and John and brought them before the Sanhedrin to find out what they were doing and put them in prison for the night.

The Sanhedrin met the following day and the apostles were asked by what power or by what name had they done these things. Peter, and not John, responded and Dillon[29] argues that his first speech before the Sanhedrin (like the second in 5:29–32) is an apologia rather than a sermon. Peter boldly seizes on the moment to defend the gospel by explaining the power behind the miracle. Barclay[30] notes that by being so confident he was taking his life in his hands because this was the same court that had condemned Jesus to death.

It is significant that Peter was inspired by the Holy Spirit as he addressed the council. Throughout the book of Acts the role of the Holy Spirit is referred to many times. As this topic will be looked at in more depth later it would be useful for you to take note of the situations when the Holy Spirit is mentioned.

Peter's speech before the Sanhedrin

- Peter is quick to point out that the reason they are gathered is due to a good deed being carried out to someone in need.

- He boldly proclaims that the miracle is to be credited to the power of the name of Jesus Christ of Nazareth.

- The blame for Jesus' death is again put on the Jews and it is emphasised that God raised him from the dead.

- Peter then uses a metaphor by quoting the language of Psalm 118:22 to make his point. Jesus is the *"stone which was rejected"* by the Jews, *"you builders"*. But Jesus has become *"the head of the corner"* or cornerstone/capstone. Guy[31] explains that when men build a house they place on one side a stone which they don't need. Later, however, they find that this is the stone necessary for a cornerstone at the junction of two walls.

- It was Jesus then who saved the lame man and through Jesus they also could be saved.

Dillon[32] comments that "the little speech" gives a precise answer to the question put by the interrogators (v 7). The members of the Sanhedrin were amazed because the apostles were 'unschooled', meaning that they were not well-read men; they didn't speak with big words but rather in a simple way.[33] The speech put the Sanhedrin in a dilemma (v 16) and they were content to let Peter and John go with a warning, to which Peter replied that they would proclaim their faith regardless of threats.[34]

TASKS

a) Give an account of the events leading up to Peter's speech before the Sanhedrin, the speech itself and the aftermath.

- Summary of healing of lame man; the speech:
- Good deed carried out in name of Jesus
- Jesus' death blamed on Jews
- They could be saved
- Aftermath: reaction of Sanhedrin; let go with a warning

b) Comment on claim that Peter's words can be described as a defence speech

- Answers their question on authority
- Defends the gospel through an account of Jesus' death

Peter as disciplinarian

Ananias and Sapphira (Ch 4:32–5:11)

This story has been described as both a "chilling tale"[35] and "a sordid episode".[36] It might well have been left out of the book of Acts because it reveals that even in the early church there were imperfect Christians.[37] By including the account Luke shows us how honest he was in his writing, which supports the historical accuracy of Acts discussed in Chapter 1 of this book.

Luke describes how a married couple tried to deceive the apostles by claiming to have made a much greater financial sacrifice for the church than they actually had. Ananias and Sapphira sold property and gave part of the proceeds to a voluntary common fund established by the apostles.[38] In itself this action of only giving part of the money to the church was not wrong. However, they pretended to have given all the money from the sale to the apostles. Perhaps before the sale Ananias and Sapphira had entered into some kind of contract to give the church the total amount raised.[39] Their sin was one of deception. It was not that they withheld part of their property but that they lied about it and sought credit for having given their all.[40]

Perhaps they wanted to look good in front of the other believers. Bruce[41] suggests they did it to gain a reputation for being more generous than they actually were. Another suggestion is that Ananias and Sapphira might have noticed how well thought of Barnabas was when he sold his property for the church. They may even have been jealous of his popularity.[42]

69

Peter seems to be able to read minds as he knows he is being lied to. Perhaps he had "the power of spiritual insight".[43] He is clear in stating that the money was not the issue (v 4); the lie was (v 5). Ananias immediately dropped dead which many scholars regard as divine judgment for his sin.[44] However, it is important to note that there is no reference to any such death sentence in Peter's words. Peter had only intended to rebuke Ananias for his awful sin, and hope for repentance. He was probably as shocked as anyone that Ananias dropped dead before his eyes. Could it have been the result of a heart attack due to the shock of being exposed as a liar? The lie was to the Holy Spirit himself.[45] Dunn[46] comments that "to offend against the Spirit of this community was for the superstitious a fearful and terrifying thing".

In 5:11 the word "church" is used for the first time in the Book of Acts to describe the community of believers.

Ananias was buried immediately. Bruce[47] points out that burial in that climate quickly followed death. Three hours later Sapphira is presented as being oblivious to what has happened. Peter's action may be regarded as being insensitive for instead of telling her of the death of her husband, he tackles her about her deception. Sapphira is given the chance to tell the truth (v 8), although some scholars see this as merely encouraging her to implicate herself in the lie. Her only hope was to admit the truth of the matter. When she failed to do so, it was plain that she would suffer the fate of her husband. She, too, collapses to the ground and dies. While this might seem too much of a coincidence for some, it must be remembered that she suffered a double shock – that of being found out and of being told of her husband's death. Marshall[48] comments that "this double punishment deeply affected both the Christians and everybody who heard of it." Fernando[48a] comments that those who witnessed their deaths must have been surprised to see Peter, not a rich man, rebuking the rich giver of a large contribution.

The hypocrisy of Ananias and Sapphira was not allowed to spread, for God's judgement fell on them.[49] Many are shocked by the severity of God's judgement resulting in their deaths and have questioned Peter's ethics in not giving them an opportunity for repentance and in not telling Sapphira of her husband's death. Browne points out that we cannot imagine Christ acting towards sinners as Peter is here represented as doing.[50] Jesus' reaction to Judas, whose sin was a thousand times worse, is certainly not on this level. However, it should be taken into account that he was not handing out a curse of death to either Ananias or Sapphira. They died because God, not Peter, wanted it to happen. Paul's letter to Hebrews tells us that while God is infinite love and has tremendous patience, there is also a judgment of God – and it is a fearful thing to fall into the hands of God. Knox[51] adds that some even hope that the story is fictitious. If you check 'Google' you will find a number of interesting discussions on this issue.

TASKS

a) Give an account of the story of Ananias and Sapphira.

- Common fund
- Deception of Ananias and Sapphira
- The reason for their sin
- Peter's spiritual insight
- Death of the couple and surrounding discussion
- The significance of Luke including this story in his book

b) Comment on the claim that God's judgement on Ananias and Sapphira was too severe.

- Christ's message of forgiveness
- Peter's neglect in not telling Sapphira in a sensitive manner that her husband was dead
- Discussion concerning whether or not this is a true story

 OTHER ASPECTS OF HUMAN EXPERIENCE

Discipline

Even in the early and enthusiastic days there was a combination of good and bad in the Church. Stott[51a] believes that the incident teaches the necessity of church discipline, commenting that the church has tended to alternate in this area "between extreme severity (disciplining members for the most trivial offences) and extreme laxity (exercising no discipline at all, even for the most serious offences)."

Research some answers to the following questions:

a) How did the church deal with sin then?

b) How does it deal with sin now?

Penance

Another aspect of human experience you could research is that of the development of penance in the early church (See Banks, The Early Church, pp122–136).

a) What were the advantages and disadvantages of such a system?

b) How is penance carried out in the Catholic Church today?

c) Research the term to 'fence the table' in the Presbyterian Church. What does this mean regarding those who have sinned?

Money

Something that arises from the deceit of Ananias and Sapphira is the use of church funds. In the church today scandals over how funds are misused are common. Christian workers may be tempted in the following ways:

- To receive financial help by pretending to need more money than they actually do
- Accepting more funds than are actually needed for a project
- Letting funds be used for something other than the money was given for
- Allowing themselves unnecessary expenses, eg expensive lunches
- Avoiding tax

Avoiding such temptations can be helped by being accountable to someone about the use of money. This means keeping someone else informed about all financial dealings. If a Christian does give into the temptation, being accountable to someone can help them to make a determined effort to avoid similar temptation in the future.

Read 1 Cor.5:5 and Matt. 18:15–17

a) What advice do Jesus and Paul give concerning someone who sins?

b) How relevant is this advice for Christians today?

Peter as Miracle Worker

Many Healed (Ch 5: 12–16)

Luke gives another summary, presenting the church as having a powerful healing ministry.[52] It seems the unbelieving Jews left the Christians alone as they met together in Solomon's Colonnade. Bruce[53] suggests that the death of Ananias and Sapphira had scared off all but the totally committed Christians. They realised that "the awesome power of the Spirit that judges also demands commitment and responsibility."[54] Despite some being deterred, many became Christians and others looked for healing of their sickness from Peter. Packer comments that the power of the Spirit is again apparent, working through Peter as the leader.[55] His reputation for healing was so exceptional that people believed even his shadow could heal them. This notion that shadows had magical powers was a common belief at that time.[56] Fernando[57] comments that this is the closest we have in the Bible to a modern-day healing campaign.

Peter as Leader and Evangelist

Reaction to Persecution (Ch 5: 17–42)

Motivated by jealousy, the Sadducees arrest the apostles and throw them into prison. Fernando[58] comments that this is not surprising given the spectacular ministry of the apostles. No reason is given for the arrest except disobedience of an earlier command not to preach.[59] However, during the night the apostles escape with the help of an angel of the Lord. Neil[60] speculates that this was "a sympathetic warder" who came later to be seen as "an angel in disguise". As God's spokesman, the angel tells the apostles to go and preach in the Temple.

Meanwhile the council's officers were sent to the prison where they realised the prisoners had gone, even though all the doors were secure. Marshall[61] comments that the guards must have been unconscious during the escape and the doors were re-locked. Therefore they did not realise that anyone had escaped until they checked inside. It is no wonder the council was confused about what was going on. It is at this moment that the news comes of the apostles preaching in the Temple area.

A peaceful arrest followed. Fernando[62] comments that it is ironic that those who probably had wanted to stone the apostles for blasphemy were now afraid that they themselves would be stoned by the people. The apostles were reminded by the High Priest that they were already forbidden to preach about Jesus. However, they had ignored him. Not only that but they had tried to put the blame of Jesus' death on the Jewish authorities. The role of Peter as a strong and fearless leader is evident in his direct reply to the council (v 29). He was the spokesman for the group with the others in some way indicating their agreement.[63] The response is not really a defence speech as you might expect. Rather Peter points out that God's commands have priority over human commands. He then steps into his evangelist's shoes as he takes the opportunity to briefly preach the gospel. He agrees that yes, the Jews had killed Jesus, describing him as "prince and saviour". For them to have done this was "to act against the God whom they claimed to worship".[64] This Jesus who was crucified was the one that God had exalted to sit at his right hand. He was the Saviour through whom the Jews would have the chance to repent and receive forgiveness.

The Sadducees were furious and even thought about having the apostles put to death. However, just in time, Gamaliel, a leading Pharisee "rose with quiet dignity"[65] and intervened with a speech, which is renowned "for its sound sense and friendliness".[66] He warned against such extreme action and advised the court to go into closed session to discuss the matter. Fernando[67] suggests that the apostles' miracles and escape from prison presumably made him suspect that God might indeed be blessing this new movement.

Gamaliel has been described as "a respected teacher and a firm upholder of the law".[68] He was a tutor of Paul[69] (Ch 22:3) and as a Pharisee, would have exhibited a more tolerant spirit than the rival party of the Sadducees.[70] Gamaliel used reason in his advice to the Sanhedrin. Using two examples,[71] he argued that movements which were human in origin would die out themselves so they should waste no time on it. Movements, however, which were inspired by God needed to be approached with caution as there is a danger of opposing God. In any case, often with mass movements once the leader was dead the movement soon lost momentum. As Jesus was dead they should wait to see what happened.

Gamaliel's words managed to calm down the Sadducees. When the apostles were brought back in they were again warned not to speak in the name of Jesus and were released following a beating. Ironically this punishment filled them with joy. Perhaps they felt that they had been regarded by God as worthy to take their share of suffering for the sake of the gospel.[72]

"We should not be too ready to credit Gamaliel with having uttered an invariable principle".[73] In other words, should we always follow the rule that if a religious group of people succeeds in the long run, then the group must be from God? What do you think?

 OTHER ASPECTS OF HUMAN EXPERIENCE

Persecution

These first two waves of persecution were unfortunately only the beginning for the Christian Church. In the first three centuries in particular the church suffered much persecution in the Roman Empire.

The following are brief statements about what happened. Find out more using Banks' book The Early Church (Colourpoint, 2003):

- Nero: Christians were imprisoned and executed. Peter and Paul were probably martyrs
- Domitian: demanded Christians worship him. Those who refused were oppressed
- Marcus Aurelius: allowed outbreaks of violence to take place against Christians
- Decius: thousands died
- Diocletian: issued four edicts to try to destroy Christianity

In making connections with these other aspects of human experience it would be helpful to explore the 'attitude' of the Christians to persecution and compare to that of the apostles in Acts. For example, compare the attitude of Ignatius of Antioch to martyrdom with that of the apostles following their beating in Acts 5:40–42.

Peter as Evangelist and Miracle Worker (Ch 9:32–43)

Here we see Peter "engaged in an itinerant ministry".[74] This simply means he was not settled in one place in the way that a priest or minister might be today, but that he travelled around the country. Marshall comments that "his activity, however, is not confined to teaching the Christians, but also includes evangelism".[75] This means he was concerned with attracting new converts to the Christian faith. Miracles were also a feature of his ministry, which helped to arouse the interest of unbelievers.

One such incident is the healing of Aeneas. He had been confined to bed for eight years. Peter's ability to heal in the name of Jesus is again evident here when he announces "Jesus Christ heals you" and tells him to get up out of his bed. Many of the local community became Christians when they saw the healed man, which shows that this event was not just important as a healing but also as a tool for evangelism.

Twelve miles away in Joppa a woman called Tabitha, who was known for her good works, fell ill and died. However, her friends did not bury her body but washed it and laid it out on a bed in an upper room. This may have been because they hoped she would be raised from the dead.[76] The Christians sent for Peter to come immediately.

Peter was taken to see Tabitha in the house which was by now full of mourners. His actions are reminiscent of Jesus' (Mk 5:40) in that he sent everyone out of the room and then prayed. When Peter spoke to her by name and told her to get up she did so. Marshall[77] comments that this miracle came about purely by prayer and "the word of command". As with the previous healing, this too led to many conversions.

Peter as Leader and Evangelist: Breaking with Jewish Traditions

The Conversion of Cornelius (Chs 10: 1–11:18)

It is at this stage that events in the early church turn a corner which eventually leads to the entry of Gentiles into the church. As Marshall[78] comments "The church did not simply stumble upon the idea of evangelizing Gentiles; it did so in accordance with God's deliberate purpose."

The key event is the conversion of Cornelius, a Roman centurion, the first Gentile to become a believer. Marshall[79] comments that "the sheer length of this story and the way in which it is told twice over indicate the very great importance which Luke attaches to it in the context of Acts as a whole". The story may have been of particular interest to Theophilus. Its length adds to the argument that Luke was writing to try to convince Theophilus of the validity of the Christian faith.

To simplify such a long story it is probably best to divide it up into the following four sections:

- 10:1–8:   Cornelius' vision
- 10:9–23a: Peter's vision
- 10:23b–48: Peter's speech and results
- 11:1–18:   Effects of the conversion of Cornelius and his family

Ch 10:1–8 Cornelius' vision

Caesarea was a Roman government centre for the administration of Judea. A centurion (soldier) named Cornelius lived there with his family. He belonged to a body of troops known as the Italian Regiment, so called because they had been recruited in Italy. Hewitt[80] comments that "the captain of such a regiment would be a man of importance and some standing". More important than his career is Cornelius' religious outlook. Like many other Romans he had become interested in local religions. However, he was not a Jew or even a proselyte. Instead he had attached himself to the group called 'God-fearers'. The strength of his respect for the Jewish faith is evident from his actions (v 2, 4).

At around 3 pm Cornelius had a vision. This was the hour of prayer in Jerusalem so Cornelius was probably praying. In the vision an angel spoke to Cornelius, addressing him by name. Naturally he was terrified, but the angel assured him that his prayers and gifts to the poor had been acknowledged by God. He was then told to send to Joppa for a man called Simon (Peter's Jewish name). As would be expected of a man with such great faith, he responded immediately by sending a group of three messengers to find Peter.

Ch 10: 9–23a Peter's vision

In Joppa Peter had gone up on the roof at noon to pray in private. Peter was hungry and his thoughts may have been drifting from his prayers.[81] He fell into a trance and had a strange vision of a sheet containing living creatures. Peter then heard a voice telling him to kill and eat. But the sheet carried animals that would have been considered unclean in the Jewish religion. Peter protested strongly that he had never eaten anything unclean. However, the voice told him that if God had cleansed something people should no longer consider it unclean. Stott[82] comments that although the vision was challenging the basic distinction between clean and unclean foods, which Peter had been brought up to make, the Spirit was relating this to the distinction between clean and unclean people, and telling Peter to stop making it. After the vision was repeated twice the sheet disappeared.

As Peter was coming to terms with what had happened Cornelius' messengers arrived at the door to find him. What seems to be an inward prompting by the Holy Spirit led Peter to go down to these messengers and introduce himself. They repeated their message in such a way as to impress him about Cornelius' faith. As it was late Peter invited them to spend the night.

Ch 10:23b–48 Peter's speech and results
The next day Peter and a number of Christians set off for Caesarea. Cornelius and his family were waiting for them and when he first saw Peter he knelt before him as a sign of reverence. Peter believed that such respect should only be given to God

and told him to get up. Peter and Cornelius went into the house "as equals".[83] Peter announced to those gathered of his new willingness to meet with Gentiles (v 28) and asked why he had been called there.

Cornelius' reply (v 30–33) is a repeat of the events that occurred the previous day. There are some differences between this account and that of verses 1–8 but Marshall[84] argues that this is more to do with the fact that New Testament writers were not concerned to give a word-for-word account of conversations and speeches. Cornelius thanked Peter for coming and invited him to speak to those gathered.

Peter's speech is significant for the spread of the gospel:

- He explains how he has realised that "there is no racial barrier to Christian salvation".[85] In other words, God doesn't have favourites and will accept anyone who worships him regardless of their race or background. Peter continues by preaching the gospel.
- Peter adds some extra material about Jesus' ministry, perhaps because he was speaking to non-Jews.
- The death of Jesus at the hands of the Jews is briefly mentioned, but it is quite unlike his addresses to the Jews themselves.
- Jesus was raised from the dead on the third day.
- God allowed him to be seen by a select group of people.
- Jesus commanded his apostles to preach to the people, ie the Jews.
- Finally Peter proclaims that everyone who believes in Jesus can receive forgiveness.

Before Peter had a chance to finish his speech, the Holy Spirit came upon all those who were listening. This implies that they all had faith and that God had accepted them – the proof being the gift of the Holy Spirit.

There was no doubt that these Gentiles had received the gift of the Holy Spirit – the same gift that had been given to the apostles on the Day of Pentecost. Marshall[86] comments that their receiving of the gift of the Spirit on this occasion stressed the reality of the conversion of the Gentiles "over against all possible doubt". The next step for these new Christians was baptism, the outward sign of acceptance into the church. Peter stressed the need for them to be baptised and no one objected.

Important note!

The story does not suggest that Cornelius and his family were circumcised. In fact Ch 11:3 rules circumcision out. It can be concluded that God himself was saying that circumcision was not necessary to becoming a Christian. Hewitt comments that the church was not to be a sect within the narrow limits of the Jewish race, but a world-wide fellowship of believers.

Ch 11:1–18 Effects of the conversion of Cornelius and his family

This final section describes the effects of the conversion of Cornelius and his family. "The apostles and the brothers throughout Judea" refers to the Jewish Christians and it is their reaction to the events concerning the conversion of these Gentiles that is now all-important for the spread of the gospel. Not surprisingly, it was the circumcision party who questioned Peter about what had happened. These Christians would have originally been strict Jews who had strongly upheld Jewish laws and traditions. Guy[87] argues that the objection seems to have been that Peter stayed with Gentiles and ate with them rather than that he had preached to them and baptised them (v 3). Bound by Jewish food laws, they would have believed it wrong to eat with Gentiles unless the Gentiles were circumcised and also kept the food laws.

Peter explained the whole story to them, beginning with his own experience of the vision of the sheet. He had come to realise that the sheet was the church, which would contain all races and classes without any distinction at all.[88] Peter's finishing comments (v 16–17) stress that the Gentiles had the same experience as those in the upper room on the day of Pentecost. If they had been baptised with the Holy Spirit then they should also receive water baptism. His argument convinced those listening. In fact the audience praised God that he had allowed the Gentiles the opportunity to be saved.

 TASK

Find out what is meant by the following statements:

- As well as dealing with the issue of circumcision, these events had implications for the keeping of Jewish Laws, such as those concerning clean and unclean food. "But this was an earth-shattering idea for Jews, and was not to be accepted without much heart-searching controversy."[89]
- "The objectors eventually agreed on the admission of these Gentiles (v 18) but the question of the terms on which they were to be recognised was not settled and was to cause trouble later on."[90]
- The main point of Acts 10 is not as much the conversion of Cornelius as the conversion of Peter! Do you agree or disagree?

OTHER ASPECTS OF HUMAN EXPERIENCE

The unity of the church

Since God does not make distinctions, Christians today should not either. However, in the history of the church the sin of discrimination has crept in. Some examples are:

- Social snobbery
- Racism
- Nationalism
- Tribalism in Africa (see example)
- Sexism against women

Choose one of these to explore and apply the lessons from the story of Peter and Cornelius to what the church can learn today.

 TASK

Tribalism in modern African Churches

Fransuer Makula is a teacher of Religion in Belfast. He is originally from Kenya. He has provided the following account:

"There are many different tribes in Africa. Every tribe has positive and negative features. For example, I grew up in Kenya and my tribe, which the is Kamba tribe, was, and still is, renowned for long distance trading on foot. This is well documented by a man called Chief Kivoi, who is famed as being the key long distance traveller and an ancestor in the tribe. On the other hand my tribe, especially the people from the Kitui countryside, is well-known for witchcraft, which is a negative feature.

Another tribe, the Luo, is described as having very strong men. However they are also reputed to be arrogant and violent. A third tribe, the Kikuyu, has always been regarded as being made up of good businessmen and conversely as thieves.

These distinctions are based on African traditional life. With the introduction of Christianity and rural-urban migration, distinctions between tribes should not count. However, I have come across many Christian young people whose wedding plans have been disrupted because the couple came from two tribes who despise each other. In cases where the marriage does go ahead, the couple faces problems if one of the partners dies because at times the family of the surviving spouse and the family of the deceased do not agree on funeral arrangements due to tribal distinctions that discriminate against the other spouse's tribe.

Using the internet, find out how African Christians face difficulties due to the existence of different tribes.

79

 TASKS

a) Give an account of the Peter-Cornelius story.
- Cornelius' call for Peter
- Peter's vision
- Peter at Cornelius' house
- Peter's explanation

b) Comment on the claim that 'God does not have favourites'. Justify your answer.
- Luke's universalism
- Ongoing activity of the Holy Spirit in accepting all sorts of people
- Peter's steep learning curve
- Gospel preached to all

c) With reference to other aspects of human experience, comment on the claim that this story is not only of historical interest but also has long-lasting significance for the Christian church.
- Lessons to be learned about accepting all into the Christian church, regardless of background
- Examples of religious and racial prejudice throughout churches in the world, eg Northern Ireland, Africa
- Cultural prejudice within some Christian communities

The miracle of Peter's escape from prison (Ch 12:1–19)

Herod tried to please the Jews by murdering James, the son of Zebedee and trying to kill Peter. It is possible that he was plotting with the Sanhedrin who were also in strong opposition to the church. However, as we shall see his plan was stopped by "the direct intervention of God."[91]

Peter was arrested just after the Passover. He was well guarded with four groups of soldiers working in shifts. The Christians, however, strong in their faith, continued to pray for his release.

The night before Herod's planned execution Peter was asleep, handcuffed between two guards, and the door was also guarded by soldiers. However, during the night an angel of the Lord entered the prison and a light shone in the cell. The fact that Peter was asleep shows that he was not too worried about the events that lay ahead. The angel had to wake him up to tell him to get ready to leave the prison. Peter, not sure whether he was dreaming or not, followed the angel past the guards and out the three doors of the prison. Presumably the guards were asleep. Immediately after, the angel disappeared and Peter realised he was free. Marshall[92] believes this story to be "miraculous at every point".

Peter moved quickly to tell his friends what had happened. He went to the home of Mary, the mother of John Mark where he knew he would find them. Although late, many were gathered in prayer and when Peter knocked the door a servant girl was sent to see who it was. She was so excited when she realised that it was Peter that she ran back into the house to tell the others without letting Peter in. They thought she was mad and when Peter eventually did get in he explained how the miracle had happened and asked them to inform James and the rest of the believers. Peter then left and went to a secret hiding place.

 TASK

Explore the view that the early chapters of Acts are concerned with the opposition which surrounds the spread of the gospel. Justify your answer.
- Accusation of drunkenness on Day of Pentecost (2:13)
- Arrest (4:1–22)
- Arrest (5:17–28)

Chapter 12:24 shows us the tremendous spread of the gospel at this point, which is not hindered by the imprisonment or death of the apostles.

The last we hear of Peter in Acts is in Ch 15 which is an account of the 'Council of Jerusalem'. This will be studied at A2 level.

 TASKS

Overview questions on the role of Peter in Acts

a) Explore the claim that Peter's activity caused great excitement in Jerusalem. Justify your answer.

b) Describe the evangelising activity of Peter as found in Acts.
- The miracles of Peter
- Speeches
- Cornelius incident

c) Give an account of one of Peter's speeches as recorded in Acts.
- Solomon's Colonnade
- First speech before Sanhedrin

d) Describe the main features of Peter's speeches as presented in the early chapters of Acts, commenting on his understanding of the Person of Christ.

- Apostolic kerygma: the dawn of the Messianic age, the death and resurrection of Jesus, call to repentance, baptism and gift of the Holy Spirit

e) Explore the view that Luke portrays Peter as a strong leader. Justify your answer.

- This question is an opportunity to consider the role of Peter as leader, miracle worker, evangelist and disciplinarian, and to highlight Peter's strengths using different examples.

f) Explore the statement that during the years covered by the early chapters of Acts, Peter fulfils the prophecy that he will be the 'Rock' on which the church will be built.

- Refer to Matt 16:13–20
- Evaluate the role of Peter in light of Jesus' statement.
- Would the church have survived without Peter?
- Were others just as significant?

 # OTHER ASPECTS OF HUMAN EXPERIENCE

How necessary is the role of an important leader?

According to the Roman Catholic Church Peter went on to found the church at Rome and became the bishop of Rome or the first 'Pope'. This means that all succeeding bishops of Rome automatically became the leader and focus of the Christian Church.

Other denominations, while not having a leader who is deemed to be infallible (regarding pronouncements on matters of faith or morals), also have a type of leader to represent the people. For example, the Presbyterian Church has a moderator who is elected once a year.

Beyond the church, schools have principals, businesses have managers etc. Once in these positions these people are given respect, whether they deserve it or not. Most of the time leaders of various organisations are successful due to hard work, skill and determination. However, sometimes they fail and the organisation falls apart.

See if you can find examples of successful leadership and of failed leadership, religious or secular.

Use the examples to illustrate the importance of strong leadership in the church, linking your response to the leadership of Peter in the early church.

PHILIP AND STEPHEN

Up until now the church has been made up only of Jewish Christians and has been limited to Jerusalem. With the introduction of Stephen and Philip onto the scene Luke turns a page in the book of Acts. Through the next few chapters he describes how the foundations of the Gentile mission are laid by them.

The Choosing of the Seven (Ch 6:1–7)

As the church in Jerusalem grew to include Greek-speaking Jews (Hellenists) a practical issue arose that needed to be sorted out as soon as possible. Following the example of Jewish society, the care of poor widows was an important aspect of church life. The Greek-speaking Christians however, felt hard done by, in that their widows were not receiving the same help as the Judeans (Hebrews). They were particularly needy as unlike the native Judean widows, they did not have relatives to care for them.[93] Barclay[94] suggests there was a deeper problem in that the Hebrews looked down upon the Hellenists.

Hebrews and Hellenists

The name 'Hebrew' refers to Jews. It describes someone who is totally Jewish in all aspects of life; someone who observed the Law of Moses and lived according to Jewish traditions.

The 'Hellenists' were Jews who came out of the Dispersion. They were much more accepting of Greek ideas. Hellenists may not have totally observed ceremonial law and there may have been cultural differences between them and the Hebrews.

The Hebrew Christians probably refused to have full table fellowship with the Hellenists. A result may have been the inequality in the distribution of food to the poor Hellenist widows. This may have caused more division in the fellowship.

Up until now the administration of aid had been part of the responsibility of the twelve apostles but they were overworked and such a practical issue was taking them away from their main job of evangelising. Therefore, seven men were appointed to take charge of the distribution of food. Even with what some might consider being low order responsibilities, spiritual qualifications were vital (v 3). They were to possess wisdom and the Holy Spirit. Stott[95] emphasises that "there is no hint whatever that the apostles regarded social work as inferior to pastoral work, or beneath their dignity."

The appointment of the seven was a huge step forward in terms of church organisation which was to develop significantly in the first three centuries.

Marshall[96] believes that the seven may have been chosen from the Greek-speaking part of the church that had raised the original complaint. The seven names were all Greek. However, Stott[97] sees this as speculative, agreeing with Lenski[98] that "some of both classes of Jews were elected". Some scholars would even go as far as to say that the seven were appointed as leaders of the Greek-speaking part of the church, separate to the rest of the church Two of the seven, Stephen and Philip, emerge as having the same evangelistic ability as the Twelve. Marshall[99] points out that Stephen is given a fuller description as a man full of faith and the Holy Spirit, which prepares us for the next section. The seven received the laying on of hands by the apostles, which indicates that authority has been passed onto them.

The effect of the appointment of the seven was positive as there was an increase in the preaching of the gospel and subsequently more converts.

 ## OTHER ASPECTS OF HUMAN EXPERIENCE

Church Issues

1. It seems the Twelve realised their own limitations in that they recognised that the task of teaching, and administering poor relief was too great for them. They were probably not able to do either task properly.
   Discuss how the church today could learn from their attitude.

2. God calls different people to different roles in the church. Some are called to preach while others are called to do pastoral or social work. Neither work is superior to the other.
   Do you agree or disagree?

3. Clearly the early church had problems of disunity. A good example to follow is how they dealt with such problems immediately.
   Discuss the sort of problems the church faces today — where it would be wise to follow the example of the early Christians.

4. The early church did not divide into two separate churches – one for the Hellenists and one for the Hebrews. Rather they made sure the Hellenists were cared for.
   Discuss the difficulties of having one Christian Church today.

Stephen Seized (Ch 6:8–15)

Stephen is described as being full of God's grace and power, which reminds us of the apostles (Ch 4:33). His ability to preach and heal was obviously due to being filled with the Holy Spirit. However, his ministry provoked opposition from members of various synagogues. The Freedmen were Jews who had been taken prisoner by the Romans and later given their freedom. They argued with Stephen but were unable to get the better of him. So they persuaded some people to publicly complain that they had heard Stephen blaspheme against Moses and God. Stott describes this as "a smear campaign against him".[100] The people were furious and along with the religious leaders they arrested Stephen and brought him before the Sanhedrin. False witnesses were set up to testify against Stephen, saying that he was always attacking the Temple and the law. In particular they claimed that he said Jesus would destroy the Temple and change the customs handed down by Moses.

Customs handed down by Moses were the oral traditions which interpreted the Law of Moses. An attack on the oral law would have been considered as just as serious as an attack on the whole law.

What were the accusations against Stephen?

The formal charges against Stephen were twofold:

1. Speaking against "this holy place" (6:13) seems to be summed up by "Jesus will destroy this holy place".
2. Speaking against "the Law" (6:13) is equivalent to "altering the customs which Moses handed down to us" (6:14).

When the Sanhedrin looked at Stephen for a response they realised that he seemed to have the face of an angel. Marshall[101] explains that this describes someone who is close to God and reflects some of his glory as a result of being in his presence. Stott[102] explains that the same thing happened to Moses' face when he came down from Mount Sinai with the law (Ex 34:29ff): "Was it not God's deliberate purpose to give the same radiant face to Stephen when he was accused of opposing the law as he had given Moses when he received the law? In this way God was showing that both Moses' ministry of the law and Stephen's interpretation of it had his approval."

Stephen's Speech to the Sanhedrin (Ch 7:1–53)

Stephen's speech is the longest speech in Acts. It is not a defence in the sense of an explanation or apology calculated to win an acquittal.[103] Rather it is mainly a recital of Old Testament history and can be described as a tedious read, with many seemingly irrelevant points. As good debaters do, Stephen avoided the question and did not directly address the charge that he had blasphemed against Moses and God.

Neil,[104] however, calls it "a subtle and skilful proclamation of the gospel". The detail of Israel's history that Stephen recited was completely familiar to his listeners. His approach would not have been regarded as unusual because it was common practice among Jewish rabbis to recite elements of the history of Israel. Lenski[105] explains that through telling the story of the Old Testament Stephen "first refutes the charge that he blasphemed God; secondly, he blasphemed Moses and the law; thirdly, that he blasphemed the Temple. In fact, he proves that he does the very opposite."

Before discussing the purpose of the speech it is worth taking a detailed look at its content. Stephen retells the Old Testament story "in such a way as to draw lessons from it which they had never learned or even noticed".[106]

Overview of Speech:

Throughout history God sent deliverers to his people but the Jews rejected them and broke God's law.	(v 2–8) The Call of Abraham and promises made to him (v 9–16) Joseph, rejected by his brothers but rescued by God (v 25, 39–43) Moses, sent to deliver his own people from Egypt but rejected by them	Stephen had not spoken against the law. The truth is that in the past the Jews themselves had rejected Moses, worshipped idols, killed prophets and failed to keep the law.
The Jews had the tabernacle in the desert and then Solomon's Temple.	They committed idolatry (v 39–43) and came to believe that God actually lived in the Temple (44–50).	While the Jews had the tabernacle and the Temple, God was not restricted to them but was everywhere.

Abraham: v 2–8

Stephen responded immediately to the invitation from the High Priest to speak. His speech lacks an introduction as he launches straight into an account of how God called Abraham to be the father of the nation. It is significant that he mentions how God appeared to Abraham in Mesopotamia,[107] outside the land of the Jews.

Stephen's main focus is God (7:2) and God's actions dominate this section. God appears (7:3), speaks (7:3, 6), moves (7:4), gives an inheritance (7:5), promises (7:5), judges (7:7), gives a covenant (7:8). Luke does not even mention Abraham's faith. Abraham merely goes and dwells (7:4), and circumcises (7:8). The focus is on God's promise and the way it will be fulfilled in a time beyond Abraham.[108]

Abraham only leaves his home because he is promised a land of his own (7:3). Although he possessed none of it, the same land was promised to his descendants (7:5). Abraham went on to settle in Haran but his destination was "this land where you are now living" (7:4). God's promise that Abraham's descendants would live in the promised land was fulfilled. The point is that long before there was a holy place, there was a holy people, to whom God had pledged himself.[109]

Stephen next describes the giving of the covenant of circumcision to Abraham.

Abraham was told that before his descendants received the promised land they would be slaves in a foreign land for 400 years. The covenant was a symbol of the promise given to them.

Joseph: v 9–16

In this section Stephen begins to show the pattern of opposition to God's leaders. Here Stephen is showing how the prophecy in v 6 has been fulfilled. Stephen showed Joseph to be a man of faith. Joseph's brothers were jealous of his dreams which showed his future role (Gen 37:5–11). Stephen relates how they rejected Joseph (which corresponds to the attitude of the current leaders towards Jesus) and sold him as a slave but God was with him and saved him from any trouble, even enabling him to become ruler over Egypt. Then Joseph's family came to Egypt because of the famine, hoping to buy corn. Once introduced to Pharaoh they became acquainted with him and were invited to settle in Egypt, where they ended their days.

In the previous section concerning Abraham, Stephen had shown God acting outside of the Holy Land, in Haran. Now he points out that God was with Joseph and his brothers in Egypt, again outside the Promised Land.

When Joseph's family died they were buried in Abraham's tomb. Stephen may have deliberately singled out the fact that Shechem was the burial place because it was located in despised Samaritan territory. His audience held their land in great esteem. If the respected patriarchs of Israel had been buried in Shechem (and proper burial was important to Jews), this implies again that God can work anywhere.

A type of Jesus can be seen in the story of Joseph:

- Joseph was rejected by his brothers, just as Jesus was rejected by his own people (John 1:11).
- Joseph was thrown into a pit but God rescues him out of it. Jesus was buried in a tomb and rose from the dead.
- Though Joseph was rejected by his own, strangers received him. Jesus was accepted by the Gentiles.
- Finally, Joseph was raised up to be the ruler of Egypt, just as Jesus has been glorified by God.

Moses: v 17–43

It has been suggested that Stephen's handling of Moses' career is longer and fuller than his account of the others because he had been accused of speaking against Moses.[110] In the speech, Stephen turned the accusation of speaking against Moses towards those who had accused him. It was not Stephen but the nation of Israel that had rebelled against Moses (7:9, 35, 39, 51, 52). He discusses Moses' life *in three parts*, each one totalling forty years (7:17–29; 30–35; 36–43):

The first forty year period (Ch 7:17–29):

First he describes Moses' early life in Egypt, dealing with his birth, upbringing and education. Having been rescued from the Nile, Moses was brought up by Pharaoh's daughter. When Moses was around forty he attacked and killed an Egyptian who was ill-treating an Israelite. Moses hoped that the Israelites would realise that he could be trusted. When he came upon two Israelites arguing he attempted to intervene. However, this backfired on him and the perpetrator asked him who did he think he was by setting himself up as ruler and judge over them. Moses realised that they knew he had killed an Egyptian so he fled to Midian where he married and had a family.

The second forty year period (Ch 7:30–35):

After another forty years Moses had a vision of an angel at Mount Sinai in a burning bush. God spoke to him commanding him to treat the place as holy ground. Stott[111] highlights that as Mount Sinai was not in the promised land this statement shows that there was holy ground outside the holy land; that the presence of God is not confined to Palestine. Through Moses God promised to save his people from their suffering in Egypt. God was sending Moses back to save the very people who had rejected him.

The third forty year period (Ch 7:36–43):

Moses led the Israelites out of Egypt and received the law as a sign of the covenant God had made with his people. By obeying the law the Israelites would continue to be his people. There is now a turning point in Stephen's speech. He describes Israel's reaction to Moses' teaching and law: "Our fathers refused to obey him" (7:39), which was really a rejection of God himself. Stephen then outlines a series of disobedient acts by the nation in the wilderness:

- They rejected Moses (and so God), made an idol of a golden calf and worshipped it.
- In their hearts they turned back to Egypt.
- They forced Aaron to make gods and had committed idolatry by worshipping a golden calf. Stephen quotes Amos 5:25–27 to support his firm belief that this despicable form of idolatry caused God to hide himself from Israel.

Stephen's audience claimed he had spoken against the law, saying it would be removed by Jesus. Ironically, Stephen points out that it seemed his audience belonged to a nation who had rejected the law right from the start. "So far from speaking against Moses, Stephen accuses his hearers of failing to obey the laws which God gave through him to Israel".[112]

To sum up, the Jews might offer sacrifices and offerings at the temple, considering it to be the place of God's presence; they might hold the law in the highest regard and be quite fanatical about it. But Stephen seems to be suggesting that the Jews are not really God's people after all.

God's presence

Throughout the Moses section Stephen emphasises that God was present outside of Palestine. Here he stresses this point by echoing a number of locations outside the Holy Land where God interacted with Moses:

- God raised up the deliverer Moses in Egypt (7:17–22);
- He provided for the rejected Moses in Midian (7:29);
- He commissioned Moses in the desert near Mount Sinai (7:30–34);
- God pronounced Mount Sinai to be 'holy ground';
- Moses was sent back to Egypt, not Israel, to do God's will. God delivered his people from this pagan nation, as well as at the Red Sea and the wilderness (7:35–36).

As in the case of Joseph, Moses can be compared to Christ in Stephen's account:

- Just as Moses narrowly escaped death at the hands of Pharaoh (7:21), so the infant Jesus was saved from King Herod.
- Moses was described as being "no ordinary child" (7:20). The same can be said of Jesus (Luke 2:52).
- Moses grew in wisdom and stature (7:22); as did Jesus (Luke 2:52).
- Moses was mighty in word and deed. Luke describes Jesus in a similar way (Luke 24:19).
- Stephen said that Moses thought that his own people would realise that God was using him to rescue them, but they did not (7:25–28). Like Moses, Jesus was sent to save his own people but they rejected him.

Solomon: v 44–50

The 'tabernacle of the Testimony' was a moveable place of worship carried by the Israelites in the desert. The tabernacle had been the focus of national worship in Israel from the beginning of the wilderness wandering until David's reign. It was passed on to the next generation under the leadership of Joshua and then until the time of David. He wanted to find a more permanent dwelling place for God but this privilege was given to Solomon.

The point of Stephen's discussion on the tabernacle seems to be discouraging the institutionalising of worship by saying that God was better served when his presence was focused upon a moveable structure: "The Most High does not live in houses made by men" (7:48).

Barclay[113] points out that the Temple, which should have become their greatest blessing, was in fact their greatest curse; they had come to worship it instead of worshipping God. Stott[114] agrees: "they conceived of Yahweh (God) as so completely identified with the temple that its existence guaranteed his protection of them, while its destruction would mean that he had abandoned them". The Jews had made the temple their safeguard. They were left with a Jewish God who lived in Jerusalem rather than a God of all men whose dwelling was the whole universe. Scott[115] agrees commenting that the Judaism of Stephen's day had become increasingly "place-conscious, provincial and localised in its view of God". Palestine in general, and Jerusalem in particular, had come to be looked upon as the only places where God could be found. With God being limited to Jerusalem and its institutions, the implication was that the only way to be saved was to become a Jew first.

Stephen, however, "was striking at the very roots of Jewish nationalism. He was saying, in effect, that God could get along without either the Temple or Judea (the Holy Land), and from now on the world was God's parish. Here we have universalism".[116]

Conclusion: v 51–53

Stephen suddenly seems to break off from his recital of Israel's history. Rather he begins a scorching attack on his audience for having the same attitudes as their ancestors. He portrays them as stubborn people. "Uncircumcised hearts and ears" refer to the fact that they have failed to 'cut away' pride and sin from their lives and were deaf to the truth. They always resist the Holy Spirit who spoke to them through the Old Testament prophets, through Jesus, and now through the new Christian community. Stephen insisted that the Sanhedrin's refusal to acknowledge Jesus as Messiah, and to have him killed, reflected their negative attitude towards God's messengers in general throughout Israel's history.

His audience resist the Holy Spirit. They betrayed and murdered "the Righteous One" (Jesus). Finally, they had failed to keep the divine law. Stephen had now put the blame of Jesus' death on the shoulders of the Sanhedrin, the spiritual leaders of the nation (Luke 24:20; Acts 4:10; 5:30).

The Stoning of Stephen (Ch 7:54–60)

Not surprisingly, the Sanhedrin's response to Stephen's speech was one of absolute fury (7:54). The term "gnashed their teeth" was a sign of rage. Claiming to have a vision of Jesus standing at the right hand of God made matters worse and violence broke out among the council. Some scholars suggest that Christ stood up to welcome his first martyr.[117] Stephen was dragged out of the town and stoned to death. His final words were a prayer for himself and for those killing him. Then he "fell asleep". Bruce[118] regards this as "an unexpectedly beautiful and peaceful description of so brutal a death." They are similar to the words spoken by Jesus before his death (Luke 23:34).

There appears to have been no formal trial. Even if there had been the Sanhedrin had no legal right to put anyone to death, and was supposed to liaise with the Romans regarding cases of capital punishment (John 18:31). However, a Roman form of execution was not used, as Stephen was stoned. This stresses the intense anger of the Sanhedrin. As Stephen lay dying, he asked the risen Jesus to receive his spirit, and that his killers be forgiven. It has been stressed that Stephen was following Jesus' example as he also wanted forgiveness for his executioners (Luke 23:34).

Saul, who belonged to the group of Stephen's enemies, was there. While he did not actually take part in the murder, he did approve of what was done and seemed unmoved by the horror of it all. This is in striking contrast to the man he was to become following his conversion. Perhaps Luke includes this comment here to demonstrate how amazing the conversion of Saul was in the early church.

Stephen as "a type of Christ"

The way Luke moulds the story, Stephen emerges as "a type of Christ".[119] Various parts of Stephen's speech and details of his death remind us of the last days of Jesus:

- Like Jesus, Stephen has grace and power, and works wonders and signs among the people (6:8).

- Both enter into debate with those who challenge them (6:9; Luke 20:1–7), including those who are sent as spies (6:11; Luke 20:20).

- Both are arrested (6:12; see Luke 22:54), and brought to trial before the Sanhedrin (6:12–15; see Luke 22:66–71).

- Stephen has false witnesses accuse him (6:13); while this is left out of Luke's passion narrative, it can be found in the Synoptic parallels of Mark 14:56 and Matthew 26:59.

- Both are taken out of the city to be executed (7:58, Luke 23:32).

- At his death Stephen prays that his spirit be accepted (7:59) as did Jesus (Luke 23:46).

- Stephen asks forgiveness of his murderers (7:60) as did Jesus (23:34).

- Stephen is buried by pious people (8:2) as was Jesus (Luke 23:50–55).

Significance of Stephen's speech and martyrdom

1. In the book of Acts, Stephen's speech and martyrdom stands between the spread of the gospel in Jerusalem (Acts 1–5) and its spread to the rest of the Roman world (Acts 8–14). It was a timely event. If Stephen's martyrdom takes place around AD35, then Peter's vision in Joppa would be around six years later in AD41, with the Council of Jerusalem occurring in another eight years or so in AD49.

2. His speech led to a rejection of the Law and the Temple.

3. It resulted in a move away from the Jewish people and Jerusalem. The persecution which led to the spread of the gospel outside of Jerusalem is a direct result of the events in Acts 7.

4. The death of Stephen provided Luke with an important literary transition. Luke has shown how the apostles and others were witnesses in Jerusalem. But the story of the Jerusalem church was complete. Now it was time for Luke to show the gospel spreading out to "Judea and Samaria, and to the ends of the earth" (1:8).

 OTHER ASPECTS OF HUMAN EXPERIENCE

There may be a lesson here for all religions – with their own churches, temples, holy places, systems of worship, creeds and theology. God can work outside of established religion; He works wherever and however he pleases, and it is important not to limit him in the human mind.

What do you think?

 TASKS

a) Describe what is known from Acts about Stephen and the charges brought against him.

- Stephen's career as recorded in Acts.
- Institution of the Seven, Stephen's arrest and charges (6:8–15), Stephen's speech and the stoning of Stephen.

b) Explain the relevance of Stephen's speech in light of the charges brought against him.

- The charges brought against Stephen (6:8–15).
- Stephen's speech in response to these charges (7:1–54). Either tell the speech in

chronological order or pick out Stephen's response in relation to the charges that he spoke against the law, Moses and the Temple.

c) With reference to other aspects of human experience, comment on the claim that it is important that Stephen is remembered as a significant Christian martyr. Justify your answer.

- Stephen is known to be the first Christian martyr.
- His death serves as an example of the ultimate devotion to God.
- While his death was horrific, others suffered worse fates and are not well known in the Christian Church, eg Blandina.
- Many are martyred today in China and other places and they are not remembered the way Stephen is.

The Evangelising Activity of Philip

After the burial of Stephen persecution broke out against the church in Jerusalem and many Christians were scattered to the countryside of Judea and Samaria. On a positive note, this led to widespread evangelism.

The Gospel Spreads to Samaria (Ch 8:4–25)

As the Christians moved to new areas they found a welcoming response to the gospel.[120] An example of this is the reaction of the Samaritans to Philip's preaching and miracles. Philip was another member of the Seven (6:5), who took the brave step of taking the gospel to Samaria.

Stott[121] points out that hostility between the Jews and Samaritans had lasted a thousand years. In the eighth century BC, Samaria was destroyed by the Assyrians and most of the people were deported to parts of the Assyrian empire (2 Kings 17:5–6). The area of Samaria was resettled by a mixed group of peoples from other parts of the empire. The resentment between Samaritans and Jews was centuries old, and may have dated back to this time. It was deepened when the Samaritans opposed the rebuilding of the Jerusalem temple in the fifth century BC. This led to bitter hatred between Jews and Samaritans which grew worse through the passage of time. However, in 63BC the Romans occupied Palestine and the Jewish republic. The Samaritans were freed from Judean domination, but the bitterness between the Jews and Samaritans continued. For Jews to evangelise the people of Samaria and bring them into fellowship with Jewish Christians was a very brave step.

On the surface it looks as if the mission to Samaria was the first step in the evangelisation of Gentiles. However, to Jews the Samaritans were considered more as schismatics (those who split away from the main group) than Gentiles. Peter, for example, had no problem visiting the Samaritans, but he needed a life-changing vision before visiting the Gentile Cornelius. You could say that the Jews considered Samaritans to be 'half-Jews' or 'half-breeds', both religiously and racially. However, they were regarded more as heretics from the faith rather than outright pagans.

The Samaritans were also hostile towards the Jews. In his Gospel Luke describes an incident which shows their hostility when a small village of them refused to welcome Jesus and his disciples, because it was known that they were travelling to Jerusalem (Luke 9:52–56).

Yet, the Jews and Samaritans did have a lot in common. Philip's preaching would have been particularly attractive to them as the belief in a coming 'restorer' was part of their theology. Philip, as a Hellenistic Jew, also found himself on common ground with the Samaritans because he, too, was an outcast from Jerusalem. By now the news of the persecution suffered by the Christian Hellenistic Jews may have reached Samaria, making the Samaritans more willing to receive the missionaries.

Many were in awe of Philip as they heard his message. Like Jesus[122] and the apostles, he also had the ability to exorcise evil spirits and heal people. It was God's power that got the attention of people so that some might become receptive to the gospel message. Johnson[123] comments that as Philip evangelised the Samaritans he continued "the work of Jesus in reaching out to the marginal and outcast among the people and inviting them to a full participation in the restored people of God".

Luke combined his story of the Samaritan mission with that of a notorious local religious personality named Simon Magus or Simon the Sorcerer (Magician). He features in the writings of second-century Christian writers as the first heretic (false teacher) of the church, and founder of gnostic Christianity. The early Christian theologian Irenaeus[124] (AD120–202), bishop of Lyons, France, refers to Simon as the originator of a number of heresies.

Before the arrival of Philip in Samaria, Simon had astounded the people by his magic powers. The people were taken in by him, even calling him the 'Great Power'. It seems that Simon claimed to be divine (from God) but Luke simply presents him as a magician who deceived the people by his tricks.

Philip's preaching, however, was so powerful that the people listened to him instead of Simon. Many, both men and women, went on to believe and be baptised, as did Simon who stuck by Philip's side from then on. However, whether or not his conversion was real is questionable because he was preoccupied by Philip's ability to perform miracles and longed to be able to do the same. Luke does not say what exactly these miracles were but it seems that when people were converted to Christ the Holy Spirit was given to them in such a way that greatly impressed Simon. Hewitt[125] suggests that they may have engaged in Glossolalia, although this is not stated.

The apostles at Jerusalem sent two delegates, Peter and John, to assess what was happening at Samaria. The spread of the gospel to the Samaritans represented such a dramatic step that the apostles were bound to be intrigued by what was going on. The Jerusalem church also needed to satisfy itself of the genuineness of the Samaritan conversions. Once they did so, there would be no question of the mother church accepting these new converts. By going to Samaria, Peter and John were also confirming the validity of Hellenistic Christians' ministry of evangelisation.[126] It was a mission of goodwill by the Jerusalem Church, showing that the church was one body, and demonstrating their brotherly bond with the Samaritan converts.

Peter and John were satisfied that the gospel had been received favourably but discovered that the new converts had not yet received the Spirit. This seems strange as Luke did not hint at any deficiency in the Samaritan believers' faith. So they prayed for them, laying hands on them. Up until this point they had only been baptised in the name of Jesus. Many wonder why they had not received the Spirit following baptism. Lampe[127] suggests God withheld the Spirit until this point so that the Samaritans would be seen to be fully part of the community of Jerusalem Christians, and not only the Hellenistic branch of the church.[128] Others argue that the conversion of the Samaritans was not real and that was why they had not received the Spirit.[129] However, Luke tells us none of this.

Simon keenly observed the apostles' ability to bestow the Spirit on people[130] and longed to be able to do the same. However, this desire was clearly for the wrong reasons for he offered to pay for the gift. Here we again see the role of Peter as a disciplinarian. Peter gave Simon a scathing rebuke about his spiritual blindness. The Phillips translation of Philip's reply catches the sense of his grim reprimand of Simon: "To hell with you and your money!" (8:20). It is a curse against Simon or a warning that he must change his ways. It shows how serious the church took Simon's misunderstanding of the gifts of God. Unlike Ananias and Sapphira, he was given the chance to repent and seek forgiveness because he was "full of bitterness and captive to sin" (8:23). However, Simon lacked understanding and had his mind only on physical consequences. Stott[131] comments that instead of praying for forgiveness, Simon asked Peter to pray for him that none of these awful things would happen to him (8:24). He argues that he was more concerned with God's judgement than receiving forgiveness.

He then disappeared from the story, and that is the last we hear of him in Acts, or anywhere else in the New Testament.

 TASK

The term 'simony' originates from this story.
Find out why.

Significance of the story:

1. It gives an account of the conversion of the Samaritans, people whom the Jews hated. The story hints at the overcoming of the resentment between the Jews and Samaritans through a common Christian faith.

2. It shows an early indication of bringing Jews and Gentiles together.

3. It suggests that there is the possibility of forgiveness, even for serious sin committed by a baptised person.[132]

◎ OTHER ASPECTS OF HUMAN EXPERIENCE

The elapsed time between the Samaritan's baptism and receiving of the Spirit has led to two widely held beliefs in the Christian Church. One is the doctrine of 'confirmation' and the other is 'the baptism of the Spirit', as a second work of grace following conversion.

In some Christian circles a person is baptised, perhaps as a baby, and later in life is confirmed in the church. In a few other denominations, a person may be regarded as converted but later be 'confirmed' by exhibiting a special outward expression of charismatic gifts, such as speaking in tongues.

Philip and the Ethiopian (Ch 8: 26–40)

A second story in Acts highlighting the missionary activity of Philip is that of the conversion of the Ethiopian. It begins with Philip receiving a divine command from an angel to go to a remote place. This might have seemed strange considering the extent of Philip's involvement in evangelism in Samaria. This, however, was obviously God's intention so he obeyed the command to go south and found himself on a desert road. It was also the last community before a traveller encountered the desert waste stretching to Egypt.

It would have been highly unusual to meet anyone on such a remote road so it is surprising that he met the Ethiopian at all.[133] Luke's narrative is formed in such a way to stress this. The man was a Eunuch (meaning he was castrated), employed as the royal treasurer by the queen mother, who was the ruler of Ethiopia. Stott[134] suggests that he may have actually been Jewish, either by birth or conversion, for the Jewish dispersion had reached Egypt and beyond. Other scholars disagree, however, believing him to be a Gentile. He had been in Jerusalem 'to worship', probably at one of the pilgrim festivals, so he was most likely a God-fearer. As he traveled home he put the journey in by reading from the Jewish Scriptures. Some scholars believe it would have been difficult for a non-Jew to get a copy of the Isaiah scroll.

Philip receives a second divine command telling him to stay close to the Ethiopian's chariot. As he went near he heard someone reading and recognised the words. He asked the Ethiopian if he understood what he was reading. He admitted that he was having difficulty and asked Philip to interpret the passage for him. "The passage which the eunuch was reading provided a golden opportunity for an evangelist".[135] Isaiah 53 is a prophecy which describes a Servant of God who suffers and bears the consequences of the sins of others. Jesus had quoted from Isaiah 53, saying it had been fulfilled in his death (Luke 22:37). Now, Philip was preaching the same message. The Eunuch was concerned with who the prophet was describing. Philip uses this as an opportunity to show that Jesus was the one who fulfilled the prophecy.

When the two men reached a stream the eunuch asked for baptism. At this point the eunuch must have given Philip some indication of his new faith in Jesus for he agreed to baptise him in a nearby stream. The phrase "went down into" implies that baptism was done by immersion, not sprinkling. Jesus himself was baptised this way, setting the example (Mark 1:9–10).

The story ends abruptly with a description of how the Spirit took Philip away as the two men came out of the water. The eunuch returned home rejoicing, which suggests that he had also received the Holy Spirit (8:39). Africa had now been penetrated by the gospel in the person of the Ethiopian eunuch. This signified another small step in the advance of the gospel from its Jewish confines to a wider Gentile world.

However, the church was still far from engaging in a direct effort to bring the gospel to purely pagan Gentiles. While this event may describe the conversion of a Gentile, the fact that he returned to his own country, means that the church was not at this point forced to consider its views on the acceptance of Gentiles. Johnson[136] concludes that "as with the Samaritans, the conversion of the Ethiopian does not yet represent a formal opening to the Gentiles, but rather to those who were marginalised within the people of God".

Meanwhile Philip turned up in Azotus, preaching as he made his way to Caesarea, his hometown. He probably spent considerable time in each of the towns. Luke, however, passes over the details of what may have a number of months' work in a sentence.

Philip's final destination was Caesarea, which was either where he then lived or later settled. After arriving in Caesarea, he disappears from Luke's account. However, Philip made a sudden reappearance about 20 years later, as Paul's host (21:8–9). By this time he was the father of four unmarried daughters, who were all prophetesses.

TASKS

a) Describe the role of Philip in the Acts of the Apostles.

  • One of the seven (6:5)
  • Mission with Samaritans
  • Conversion of Ethiopian
  • Evangelist (8:40)

b) Give an account of the story of the encounter between the Ethiopian and Philip as recorded in Acts.

  • Divine command
  • Discussion of religious outlook of Ethiopian
  • Interaction with Philip
  • Results
  • Implications

c) Describe Philip's activity in Samaria.

  • History of relationship between Jews and Gentiles
  • Significance of Philip's step in taking the Gospel there
  • Religious outlook of Samaritans
  • Reaction to Philip's ministry
  • Simon the magician – a genuine conversion?
  • Visit by Peter and John – reasons

d) Comment on the claim that Philip was a forerunner of Paul in accepting Gentiles into the church

  • Explore the consequences of Philip's opening out of the church's mission to non-Jews.
  • Philip's activity eventually led to the Council of Jerusalem (Ch 15) and the acceptance of Gentiles into the church

e) Explore the claim that Philip was a successful preacher. Justify your answer.

  • Examples of his ministry – preaching and miraculous signs
  • Evidence from Samaria
  • Ethiopian eunuch
  • Fact that he was still an evangelist 20 years later and had a positive influence on his daughters

f) Explore the claim that from the beginning baptism was essential for entry into the Christian community.

- Peter's call for baptism of the believers (Acts 2)
- Philip, Peter and John and the Samaritans
- The conversion of the Ethiopian (Acts 8)
- The Gentile Pentecost (Acts 10)
- Peter's report to the Church at Jerusalem (Acts 11)
- An exploration of the link between baptism and the reception of the Holy Spirit

g) Comment on the claim that it is easy to overlook the importance of the role of Philip in the spreading of the Good News. Justify your answer.

- Space taken up by Philip in Acts compared to that of Peter and Paul
- Silence of Philip's activity from Acts 8 until Ch 21
- Luke's focus on Paul's missionary journeys and stay in Rome dominate the book of Acts
- On the other hand, Philip laid the ground work for Peter and Paul and has not been forgotten for this.

LEARNING INTENTIONS CHECKLIST/ TARGET SETTING

By the end of this unit I will be able to:	Yes	No	To be achieved
• understand the different roles carried out by Peter in the book of Acts, with at least one example of each			
• explain the significance of Matt 16:17–19 for the role of Peter in Acts			
• understand what is meant by the terms 'miracle' and 'evangelist'			
• be aware of the main features of early Christian preaching			
• know the details of at least one of Peter's speeches			
• describe the story of Ananias and Sapphira			
• comment on the suggested severity of God's judgement of them			
• understand the significance of the story of Peter and Cornelius for the growth of the church			
• outline why it was necessary to appoint the 'Seven' and explain the deeper reasons for discontentment			
• summarise Stephen's speech using the headings: Abraham, Joseph, Moses and Solomon			
• explain the real meaning behind Stephen's speech			
• describe the evangelising activity of Philip			
• show how various incidents concerning Peter, Stephen and Philip are relevant to other aspects of human experience.			

Endnotes

[1] Nelson, J & McNeice, J, *The Challenge of Jesus*, Newtownards: Colourpoint, 1999. Note that a number of scholars disagree that Jesus was referring to Peter in this statement.

[2] Stott, *op cit*, p53

[3] Lewis, *op cit*, p25

[4] The habitation is the field which Judas bought and over which a curse will rest; nobody will live in it (Marshall, IH, *Tyndale New Testament Commentaries, Acts*, IVP, 1980, p63)

[5] The Psalmist utters a string of curses against his enemy and wishes that somebody else may take over his occupation. This is used as justification for handing over the office of Judas to somebody else (Marshall, IH, *Tyndale New Testament Commentaries, Acts*, IVP, 1980, p63)

[6] Bruce, *op cit*, p44

[7] Guy, *op cit*, p26

[8] Bruce, *op cit*, p47

[9] Marshall, *op cit*, p66

[10] Nothing further is mentioned in the New Testament about either Matthias or Barsabbas.

[11] Stott, *op cit*, p59

[12] Dillon, *op cit*, p735

[12a] Marshall, *op cit*, p86

[13] Scholars are not sure which temple gate this happened to be, as neither the Talmud nor Josephus mention a "Beautiful Gate." The Nicanor and Shushan gates have been suggested as possibilities.

[13a] Marshall, *op cit*, p86

[14] Dillon, *op cit*, p735

[15] Harnack, A, *Luke the Physician*, London: ET, 1907, p191

[15a] Marshall, *op cit*, p86

[16] Barclay, *op cit*, p28

[17] *ibid*, p29

[18] The Online Members' *Magazine of the Law Society of Scotland*, 5 Jan 2005, http://www.journalonline.co.uk/news/1001379.aspx

[19] Story from BBC NEWS: http://news.bbc.co.uk/go/pr/fr/-/1/hi/northern_ireland/6332323.stm, Published: 2007/02/05 14:08:18 GMT

[20] Barclay, *op cit*, p30

[20a] Tannehill, RC, *The Narrative Unity of Luke-Acts: A literary interpretation*, Vol 2 *The Acts of the Apostles*, Minneapolis: Fortress, 1994, p58

[21] Stott, *op cit*, p92

[22] Dillon, *op cit*, p735

[23] Hewitt, *op cit*, p49

[24] Marshall, *op cit*, p95

[25] Bruce, *op cit*, p83

[26] Marshall, *op cit*, p86

[27] Barclay, *op cit*, p34

[28] Stott, *op cit*, p95

[29] Dillon, *op cit*, p737

[30] Barclay, *op cit*, p36

[31] Guy, *op cit*, p30

[32] Dillon, *op cit*, p737

[33] Gutzke, MG, *Plain Talk on Acts*, Zondervan Publishing House, Michigan, 1966, p59

[34] Lewis, *op cit*, p32

[35] Dillon, *op cit*, p738

[36] Stott, *op cit*, p109

[37] Barclay, *op cit*, p42

[38] Guy, *op cit*, p31

[39] Stott, *op cit*, p109

[40] Lewis, *op cit*, p33

[41] Bruce, *op cit*, p105

[42] Gutzke, *op cit*, p63

[43] Marshall, *op cit*, pp111–112

[44] *ibid*, p112

[45] Packer, *op cit*, p43

[46] Dunn, JDG, *Jesus and the Spirit*, NLT, London: SCM, 1975

[47] Bruce, *op cit*, p106

[48] Marshall, *op cit*, p113

[48a] Fernando, *op cit*, p197

[49] Guy, *op cit*, p31

[50] Browne, LE, *The Acts of the Apostles*, London: Indian Church Commentaries, SPCK, 1925, pp83–84

51 Knox, WL, cited in Haenchen, E, *The Acts of the Apostles: A Commentary*, Oxford: Blackwell, 1971, p237

51a Stott, *op cit*, p112

52 Marshall, *op cit*, p114

53 Bruce, *op cit*, p109

54 Pohill, *op cit*, p164

55 Packer, *op cit*, p46

56 P.W. van der Horst, *Peter's Shadow: the Religio-Historical Background of Acts 5:15*, NTS 23, 1976–77, pp204–212, cited in Marshall, *op cit*, pp204–212

57 Fernando, *op cit*, p210

58 *ibid*, 210

59 Lewis, *op cit*, p33

60 Neil, *op cit*, pp96–97

61 Marshall, *op cit*, p118

62 Fernando, *op cit*, p211

63 Longenecker, RN, *The Acts of the Apostles*, The Expositor's Bible Commentary, Grand Rapids: Zondervan, 1981, p320

64 Marshall, *op cit*, p119

65 Packer, *op cit*, p47

66 Lewis, *op cit*, p34

67 Fernando, *op cit*, p213

68 Marshall, *op cit*, p117

69 Packer, *op cit*, p47

70 Stott, *op cit*, p116

71 There is some confusion over the two examples used by Gamaliel. According to Josephus (Antiquities xx.5.1) the rebellion of Theudas took place later, about AD44–45.

72 Marshall, *op cit*, p124

73 Stott, *op cit*, p118

74 Stott, *op cit*, p182

75 Marshall, *op cit*, p178

76 *ibid*, p179

77 *ibid*, p180

78 *ibid*, 180

79 *ibid*, p181

80 Hewitt, *op cit*, p94

81 Marshall, *op cit*, p185

82 Stott, *op cit*, p187

83 Marshall, *op cit*, p188

84 *ibid*, pp188–189

85 Haenchen, E, *The Acts of the Apostles*, KEK, Eng tr, Oxford: Basil Blackwell, 1971, p351

86 Marshall, *op cit*, p194

87 Guy, *op cit*, p44

88 Rackham, RB, *The Acts of the Apostles: An Exposition, in the Westminster Commentaries Series*, London: Methuen, 1901; 4th edition, 1909, p153

89 Marshall, *op cit*, p198

90 Guy, *op cit*, p144

91 Marshall, *op cit*, p206

92 *ibid*, p209

93 Fernando, *op cit*, p225

94 Barclay, *op cit*, 51

95 Stott, *op cit*, p121

96 Marshall, *op cit*, p125

97 Stott, *op cit*, p122

98 Lenski, RCH, *The Interpretation of the Acts of the Apostles*, Minneapolis: Augsburg, reprint of 1934 ed, p246

99 Marshall, *op cit*, p127

100 Stott, *op cit*, p127

101 Marshall, *op cit*, p131

102 Stott, *op cit*, p129

103 Fernando, *op cit*, p246

104 Neil, *op cit*, p107

105 Lenski, *op cit*, p256

106 Stott, *op cit*, p130

107 This land is now covered by modern Iraq, and north-eastern Syria.

108 Johnson, *op cit*, p121

109 Stott, *op cit*, p132

110 *ibid*, p134

111 *ibid*, p137

112 Marshall, *op cit*, p147

113 Barclay, *op cit*, p61

114 Stott, *op cit*, p130

115 Scott, JJ, *Stephen's Defense and the World Mission of the People of God*, Journal of the Evangelical Theological Society 21, 1978, p133

116 Hewitt, *op cit*, p70

117 Stott, *op cit*, p141

118 Bruce, *op cit*, p160

119 Johnson, *op cit*, p143

120 Marshall, *op cit*, p152

121 Stott, *op cit*, p147

122 Luke 4:33, 36; 6:18; 7:21; 8:2, 29; 9:42; 11:24

123 Johnson, *op cit*, p151

124 Irenaeus, *Against Heresies*, 1:23

125 Hewitt, *op cit*, p77

126 During the early years of the church, the apostles seemed to exercise a supervision over the progress of the gospel in general (11:22).

127 Lampe, GWH, *The Seal of the Spirit*, London, 1967, p70

128 This is not to say the converts could receive the Holy Spirit only through the apostles. Ananias, who had no known ministerial role and was certainly not an apostle, was the instrument through which the Holy Spirit was given to Paul (9:17).

129 Dunn, JDG, *Baptism in the Holy Spirit*, London: SCM, 1973, pp63–68

130 Some speculate that the original Pentecost charismatic gifts were in evidence, such as speaking in other languages. Perhaps the Samaritan converts outwardly exhibited a sense of spiritual joy, which is a gift of the Holy Spirit (Galatians 5:22).

131 Stott, *op cit*, p151

132 Marshall, *op cit*, p160

133 Not to be confused with the modern nation of Ethiopia; it was then the Upper Nile region.

134 Stott, *op cit*, p160

135 Marshall, *op cit*, p163

136 Johnson, *op cit*, p160

Chapter 4

Paul the Apostle

THE CONVERSION OF SAUL (PAUL) (Ch 9:1–19)

Introduction

THE CENTRE OF INTEREST now moves away from Peter and the other disciples of Jesus to one of the most significant conversions in the early church – that of Paul the Pharisee (previously called Saul).[1] Stott argues that his conversion on the road to Damascus is the most famous conversion in church history. Luke is so impressed with its importance that he includes the story three times, once in his own narrative (Acts 9) and twice in Paul's speeches. The story is told as part of Paul's speech before a Jerusalem crowd (Acts 22:5–16) and his words before Agrippa and Festus (Acts 26:12–18). Willimon[2] adds that "only an event of greatest importance would merit such repetition by an author whose hallmark is brevity and concision". In other words, Luke was known not to waste words; he kept his work brief and to the point. So to repeat an event three times shows the importance he attached to it. Johnson[3] agrees, commenting that the turning of a Pharisaic persecutor into the apostle of the Gentiles is a paradox so profound that it requires multiple retellings.

There are slight variations between the three accounts, mainly concerning what each adds or leaves out from the basic story, with each version bringing out some further nuance of significance.[4] Marshall[5] comments that "Luke is not trying to give us an account of what happened in precise detail but rather the general nature and significance of the event". It might be useful to refer to a few of these differences in this section, and also at A2 level, when we discuss chapters 22 and 26. However, it is not necessary to know the exact details of these for your AS examination.

As well as the conversion story being told three times in Acts, Paul mentions three times in his letters that he was "once a blasphemer and a persecutor and a violent man", who "persecuted and tried to destroy" the church of God, and therefore he was "the least of the apostles." In Paul's letter to the Galatians, which you will study at A2, Paul highlights the importance of his encounter with the risen Jesus: "God, who set me apart from birth and called me by his grace, was pleased to reveal his Son in me"[6] (Galatians 1:16).

Detail of the story

We first read of Saul at the stoning of Stephen, which some scholars feel had a profound influence on him. Perhaps the very fact that he did not himself take part in the stoning of Stephen may suggest that he had an uncertain sympathy with what was being said. However, Lewis[7] feels we only guess what effect the martyrdom of Stephen must have had on Saul, for when we next meet him Luke is describing his persecution of the Jerusalem church, commenting that he "was still breathing out murderous threats against the Lord's disciples" (9:1). Some of the language Luke uses to describe Saul in his pre-conversion state seems deliberately to portray him as "a wild and ferocious beast."[8] Stott[9] describes Saul's heart as being "filled with hatred and his mind was poisoned by prejudice."

Saul also travelled to other towns, Damascus in particular, to round up Christians. For example, he later tells King Agrippa, "I even went to foreign cities to persecute them" (26:10). Saul regarded getting rid of the Christians as part of doing God's will. As far as he was concerned Christianity was a blasphemous heresy that threatened God's people (the Jews), the sanctity of the law, and temple.

"Damascus was an important town, about 150 miles from Jerusalem, with a considerable Jewish population."[10] It had been part of the Roman province of Syria since 64BC. At the time, Damascus was a large and thriving commercial centre and had a large Jewish population. Saul set out towards this city like an avenging prophet, carrying the necessary letters from the High Priest (a Sadducee) with authority to return any Christians he found in the synagogues. The Sadducees were, according to Josephus,[11] more heartless in their judgements than the Pharisees, and it may not have been natural for a loyal Pharisee like Saul to go and request letters from the Saducean high priest (v 2). This is an indication of how far he was willing to go to try to stamp out this threat.

Saul would then bring the Christians back to Jerusalem for punishment (9:2). The High Priest would not have had direct authority over the Damascus Christians, as they would not have been part of his jurisdiction.[12] So it is more than likely that those being hunted down were the Hellenistic Christians who had fled Jerusalem, rather than Christians from Damascus.

Luke describes the Christian religion as "the Way" (9:2), which seemed to be a common description for the church. Haenchen[13] comments that this designation was probably applied to the church by the Christians themselves. The term is used several times in Acts (19:9, 23; 22:4; 24:14, 22), and has parallels with Jesus' words: "I am the way" (John 14:6). Another term used to describe the church, usually by outsiders, was "the sect of the Nazarenes" (24:5, 14; 28:22).

Saul was near Damascus when "without any previous warning he found himself surrounded by an intensely bright light and heard a voice speaking to him",[14] the shock causing him to fall to the ground. Then he heard a voice saying, "Saul, Saul, why do you persecute me?" (9:4). "The revelation was one given to Saul alone and not shared by his companions",[15] although they were witnesses that something unusual had happened. They stood speechless and saw the light, but did not see the risen Christ (9:7).[16]

In the other two accounts later in Acts, Paul describes that the bright light flashed, not at night, but at high noon. It was brighter than the sun, which made it all the more amazing (26:13). In Acts 22, Paul said the men with him did see the light, which is not mentioned in Chapter 9. In Acts 22 Paul also says that the men did not hear the sound, presumably meaning that "they did not understand the voice," as the NIV puts it (22:9). What seems to have happened was that the whole group heard a sound but only Paul understood it as speech.

The voice asked, "Saul, Saul, why do you persecute me?" (9:4). The double name was used for emphasis, and is found in other stories of divine calling, including Abraham's, Jacob's and Moses' (Genesis 22:11; 46:2 ; Exodus 3:4). Chapter 26 tells us that the voice addressed Saul in Aramaic. Scholars have speculated that this is because it was Saul's first language. Saul asked, "Who are you, Lord?",[17] as he did not yet realise it was Jesus. Saul probably discerned a divine quality about the voice as it spoke to him.[18]

Saul must have been considerably shaken when the figure answered, "I am Jesus" (9:5). It does not actually say in this verse that Saul saw the risen Christ, only that he heard a voice. However, it is confirmed afterwards, when Luke introduces Ananias (9:17) and Barnabas (9:27) into the story.

When the risen Christ told Saul he had been persecuting him, he was pointing out that Saul had not only been rejecting people by his actions, but was rejecting Christ himself (Luke 10:16). The followers of Jesus whom Saul hated were the people of God, and were not heretics. The evidence was too compelling to reject any longer.[19]

It was now obvious to Saul that the Jesus whose followers he had been persecuting was alive, and associated with the God of Israel. Saul would therefore, have had to re-evaluate his views on the life, teaching and death of Jesus.

Saul finally struggled to his feet, but he had been blinded by the light (9:8). The men with Saul took him to a house in Damascus. Stott[20] comments that "he who had expected to enter Damascus in the fullness of his pride and prowess, as a self-confident opponent of Christ, was actually led into it, humbled and blinded, a captive of the very Christ he had opposed". Dillon[21] agrees, describing Saul as "the dreaded persecutor, completely immobilised".

For the next three days the blind Saul fasted, no doubt reflecting on the meaning of his encounter with Jesus. There he stayed for three days, taking neither food nor drink. Bruce[22] believes that there is no need to regard his abstinence as an early instance of fasting before baptism; it was probably the result of shock.

Saul's future commission is not recorded in this account. However, in Acts 22:10 Paul recounts how he was told to get up and go into Damascus. "There you will be told all that you have been assigned to do." This is where Ananias is introduced to the story.

Barclay,[23] describes Ananias as "one of the forgotten heroes of the Christian church'. In Acts 9 Ananias reveals to Saul that it was "Jesus, who appeared to you" (9:17). In the later versions of this event it is clearly stated that Saul saw Christ (26:16; 22:14). Ananias was a believer and "a devout observer of the law", highly respected by all the Jews living in Damascus (22:12). He was the one through whom God would restore Paul's sight and reveal his future. In a vision from God, Ananias was told to go to the house of a man named Judas who lived on Straight Street in Damascus (9:11), where he would find Saul praying. He was not keen to meet Saul for "all that he knew of this man indicated that he was an enemy of the church".[24] He had not only heard reports about him but he knew Saul had come to Damascus with authority to arrest Christians.

Note how Ananias referred to the Christians as "saints" (9:13). This is the first time Luke used the term in describing the church community (see also 9:32 and 26:10).

However, the Lord insisted that Ananias visit Saul, even though he had persecuted the saints. Ananias was told: "Go! This man is my chosen instrument to carry my name before the Gentiles and their kings and before the people of Israel" (9:15). Having grasped what was to be involved in Saul's future role, he went to the house of Judas, met Saul, and laid his hands on him. Ananias told Saul that Jesus had sent him so that he might see again and be filled with the Holy Spirit (9:17). However, Saul's calling would be to a life of pain and distress: "I will show him how much he must suffer for my name" (9:16). Dillon[25] comments that "the fierce persecutor is now to become the one fiercely persecuted".

By placing his hands on Saul and calling him brother, Ananias was welcoming him into the community of believers. Immediately, something like scales fell from Saul's eyes, and he could see again. In Acts 22, a much fuller account of Ananias' role in Saul's conversion is described. Ananias gives Saul his commission, telling him: "The God of our fathers has chosen you to know his will and to see the Righteous One[26] and to hear words from his mouth" (22:14). Ananias also told Saul that he would be a witness to all people of what he had seen and heard. Then he instructed Saul to get up and be baptised (22:16). Saul was obedient and responded to the request to be baptised immediately; and after taking some food, he regained his strength (9:18–19). Saul had become as convinced a disciple of Christ as he had been an enemy.[27]

Marshall[28] interestingly picks up that as Saul was baptised and received the filling of the Spirit by Ananias, then there was obviously no need of an 'apostle' to perform the task. Bruce[29] agrees, describing Ananias as "an obscure disciple." This shows that God chooses people for tasks who may not necessarily stand out as obvious candidates. Ananias leaves the story at this point having played a major part in the conversion of one who was to become one of the greatest missionaries of the early church.

 ## OTHER ASPECTS OF HUMAN EXPERIENCE

Dramatic Conversions – Nicky Cruz

Nicky Cruz was one of eighteen children born to witchcraft-practising parents from Puerto Rico. Bloodshed and chaos were common occurrences in his life. He suffered severe physical and mental abuse at the hands of his parents, at one time being declared the 'Son of Satan' by his mother while she was in a spiritual trance.

When he was 15, Nicky's father sent him to stay with one of his brothers in New York. However, Nicky only stayed a short time. Instead, full of anger, he chose to make it on his own. He was tough, but lonely, and by the time he was sixteen he had joined a notorious Brooklyn street gang known as the 'Mau Maus' (called after a bloodthirsty African tribe). Within six months he became their president. Nicky fearlessly ruled the streets as 'warlord' of the Mau Maus, which was one of the gangs most dreaded by rivals and police. He became lost in a cycle of drugs, alcohol, and brutal violence. However, his life took a tragic turn for the worse when a friend and fellow gang member was brutally beaten and stabbed, dying in Nicky's arms.

As Nicky's reputation grew, so did his destructive behaviour. He was arrested countless times, and a court-ordered psychiatrist pronounced that he would probably end up in prison, or sentenced to the electric chair, and eventually in hell. No authority figure could reach Nicky – until he met a street-preacher named David Wilkerson. He disarmed Nicky by showing him something he had never known before: undying love. His interest in the young thug was persistent. Nicky beat him up, spat on him and, on one occasion, seriously threatened his life, yet the love of God remained.

Finally, Wilkerson's presentation of the gospel message and the love of Jesus got through to Nicky, melting the thick walls of his heart. Nicky became a Christian and received the forgiveness, love and new life through Jesus. Since then, he has dedicated that life to helping others find the same freedom.

He reaches today's youth because they relate to his background, trust his peer authority, and respond to the message of hope he delivers with both passion and conviction. As one teenager said after an outreach, "All I knew was he was an O.G. (original gangster) and he was having this big meeting tonight."

Nicky[30] explains: "These kids are young, hardened criminals who don't respond to parents, teachers, or the jail system. They receive a glorified message of gang activity every day in rap music, television, and films. They need to hear a different message – and they need to hear it now! They come to our 'invasions' looking for an alternative to the hopeless cycle of drug abuse, alcoholism, and violence. We must offer them an alternative source of security than the one they find in the gangs. They won't surrender to authority figures that have let them down all their lives. But, believe it or not, they will respond to a message about God if it comes from others who have survived their same living hell."

 TASKS

Dramatic conversions tend to have a huge impact on the life of an individual. Like Paul in Acts, such people often completely devote their lives to the work of spreading the gospel.

a) Find out more about the work of Nicky Cruz. Compare his work to that of Paul following his conversion. For example, think about strategies they both used or challenges and successes they both faced.

b) Try to find out about other dramatic conversions. For example, if you type 'Christian conversion from Islam' into the 'Google' search engine on the internet you should be able to access information about people who have left the Islamic faith to become Christians.

c) Talk to you priest or minister. Perhaps they will have first-hand information about someone they know who became a Christian after being involved in a terrorist organisation in Northern Ireland.

 DISCUSSION

Was Paul's conversion gradual from the time he witnessed the martyrdom of Stephen or was it really a dramatic conversion?

TASKS

a) Give an account of Paul's conversion as recorded in Acts 9.
  - The context – Paul's pre-conversion outlook
  - Events on the Damascus road
  - Role of Ananias

b) Describe the role of Ananias in Paul's conversion.
  - Background to the story
  - Details on Ananias from all three accounts which build up a complete picture
  - Significance of Paul's baptism by such an obscure character

c) Comment on the claim that Paul's conversion is a turning point in the book.
  - Evidence of Paul's involvement in the persecution of Christians before his conversion
  - The drama of his conversion
  - Paul's missionary activity; missionary to the Gentiles

d) Assess the significance of Paul's conversion for the spread of the gospel to Rome.
  - Paul's determination to reach Rome
  - Did the gospel reach Rome before Paul did?
  - Comparison with the missionary activity of others
  - Would the gospel have spread without Paul?

e) Comment on the claim that even today the more dramatic conversions leave a lasting impression on people.
  - Compare the effects of Paul's conversion with that of a Christian today who experienced a complete turn around in his or her life.

What happened next?

As this is not part of the specification, a summary of the three years of Paul's life between his conversion and first visit to Jerusalem is all that is needed:

  - Paul was converted in Damascus (9:1–19);
  - He preached in the synagogues of Damascus for a short time immediately following his conversion (9:19–22);

- He then went on a longer trip to Arabia with the purpose of preaching to Gentiles (Galatians 1:17);
- He returned to Damascus and for the rest of the three year period and again preached in the synagogues there (9:22);
- Jews tried to find and arrest Paul (9:23);
- Paul escaped from Damascus and travelled to Jerusalem (9:25).

PAUL'S MISSIONARY ACTIVITY: FIRST JOURNEY (Ch12:25–14:28)

1. Barnabas and Saul Sent off (Ch 13:1–3)

The last verse in Acts 12 (12:25) picks up the story of Barnabas and Paul's trip to Jerusalem to deliver the relief fund, which Luke mentioned in 11:30. Luke notes that the relief visit had been made, and that Paul and Barnabas had returned to Antioch, accompanied by John Mark.

Luke introduces us to the leadership of the Antioch church, commenting that the church was "worshipping the Lord and fasting" (13:2). (This gives us an insight into the workings of the church which will be explored in Chapter 5 of this book.) The Holy Spirit spoke to them, saying: "Set apart for me Barnabas and Saul for the work to which I have called them" (13:2). Guy[31] explains that the message may have come from a prophet speaking in the meeting.

This was to be the first planned overseas mission carried out by representatives of a particular church, begun by a deliberate church decision.[32] Through the missionary activity of Barnabas and Paul, we see how the gospel spreads around the Roman Empire, particularly to Gentiles. However, as already emphasised, it was no mere human initiative but was guided by the Holy Spirit, who would continue to work throughout the mission.

It was through the Holy Spirit therefore, that Barnabas and Paul were sent off for the task of evangelising, following the laying on of hands by the leaders (13:3). The laying on of hands showed that the church supported these men as doing God's will, acknowledging that Barnabas and Paul had the authority to act on behalf of the Christian community at Antioch.

2. Cyprus (Ch 13:4–12)

Their destination was Cyprus, an island in the northeast corner of the Mediterranean Sea. As Barnabas' native land, Cyprus was a sensible place to begin the church's outreach. He would be acquainted with its ways, its people and would know his way around. Christian communities also probably existed on the island and could serve as bases (11:19). John Mark accompanied Barnabas and Paul on the journey as an extra helper. He may have been taken because he was related to Barnabas, and was probably familiar with Cyprus.

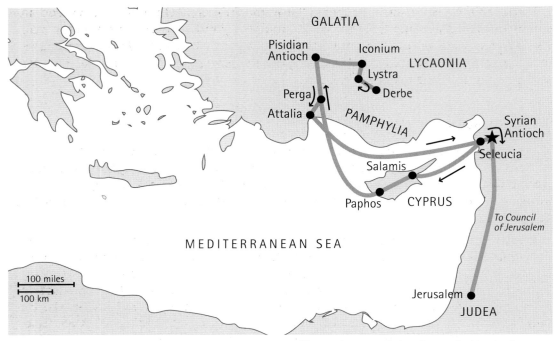

Above: A map of the first missionary journey

The first of two cities which Luke mentions in Cyprus is Salamis, the administrative centre of eastern Cyprus (13:5). Barnabas and Paul "proclaimed the word of God in the Jewish synagogues" of the city (13:5). There was probably a large Jewish population in Salamis, as there were several synagogues for Barnabas and Paul to preach in. Paul would continue this pattern of beginning his missionary work by first preaching in the synagogue (13:14, 44; 14:1, 16:13; 17:1, 10; 18:4, 19; 19:8).

The other city Luke mentions is Paphos, the provincial capital. At Paphos, the island's proconsul, Sergius Paulus, asked for a meeting with Barnabas and Paul. Presumably, they had been preaching in Paphos for some time and had come to his attention. Luke describes Sergius Paulus as "an intelligent man", in the sense that he was curious and open minded. This is one of the times in Acts where Luke presents the Roman officials as being sympathetic to the gospel. Here he said of the proconsul that he "wanted to hear the word of God" (13:7). However, it was probably more as an inquiry into the nature of what the missionaries were proclaiming in the synagogues, than a desire to be converted.[33]

There is no indication in Acts that Sergius Paulus became a Christian. Luke's main interest in him was as the setting for Paul's confrontation with Elymas (or Bar-Jesus) the sorcerer (magician), who was the proconsul's court advisor, and who opposed the preaching of the gospel (13:7–8). Bar-Jesus means 'Son of Jesus', but this name was completely inappropriate for him, as he opposed the missionaries so strongly that Paul finally confronted him.

Filled with the Holy Spirit, Paul told Bar-Jesus: "You are a child of the devil and an enemy of everything that is right! You are full of all kinds of deceit and trickery. Will you never stop perverting the right ways of the Lord?" (13:10). Paul then put a curse on the magician, saying he would be temporarily blinded (13:11). Sergius Paulus was so impressed that "he believed"[34] (13:12).

3. Significance of this story

It can be argued that Luke was interested in telling this not as the story of a conversion, but to show the superiority of God's power over the magic of the spirit world. Luke wanted to show how Paul used his apostolic authority to stop the evil influence of Bar-Jesus, proving that the power behind the gospel is superior to that of pagan magic.

It is here that Luke tells us for the first time that "Saul was also called Paul" (13:9). Luke had referred to him as 'Saul' from his first appearance in Acts (7:58), but from now on he would call him only 'Paul'. The two names are introduced casually, as though Paul already had the two names. Hanson[35] comments that "the introduction of Saul's Gentile name appropriately heralds his mission to the Gentiles". 'Saul' was a more appropriate name in the Jewish world, but now he was moving into the wider Gentile world, 'Paul' was probably regarded as more suitable.

4. Perga (Ch 13:13)

The missionaries sailed from Cyprus to Perga in Pamphylia. While describing these events, Luke for the first time, no longer speaks of 'Barnabas and Saul'. Instead, Paul is now placed ahead of Barnabas (see 11:30; 12:25; 13:2). This seems to be Luke's way of saying that Paul has taken over the leadership slot or at least the place of prominence.[36] In any case, it is clear from what follows that Paul has become the dominant partner in the missionary team.

John Mark left the evangelising team at Perga and returned to Jerusalem. Whatever the reason for Mark's departure, we later find out that Paul did not like it, referring to it as desertion (15:38). John Mark's departure led to an argument between Barnabas and Paul, and their permanent split (15:39).

5. Pisidian Antioch (Ch 13:14–15 and 13:42–52)

Paul and Barnabas travelled to Antioch in Pisidia, about 100 miles north of Perga. It was a difficult and dangerous journey, as the missionaries had to cross the Taurus mountains. The highlands were prone to sudden flooding and there was a danger from attack, as the Romans had not yet fully suppressed the bands of robbers who lived in the mountains.

When they arrived the missionaries followed the "synagogue formula".[37] The Jewish elders invited them to speak and the rest of Ch 13 is devoted to the preaching of the sermon, which will be studied in-depth at A2 level.

Summary of speech at Pisidian Antioch

In the speech, Paul gave a summary of the history of the Hebrews from the Exodus, their stay in Sinai, the entry into Canaan, the period of the judges and the monarchy as far as the reign of David. He reminded the audience of the Jewish hope of a Messiah from the line of David and declared that Jesus was this Messiah. He highlighted the condemnation of Jesus by the rulers at Jerusalem and his death, burial and resurrection. Finally Paul proclaimed the forgiveness of sins through faith in Jesus, finishing with a warning that his audience should not reject this opportunity.[38]

Synagogue

The synagogue was a place in which the Christian missionaries could find a receptive audience for the gospel message. It played a major role in Jewish life serving as a meeting place, schoolhouse, library and court. It was a centre of religious education and learning and the place where all Jews came to worship. Even more significant was the fact that Gentile proselytes and God-fearers attended the synagogue as well as Jews.

Paul's speech aroused a lot of interest and many who had heard it spoke to Paul and Barnabas after the synagogue service, to discuss the topic of salvation further (13:43). Word must have travelled during the week among the Jews and Gentiles about Paul's message because "the next Sabbath almost the whole city gathered to hear the word of the Lord" (13:44).

However, conflict with the synagogue leaders was imminent. They were irritated and "filled with jealousy" (13:45) when they saw the large crowd of Gentiles attempting to crowd into the synagogue to hear Paul. They must have refused to allow Paul to speak during the next synagogue service. At some point, he turned to the unbelieving Jews and said: "We had to speak the word of God to you first. Since you reject it and do not consider yourselves worthy of eternal life, we now turn to the Gentiles" (13:46). This began a pattern which was repeated time and time again. Paul would begin his missionary work by preaching in the synagogue. He would be rejected by the leaders and the majority of the Jewish worshippers and would then preach to the Gentiles.

"I go to the Gentiles"

Luke records three formal statements by Paul in which he said, "I go to the Gentiles." The first one is here. It is followed by the same statement in Corinth (18:6), and a final one in Rome, which closes the book of Acts (28:28).

Paul and Barnabas must have met with great success in the area around Pisidian Antioch (13:49). When the Gentiles, listening to Paul, heard that God had planned to give them salvation, "They were glad and honoured the word of the Lord" (13:48).

However, the Jewish leaders were furious and plotted with "the God-fearing women of high standing and the leading men of the city" (13:50). These were probably Gentile women who had become adherents of Judaism with their politically connected husbands.

They were probably convinced to use their husbands' influence, to have Paul and Barnabas expelled from the area (13:50). Since Paul and Barnabas were not accepted as representing a sect of Judaism, they were regarded as nothing more than trouble-makers. As such, they should be expelled since they were disturbing the Roman peace. Following expulsion, Paul and Barnabas "shook the dust from their feet" in protest (13:51). This was a gesture Jesus had suggested his disciples practice when facing persecution (Luke 9:5; 10:11).

To shake off dust

It was a custom for Jews to shake off the dust of a pagan town from their feet when they returned to their own land, as a symbol of cleansing themselves from the impurity of sinners who did not worship God. For Jews to do this to their fellow Jews was equivalent to regarding them as pagan Gentiles. In a similar way, the Christians were indicating that Jews who rejected the gospel and drove out the missionaries were no longer truly part of Israel and were no better than unbelievers.[39]

6. Iconium (Ch 14:1–7)

Paul and Barnabas had established a congregation of believers in Pisidian Antioch However, they were forced to move on to Iconium. Following their usual procedure, they went to the Jewish synagogue to preach to those assembled for services (14:1). Their preaching was so effective that large numbers of both Jews and Gentiles believed the gospel.

As before, the unbelieving Jews caused trouble for the missionaries. They began a smear campaign to poison the minds of the Gentiles "against the brothers" (14:2). In spite of this persecution, Paul and Barnabas "spent considerable time" in Iconium (14:3). This is an example of one of the times where Luke gives few details of events, and condenses the work of several months into a few sentences.

Paul and Barnabas preached effectively in Iconium and God performed miraculous wonders through them (14:3). However, the city remained divided about them: "Some sided with the Jews, others with the apostles" (14:4). Eventually the Jews plotted with some Gentiles and political leaders of Iconium to gather a mob, beat up Paul and Barnabas, and stone them to death (14:5). The missionaries were told of the plot, perhaps by sympathetic Jews, so they quickly left Iconium before the plotters could get to them (14:6).

"Apostle'"

Hanson[40] interestingly comments that Paul and Barnabas are referred to as "apostles" in Acts only in 14:4 and 14. This will be useful information when you are studying Paul's defence of his apostolic authority at A2 level.

---

7. Lystra and Derbe (Ch 14:8–28)

Paul and Barnabas travelled to "the Lycaonian cities of Lystra and Derbe" (14:6), where they continued to preach the gospel. Luke only reports a single event in Lystra, which began with the healing of a crippled man lame from birth (14:8). Paul had been speaking to what was probably a crowd of Gentiles in a public place and he was somehow drawn to the faith of this crippled man. Suddenly Paul directed his words to the man, demanding him to: "Stand up on your feet!" (14:10). At once the man jumped up and began to walk.

This story depicts Paul as a genuine messenger of God, similar to Peter, who also healed a lame man (3:1–10). In fact, the expressions Luke uses in the two accounts are strikingly similar: "lame from birth", "looked directly at him", "jumped up and began to walk". In the same way, both Peter and Paul are shown to be exercising the same power as did Jesus, who also healed a crippled person (Luke 5:17–26).

It should be noted that the people of Lystra, were probably acquainted to some extent with three languages:

1. Latin would have been the official language of the Roman Empire.

2. Greek would have been understood to some degree by most of the Lystrans.

3. Their native dialect, the Lycaonian language.

Paul had probably preached in the Greek language, which most people would understand. It is less likely, however, that he would have understood the Lycaonian language. It seems that following Paul's healing of the crippled man the Lystrans thought that they were experiencing a divine visitation from the gods of Zeus and Hermes. When the beggar jumped up and walked, the crowd began to shout in their own language, "The gods have come down to us in human form!" (14:11). They believed that Barnabas was Zeus, and Paul, as the main speaker, was thought to be Hermes.

Zeus and Hermes

According to the legend, Zeus and Hermes (to use their Greek names) came to earth in the nearby region of Phrygia disguised as human beings. They looked for somewhere to stay but no one would show them any hospitality. Finally, an old peasant couple, Philemon and his wife Baucis, welcomed them into their home, even though they could hardly afford it. The gods were angry and destroyed all the people for their lack of hospitality, except for the gracious Philemon and Baucis. The couple's humble home was transformed into a temple, of which they were given the charge until their death.

This ancient legend was well known in southern Galatia, and it may explain why Paul and Barnabas became the objects of such a wild celebration.[41]

If their ancestors had failed to honour the gods on their previous visit, the Lystrans were determined not to make the same mistake. So the priest at the local temple arranged a sacrifice to honour the presence of Paul and Barnabas (14:13). Fernando[42] comments that when the apostles found this out "their response was swift and typically Jewish", tearing their clothes, "the usual sign of indignation".[43] They were horrified by the idea that they should be thought of as gods.

The Speech at Lystra

Paul made a moving speech (14–17) in the hope of stopping the attempt of the Lystrans to worship them. It is an example of how the gospel was introduced to purely pagan audiences. The speech differs widely in content from those delivered to Jews and Gentile followers of Judaism. Obviously, when speaking to Jews the believers had the luxury of drawing upon the Old Testament scriptures. With a purely pagan audience, however, it was necessary to backtrack to first proclaim the existence of the one true God. Therefore, in this speech to the Lystrans, Paul began by explaining that the one God was the creator of all living things (14:15).

Before this, however, Paul and Barnabas were forced to deny that they were gods. When they realised what was about to happen, that the Lystrans were going to make sacrifices to them, they raced into the crowd screaming for them to stop: "We too are only men, human like you" (14:15). Paul was saying he and Barnabas had no special qualities.

Paul and Barnabas urged the Lystrans to "turn from these worthless things to the living God" (14:15); in other words, to give up their idolatry. Paul advocated that the one true God is he "who made heaven and earth and sea and everything in them" (14:15). This was a very simple form of 'natural theology'. It means that nature itself bears witness to the existence of a creator God.

Paul and Barnabas went on to insist that the works of creation should lead us to understand that God is kind and merciful (14:17). God is not a vengeful deity who becomes angry over nothing (as Zeus and Hermes were when they destroyed those failing to show them hospitality).

The proof of God's kindness can be seen in his providing rain for crops (14:17). God shows his presence through the good things people enjoy. Since Paul's audience was probably made up of a large number of farmers, they would have appreciated the importance of food, and that they were dependent on God for its supply.

It has been suggested that this speech was incomplete because there was no mention of the death and resurrection of Jesus, and its meaning for the lives of the audience. Perhaps Barnabas and Paul's first concern was to stop the crowd from making sacrifices to them (14:18). Luke implies that the Lystrans failed to grasp Paul's message about God from natural theology. Bruce[44] comments that "they had been made to look foolish, and felt resentful".

Sometime after this turbulent event, Jews from Pisidian Antioch and Iconium, who were opposed to Paul and Barnabas, came into Lystra and began to preach against the missionaries. Eventually, they "won the crowd over" (14:19), which shows just how fickle the Lystrans were. At one time they were calling the missionaries gods. Now they had no respect for them. No doubt they were disappointed that Barnabas and Paul claimed to be no more than ordinary human beings.

As a result the crowd attacked Paul and stoned him. Thinking he was dead, they dragged his body away and dumped it outside the city (14:19). However, as the disciples gathered around Paul's body, probably to give him a decent burial, "he got up and went back into the city" (14:20). Luke does not list this event as a miracle, although Bruce[45] feels it "has a flavour of a miracle about it". It may have been that Paul was beaten into unconsciousness, and then revived. Even so, the fact that the stoning did not kill him indicated Paul was under God's protection.

Once revived, Paul went back into Lystra, and then he and Barnabas left the next day for Derbe. Luke gives no details about the activities of Barnabas and Paul in Derbe. However, their missionary work must have been successful, because their preaching won a large number of disciples (14:21). It also seems that they did not suffer any persecution in Derbe.

Paul and Barnabas prepared to return to Syrian Antioch (the sponsor church) after finishing their missionary activity. They backtracked by returning to Lystra, Iconium and Pisidian Antioch, not to preach the gospel, but for pastoral purposes. Naturally the threat of harm from Jews and city officials was still a distinct possibility. However, the missionaries probably kept a low profile by avoiding public preaching, for Paul and Barnabas were apparently able to gain entry into the cities without any bother. Bruce[46] sums up their brave determination, commenting that "tribute must be paid to the courage of the two men in returning so soon to Lystra, Iconium, and Pisidian Antioch – cities from which they had so lately been expelled with shameful brutality".

This was, in a sense, the end of the first missionary journey as far as preaching the gospel to outsiders was concerned, except for a brief mention of it in Perga (14:25).

After arriving in Antioch, Paul and Barnabas gave a full report of their activities to the church. They especially pointed out how God "had opened the door of faith to the Gentiles" (14:27). Luke ends the account by saying that Paul and Barnabas "stayed there a long time with the disciples." (14:28).

OTHER ASPECTS OF HUMAN EXPERIENCE

The Internet

Just as the printing press transformed education, learning, evangelism and communication, laying the foundations for the Renaissance, the arts, sciences, and the world as we know it today; so the digital revolution is bringing about a similar huge change in evangelism, Christian discipleship and community, in ways which are only just beginning.

Although the Internet first grew in USA and northern Europe, it is now no longer a toy for the rich West. There are internet users throughout the world. Some Christians today believe that using a computer for online religious activity could become the main form of religious experience and evangelism in the years that lie ahead.

So just how can Christians reach out to people through the internet? One suggestion, which might seem a bit odd, is: 'If you want to convince people of Christianity, don't write about the Gospel.' In other words, think about what most people are searching for online and write about the things that interest them, giving a Christian slant: sport, health, sex and relationships, advice on personal problems, films, music, news-related items and famous people.

TASKS

a) Describe the successes Paul experienced during his first missionary journey.

- Extent of ground covered
- Sergius Paulus in Paphos; power over Elymas
- Pisidian Antioch
- Initial preaching in Iconium
- Appointed elders in every church

b) Comment on the claim that the spread of the gospel owes much to Paul.

- Use examples from any of the missionary journeys to answer this question if asked in an AS examination.
- For now, however, you have only covered the first journey. You can use the information from the above answer to highlight how Paul's successes helped to spread the gospel. Evaluate the events – did Paul's actions aid the spread of the gospel or where there times when they did not?

PAUL'S MISSIONARY ACTIVITY: SECOND JOURNEY

The purpose of the second missionary journey was to revisit the churches Paul and Barnabas had established "in order to strengthen and encourage the groups of believers".[47] They were determined to make sure that the new converts would not fall away back into Judaism or paganism.[48] Paul then intended to travel to Ephesus, the great commercial centre on the coast of Asia Minor. This would be a logical step in his goal to evangelise the Roman world. However, the Holy Spirit prevented them from going into the province of Asia (16:6). Luke does not explain the reason for this. Paul instead turned north and went to Mysia. Paul wanted to circle back to preach in Bithynia, but again the Holy Spirit would not let this happen (Acts 16:7).

1. Troas

a. Disagreement between Paul and Barnabas (Ch 15:36–41)

There was a strong disagreement between Paul and Barnabas as to whether they should take John Mark along on this journey. He had abandoned the first mission, and Paul did not want to risk the same happening again. Bruce[49] comments that Luke "indicates at a later point in his narrative (15:38) that Paul regarded his departure as desertion". However, Barnabas wanted to give his cousin another chance to prove himself. In the end they decided to separate with Barnabas and Mark going to Cyprus while Paul and Silas went to Galatia. "We hear no more of Barnabas's activities"[50] as Luke concentrates on the missionary activity of Paul and Silas. Paul may have sent for Silas to join him as he had connections with the Jerusalem Church. He was also a Roman citizen like Paul, "an asset in an itinerant ministry in the Roman Empire".[51]

This disagreement reminds us that arguments can arise even between good people, causing separation. Paul and John Mark were unable to work together, therefore the decision to go their separate ways was probably best for the sake of the spread of the gospel. One positive thing that came out of it however, was the fact that now there were two missionary teams, instead of one. Barnabas and John Mark went to Cyprus, while Paul and Silas went to Syria and Cilicia.

Above: A map of the second missionary journey

b. Timothy joins Paul and Silas (Ch 16:1–5)

Paul and Silas began the journey by travelling west through the cities of southern Galatia, preaching and distributing the letter from the Council of Jerusalem (Acts 16:4). They preached in Derbe and Lystra and while in Lystra they met Timothy, who wanted to go with them. As Timothy was half-Jewish, Paul circumcised him, in order to help them with their mission among the Jews (16:1–3). As a full Jew he would be of much greater help to Paul when they went to Jewish synagogues to preach. So Paul, Silas and Timothy worked together during Paul's second missionary journey.

 TASK

In Paul's letters (1 Corinthians 7:19; Galatians 5:2,6; 6:15) he writes that circumcision is not necessary for salvation. So why have Timothy circumcised? Timothy was already saved through faith!

Paul was in fact forward thinking. He had Timothy circumcised in order that a greater number of Jews might be saved. Read 1 Corinthians 9:20 and explain what this means.

c. Paul's Vision of the Man of Macedonia (Ch 16:6–10)

In obedience to the Holy Spirit, they came to the city of Troas, which was a prominent commercial centre. We know that Paul was joined here by Luke the doctor, because a 'we section' begins at this point and continues until they leave Philippi in Macedonia.

While there, Paul had a vision one night of a man from Macedonia who said, "Come over to Macedonia and help us". "Dreams were a recognised means of divine communication in ancient times".[52] Luke explains how they immediately prepared to go there.

2. Philippi

a. Lydia's Conversion in Philippi (Ch 16:11–15)

Paul, Silas, Timothy (and Luke) travelled to Philippi, "a Roman colony and the leading city of that district of Macedonia" (Acts 16:12). It was an ancient town. There Paul followed his custom to speak first to the Jews. This occurred by the river as there were not enough Jewish men for a synagogue in Philippi. The arrival of the missionaries led to successful evangelism especially among women associated with the Jewish faith. It is interesting that women are mentioned (16:13). Lydia, a prominent dealer in purple, was converted and showed hospitality to the missionaries in her home.[53] She had been called after the region from which she came. "The act of baptism also embraced her household".[54] It was a common thing for members of a household to embrace Christianity all at one time (see Acts 11:14; 16:31, 33; 18:8).

b. Paul and Silas in Prison (Ch 16:16–40)

Paul and Silas healed a demon-possessed girl, who had the gift of second sight and made money for her owners by telling fortunes. It was not the slave girl who was doing the fortune-telling, but the evil spirit within her. When she met Paul and his companions she called after them, "These men are servants of the Most High God, who are telling you the way to be saved".[55] Marshall[56] points out that this had the effect of giving the missionaries some unexpected publicity, because she followed them for several days. As it became clear to Paul that she was possessed by an evil spirit, he went on to exorcise the spirit by using the name of Jesus. 'The exorcism deprived the girl of her ability or willingness to tell fortunes",[57] which roused the anger of her pagan owners, who dragged Paul and Silas before the magistrates. It is interesting that when the owners made their charge, their real motive fades into the background and they insist they are concerned that the missionaries were causing a public disturbance and promoting non-Roman customs. As a result, Paul and Silas were beaten[58] with rods and thrown into prison.

Following a command, the jailor placed them in the most secure part of the prison, taking the extra precaution of fastening their legs securely in wooden stocks, which would have been extremely painful. A sleepless night followed for Paul and Silas but in the midst of their suffering they sang praises to God. Suddenly, an earthquake erupted, causing the prison doors to open, and loosening the bonds securing the prisoners. Despite the possibility of freedom, the prisoners made no attempt to escape. Many ask why? We are used to thinking of prisons as places that are fairly well-kept, clean, and conducive to good treatment. However, prisoners at Paul's time did not have such privileges. As well as being dark, cramped, badly ventilated, and sweltering, prisons were breeding pits for disease. If there was any reason why the other inmates did not try to escape, it may be because, unlike Paul and Silas, they were simply too weak to go anywhere. Bruce[59] argues, however, that it may have been "the awed impression which the two missionaries' behaviour produced on the other prisoners that enabled them to dissuade those others from making their escape while the going was good".

The jailor assumed they had gone and terrified of receiving the death penalty (see Acts 12:18–19), he decided to kill himself. However, he was stopped in his tracks when he heard the voice of Paul shouting that no one had left the prison. Their joyful outlook influenced the jailor, who became a believer after this miraculous event. Nevertheless, "it took an earthquake and confrontation with death to make him take thought for his salvation".[60] Just as Lydia had done, the jailor had all of his family baptised.

The following day the magistrates authorised the release of the captives. Before leaving, however, and probably for the sake of the local church, Paul demanded an apology from the city officials, revealing that he and Silas were Roman citizens. The magistrates gave in, knowing that if word reached a higher authority they would be in trouble. After their release, the missionaries visited Lydia and some others and then headed for Thessalonica.

3. Thessalonica (Ch 17:1–9)

It is obvious from the text that Luke did not continue on the journey, as the tense in the text changes to the third person plural. Thessalonica, like Philippi, was an ancient city and had a Jewish population. While staying there, Paul supported himself financially (1 Thess 2:9; 2 Thess 3:7–9), which may have taken up valuable preaching time. However, he stayed for at least three weeks, teaching in the synagogues on the Sabbath.

Acts 17:2–3 describes the evangelistic style Paul used with the Jews. His preaching was effective and some Jews believed, as well as many God-fearers and prominent women.[61] Marshall[62] points out that many God-fearers, while attracted to the spiritual aspects of Judaism, were unwilling to take the step of circumcision. Christianity, therefore, appealed to them.

Paul's success caused jealousy among the Jewish leaders. As Thessalonica was a free city, it had an assembly before which charges could be brought. The Jews tried to bring Paul and Silas before this assembly by getting a crowd of 'wasters' to start a riot. Therefore they could argue that the missionaries were guilty of disturbing the peace. These wasters gathered outside Jason's house, hoping to find Paul, but none of the missionaries were there. In their frustration, they grabbed Jason and some of the other Christians, and instead of taking them before the assembly, they went even further by taking them before the magistrates.[63] With gross exaggeration, they argued that the Christians had been causing trouble all over the world and now they had come to Thessalonica. Furthermore, Jason was protecting the missionaries in his own home. As a result the magistrates "contracted a legal bond" with Jason not to harbour Paul anymore.[64]

As soon as night fell, the local Christians sent Paul and Silas secretly away to Berea, in the south west. Paul was forced to leave behind the young church in Thessalonica, even though it was still in need of teaching and faced the risk of persecution.

4. Berea (Ch 17:10–15)

Paul's ministry in Berea was calmer than in Philippi or Thessalonica. Here the audience in the synagogue "were of more noble character than the Thessalonians, for they received the message with great eagerness and examined the Scriptures every day to see if what Paul said was true" (17:11). Many believed, including, again, some prominent Greek women.

When the Jews in Thessalonica heard of the success of Paul's ministry in Berea, they, too, went to Berea to stir up trouble. They were so successful that Paul was forced to leave and sail to Athens. Once there, he sent for Silas and Timothy to join him.

 OTHER ASPECTS OF HUMAN EXPERIENCE

What can we learn from the example of the Bereans in dealing with new religious teaching?

5. Athens (Ch 17:16–34)

a. Paul and the Philosophers (Ch 17:16–21)

Paul began his ministry in Athens by speaking in the synagogue and the market place. There he confronted philosophers, such as the Epicureans and the Stoics. They regarded Paul as a babbler, who was preaching about strange deities and the resurrection. They decided that he should present his views to the Areopagus (the city's council of philosophical leaders). The name 'Areopagus' simply comes from the hill on which this council would often meet. Paul had the opportunity to preach to the educated pagans in Athens.

His speech, which is summarised below, will be studied in detail at A2 level.

Summary of Paul's Speech at Athens (17:22–31)

Paul's speech was spoken in an exalted rhetorical style, showing him to be well educated and intelligent. Theologically, the speech follows Paul's normal approach to pagans (eg at Lystra in Acts 14:14–17):

- God is the lord of the world
- Man is God's creation and needs him
- God and man are related so idolatry is foolish

b. Aftermath (Ch 17:32–34)

The Greeks mocked the idea of a bodily resurrection as distasteful to their traditions. However a few people were converted, including one member of the council, Dionysius. Longenecker[65] comments that from Athens Paul "was dismissed with polite contempt rather than being violently driven out". At this point Silas and Timothy arrived from Berea to join Paul in Athens. Paul sent Timothy back to strengthen the church in Thessalonica and Silas to Macedonia. They were to join him in Corinth (Acts 18:1, 5; 1 Thess 3:1–2).

6. Corinth (Ch 18:1–11)

a. Introduction

Corinth was the capital city of the Roman province of Achaia with a Jewish minority. Marshall[66] believes that Corinth was one of the most important cities visited by Paul in the course of his missionary work. Paul stayed in Corinth, a commercial city renowned for its wealth and wickedness, for a year and a half. He probably stayed so long to establish a church that would be capable of evangelising the surrounding areas.

b. Encouragement for Paul

On arrival he met a pious Jewish couple, Aquila and Priscilla from Rome, with whom he quickly formed "a firm and lifelong friendship."[67] They may well already have been believers for there was a flourishing church in Rome.[68] However, they had been expelled from Rome, along with the other Jews, by the emperor Claudius, because of Jewish unrest. As Paul shared the same job of tent making with Aquila and Priscilla, he stayed and worked with them to support himself. Every Sabbath he would preach in the synagogue to argue the Christian case to the Jews and Gentiles who attended the services.

Further encouragement to Paul was the arrival of Silas and Timothy. They brought news about the recently established church in Thessalonica. They probably also brought gifts of money which enabled Paul to preach full-time rather than having to support himself.

c. Opposition

His preaching, however, became more and more resisted by the Jewish authorities. In the end, Paul felt it best to separate from them, but not before he let them know how he felt. The fact that he shook out his clothes in protest was a sign of breaking off fellowship with them. By rejecting the Gospel, the Jews had brought upon themselves the judgement of God. So at Corinth too he would take his saving message to people who knew how to appreciate it.[69] From now on he would turn to the Gentiles. He moved his preaching next door to the house of Titius Justus (18:7). Many were converted including Crispus, the ruler of the synagogue, and Gaius (Titius Justus).

d. A Vision

At this time, Paul must have felt discouraged about his progress for the Lord appeared to him in a vision, encouraging him not to be afraid of harm, to keep on speaking, as he had "many people in this city" (Acts 18:9–10). It is clear from Paul's letters to the Corinthians that a large church did in fact develop in Corinth, and spread throughout the region.

e. Gallio (Ch 18:12–17)

An important event which occurred while Paul was in Corinth was his appearance before Gallio, proconsul of Achaia. Gallio had recently arrived in Corinth to carry out his one-year term and the Jews used the opportunity to attack Paul by bringing him before the proconsul. He would have had the power to prevent Paul from preaching, not only in Achaia, but in every province of the Roman Empire. Judaism was one of the legal religions of the Roman Empire. So the Jews charged Paul with preaching a new illegal religion and of persuading the people to worship God in ways contrary to the law (18:13). Hanson[70] comments on the vagueness of this charge. It is obvious that they wanted some sort of punishment against Paul. Gallio, however, regarded their dispute as a religious one and had them "ejected from the court".

Significance of Gallio's decision

Marshall[71] comments that "it was probably Gallio's refusal to support Jewish opposition to Paul which encouraged him to stay on in Corinth for some time." Gallio's decision not to forbid Paul to preach meant that the Christians were able to legally preach throughout the Roman Empire for the next twelve years, "until imperial policy toward Christians underwent a complete reversal."[72] This freedom ended when the emperor Nero cruelly persecuted the Christians in Rome.

7. Return to Antioch (Ch 18:18–22)

Acts 18:18–22 describes Paul's journey back to his home church at the end of the second missionary journey. He sailed from Cenchrea to Ephesus with Aquila and Priscilla. He only stopped briefly in Ephesus, although he did manage to speak in the synagogue there and promised to come back to Ephesus again. From Ephesus Paul went to Syria and then "went up and greeted the church" (v 22) in Jerusalem, before returning to Antioch, where he stayed for some months.

We can see that Paul was still willing to keep Jewish customs for he took a vow in Corinth, and in nearby Cenchrea had his head shaved when the vow was complete (18:18; 21:23–24). Jews made vows to God either in thankfulness for past blessings or as part of a petition for future blessings.[73] This is an example of Paul's determination to do what he could to win the Jews as well as the Gentiles (1 Cor 9:20).

Paul's second missionary journey was complete. To sum up, he had strengthened the churches in Galatia and planted strong churches in Macedonia and Achaia. His next mission was to establish a strong Christian centre in Ephesus.

 TASKS

a) **Give an account of the main features of Paul's work either in Athens or Corinth.**

- This answer really only requires you to recall the main events that occurred in one of these places.

b) **Describe the struggles Paul faced during his second missionary journey.**

- Argument with Barnabas over John Mark
- Prison at Philippi
- Riot in Thessalonica
- Jews in Berea

PAUL'S MISSIONARY ACTIVITY: THIRD JOURNEY (CH 18:23 – 21:16)

After staying several months in Antioch, Paul set off on his third missionary journey. This transition from the second journey to the third happens very subtly in Acts 18:23 so you should be aware that this is a new journey! This journey was the longest of the three, lasting for nearly three years. Paul's companions included Timothy and Titus. We also know that Luke was with him on the return to Jerusalem, as there is another 'we' passage in the text.

1. Revisiting the churches in southern Galatia (Ch 18:23)

At the beginning of the third Missionary Journey, Paul set out again for Galatia and nearby Phrygia to strengthen and encourage the believers he and Barnabas had established on their first missionary journey.

2. Ephesus

a. Apollos at Ephesus (Ch 18:23–28)

Marshall[74] comments that Luke's account of Paul's activity in Ephesus is "unusually full and vivid". The third Missionary journey begins with an introduction to Apollos, a Jewish scholar and a speaker of great eloquence, who was trained in the Greek Old Testament in Alexandria.[75] He knew much about Christ and powerfully preached the same message. However, Apollos had only learned about John's baptism, which John had performed in order to prepare people for Jesus (Mark 1:2–4). Bruce[76] explains that "John's baptism was one of preparation rather than one of fulfilment, as Christian baptism now was." Priscilla and Aquila, having just arrived there with Paul from Corinth, heard Apollos preach and realised that he lacked full understanding of the gospel message. So they instructed him properly about Jesus. As a result Apollos became "an effective evangelist as well as a pastor to the church".[77]

After a while, Apollos went to Corinth, where he became a preacher in the Corinthian church (18:27–19:1). Hanson[78] comments that it is worth noting that 18:27 implies that Christianity had reached Ephesus before Paul arrived there. Paul mentions Apollos several times in 1 Corinthians.

b. Paul arrives at Ephesus (Ch 19:1–7)

Paul had tried to go to Ephesus during his second journey but had been prohibited by the Holy Spirit. Finally he was able to spend some time there. On arrival, he found some disciples who, just like Apollos, had only heard about John the Baptist. After Paul preached the gospel to them, they became Christians. They were baptised and Paul laid his hands on them, probably "as a special act of fellowship,

Above: A map of the third missionary journey

incorporating the people concerned into the fellowship of the church".[79] This is the third place in Acts where Luke describes how the believers spoke in tongues after receiving the Holy Spirit (see 2:4; 10:44–46).

c. Paul's move from preaching in the synagogue (Ch 19:8–10)

About three months later there was an objection to what Paul was preaching in the synagogue. Therefore, as in Corinth, Paul separated from the synagogue and "moved to neutral ground",[80] leading the Christians to worship in the hall of Tyrannus, which he used for over two more years. Tyrannus probably taught only in the mornings, as most people slept in the afternoons due to the intense heat. This would have left the hall free for Paul to preach in the afternoons. Paul wanted everyone to hear the gospel, "and in his remarkable stay of at least twenty-seven months, he succeeded in bringing the gospel to the entire population of the province of Asia" (v 10).

d. The Sons of Sceva (Ch 19:11–22)

"Paul's preaching was accompanied by striking healings and exorcisms."[81] Even pieces of clothing that he touched were taken to the sick in the hope that they could be cured through contact with it. In the first century there were many Jewish sorcerers. When they saw Paul driving out demons in Jesus' name some of these sorcerers tried to copy him. The seven sons of a priest called Sceva, tried to use Jesus' name to cast out a demon but "with drastic consequences."[82] The evil spirit did not recognise them and attacked the seven men, sending them away bruised and naked.

"The effect among a superstitious people was to cause both fear and praise for the name of Jesus."[83] When the people saw how the demons fled when Paul used the name of Jesus, they were afraid. Many repented and accepted the gospel. They probably realised that no demon could protect them from the power of Jesus' name. All this seemed to set off a campaign against magic. At that time sorcerers used to recite 'mantras', which were meaningless words written on scrolls. Many believed that by reciting these mantras it was possible to gain great power. When some of the sorcerers themselves were even converted, they piled up their scrolls and burned them, even though they were worth fifty thousand drachmas.[84]

OTHER ASPECTS OF HUMAN EXPERIENCE

Holy Relics

The word 'relic' comes from the Latin 'reliquiae' (remains). A relic is an object, such as a piece of a body or a personal item of someone of religious significance, carefully preserved as a memorial. As well as being an important aspect of the Roman Catholic Church, relics are associated with Hinduism, Buddhism and many other personal belief systems.

One of the earliest sources used to support the value of relics is found in 2 Kings 13:20–21: "Elisha died and was buried. Now Moabite raiders used to enter the country every spring. Once while some Israelites were burying a man, suddenly they saw a band of raiders; so they threw the man's body into Elisha's tomb. When the body touched Elisha's bones, the man came to life and stood up on his feet."

These verses are cited to claim that the Holy Spirit's indwelling also affects the physical body, that God can do miracles through the bodies of his servants. Also cited is the veneration of Polycarp's relics recorded in the Martyrdom of Polycarp (written AD150–160). With regards to relics that are objects, an often cited passage is Acts 19:11–12, which says that Paul's handkerchiefs were filled by God with healing power.

In the early centuries of the church many tales of miracles were attributed to relics. These tales are collected in books of hagiography such as the 'Golden Legend' or the works of 'Caesar of Heisterbach'. Such miracle tales made relics much sought after during the Middle Ages.

There are also many relics attributed to Jesus, perhaps most famously the 'Shroud of Turin', which is claimed to be the burial shroud of Jesus, although this is disputed. Pieces of the 'True Cross' were one of the most highly sought after of such relics; many churches claimed to possess a piece of it, so many that John Calvin famously commented that there were enough pieces of the True Cross to build a ship from, although a study in 1870 found that put together the claimed relics weighed less than 1.7kg (0.04m³).

Relics are divided into three groups:

1. First-Class Relics

Items directly associated with the events of Christ's life (manger, cross, etc), or the physical remains of a saint (a bone, a hair, a limb etc.). Traditionally, a martyr's relics are often more prized than the relics of other saints. Also, some saints' relics are known for their extraordinary incorruptibility and so would have high regard. It is important to note that parts of the saint that were significant to that saint's life are more prized relics. For instance, King Saint Stephen of Hungary's right forearm is especially important because of his status as a ruler. A famous theologian's head may be his most important relic; the head of St Thomas Aquinas was removed by the monks at the Cistercian abbey at Fossanova where he died. Logically, if a saint did a lot of travelling then the bones of his feet may be prized.

2. Second-Class Relics

An item that the saint wore (a sock, a shirt, a glove, etc.). Also included is an item that the saint owned or frequently used, for example, a crucifix, book etc. Again, an item more important in the saint's life is thus a more important relic.

3. Third-Class Relics

Anything which has touched a first or second class relic of a saint.

The sale of relics is strictly forbidden by the Church. Saint Jerome declared, "We do not worship, we do not adore, for fear that we should bow down to the creature rather than to the creator, but we venerate the relics of the martyrs in order the better to adore him whose martyrs they are" (Ad Riparium, i, P.L., XXII, 907).

Importance of Relics in Medieval Christianity

Since the beginning of Christianity, believers have seen relics as a way to come closer to a person who was deemed divine and so form a closer bond with God. Since Christians during the Middle Ages often took pilgrimages to shrines of holy people, relics became a large business. The pilgrims saw the purchasing of a relic as, in a small way, a means to bring the shrine back home with him or her, since during the Middle Ages the concept of physical proximity to the 'holy' (tombs of saints or their personal objects) was considered extremely important. Now, instead of having to travel hundreds of miles to become close to a venerated saint, one could enjoy intimacy with him/her from home.[85]

The relics of Saint Therese

In 2001 the relics of Saint Therese (the 'Little Flower') toured Northern Ireland. Record numbers of people turned out to venerate them in Armagh city. St Therese is traditionally associated with roses. When she died, she is believed to have said, "I let fall a shower of roses". As a result, roses have come to be associated with the granting of favours, cures, or relief from suffering. Many people queuing up to see the relics outside churches carried roses, which they pressed against the brass and mahogany sides of the casket as they filed past. Some stopped to kiss the casket, and repeat prayers to St Therese.

From the front seat of the Theresemobile, the tour's national co-ordinator Father Linus Ryan manned three mobile phones and held press conferences on the road. "We're into our second million half way through the tour," he said. "There is a mass movement of the Irish population everywhere we go, which has to be supernatural in origin. She has got a supernatural magnetism." Father Ryan admitted that before the tour began he was concerned that after years of rapid economic growth Ireland might be losing touch with religion. Now he is drawing the opposite lesson. "We have to conclude that material things are not giving people what they hoped for", he said. "There is a great spiritual hunger out there."[86]

 TASK

Discuss the value and validity of Holy Relics.

 OTHER ASPECTS OF HUMAN EXPERIENCE

Magic

Hanson[87] comments that "The Christian church from the beginning officially disbelieved in magic and set its face against it." Many people today are fascinated by magic and ignore the dangers associated with it.

Research how the church today deals with the whole area of magic.

d. The Riot in Ephesus (Ch 19:23–41)

Towards the end of Paul's stay in Ephesus a riot was caused by Demetrius the metalworker (19:23–41). Fernando[88] comments that the riot "fits in with a theme that Luke considered important: opposition to the gospel." The Ephesians had built a huge Temple in honour of Artemis, the greatest goddess of all in Asia. The silversmiths made little silver images of Artemis and sold them for a huge profit. However, as people became Christians, and stopped worshipping Artemis, the sale of these statues fell and the silversmiths lost out financially. Demetrius tried to cover up his real worry about loss of trade with some talk about religious zeal.[89] "The ordinary people might not be too concerned that Demetrius was going out of business, but they might well take to heart the possibility that the temple of Artemis might lose its position in popular regard."[90]

A protest meeting followed, "which culminated in a protest march through the streets."[91] The instigators dragged Gaius and Aristarchus into the theatre. Paul himself wanted to appear to speak to the crowd but he was advised not to because the crowd was so angry. The meeting was disorganised and some people did not even know what it was for. The Jews present were worried "about trouble coming to them, so they wanted to distance themselves from Paul"[92] and they probably forced Alexander to come before the crowd to tell them that the Jews had no connection with the Christians. The hysterical crowd however, realised that Alexander was a Jew, and refused to listen to him.

Ephesus was a free city within the Roman Empire and so it had its own administration. The city clerk, worried that news of the riot might reach the Romans, intervened by trying to get the crowd to calm down. He reminded them that complaints should be brought before the court or legal assembly. He was probably concerned that the Romans would punish the whole city by taking their freedom away. Marshall[93] comments that the clerk was not an advocate for Christianity, but a defender of law and order, anxious that the city should not get a reputation for disorderliness and illegal action. His appeal was successful and the crowd dispersed and it seems that no further action was taken against the missionaries.

The period of Paul's time in Ephesus drew to a close. Bruce[94] concludes that "it had been a most fruitful and encouraging ministry."

 ## OTHER ASPECTS OF HUMAN EXPERIENCE

Martin Luther King's attitude to violence

Many people see riots and violence as a way to be heard; a means to an end. Martin Luther King, a Baptist minister and the civil rights leader who was assassinated in 1968, believed in the power of non-violence – not to humiliate but to win over.

Find out what you can about Martin Luther King's methods in reaching his goals.

Make comparisons with Paul's missionary work. (It is not necessary to provide biographical details for this task.)

3. Through Macedonia and Greece (Ch 20:1–6)

Paul spent about a year travelling through Macedonia and then went to Greece. From there he planned to return by boat to Syria and Jerusalem but just as he was about to get on the boat he heard that the Jews from Corinth were plotting to kill him so he changed his plans to get away from them. Paul's companions did take the boat and waited for him in Troas. Meanwhile Paul went by foot to Philippi where he met up again with Luke (notice the change of pronoun in v 5).

a. Eutychus is Raised From the Dead at Troas (Ch 20:7–12)

The believers at Troas gathered to celebrate the Lord's Supper on the Sunday.[95] A young man called Eutychus fell asleep, dropped to the ground from the third storey window and was picked up dead. As Luke the author of Acts was a doctor, he would have known for certain that the young man was dead. Marshall[96] comments that Luke would not have devoted space in his book for the raising of someone who was merely apparently dead. Paul was able to bring Eutychus back to life. Paul continued talking until daylight and then Paul's companions boarded a ship to Jerusalem.

4. Paul and the Ephesian Elders (Ch 20:13–38)

Ephesus was about thirty miles from Miletus. As the ship had to stop for several days at Miletus, Paul sent word to the elders of Ephesus to come to meet him there. All the Ephesian elders had become Christians through Paul and he had baptised most of them. In the verses that follow we have an example of Paul's preaching among Christians. This speech will be studied in detail at A2 level.

Paul's Speech at Miletus to the Elders of Ephesus

- Paul had appointed Elders to look after the churches in his absence.
- He reminded the Ephesians of his work among them.
- He defended himself against those who would slander him.
- He predicted that a disaster would come upon him at Jerusalem.
- He encouraged the elders to look after the church and to be on their guard from dangers from within the church.[97]

5. Paul departs for Jerusalem (Ch 21:1–16)

After praying with the Ephesian elders, Paul boarded the ship and sailed for Jerusalem, where he had planned to arrive in time for the Jewish feast of Pentecost. Luke describes the final stages of the third missionary journey in the form of a 'we' passage, which took the missionaries to Cos, Rhodes and then Patara, where they found a ship bound for Phoenicia. This ship brought Paul to Tyre, where the believers pleaded with Paul not to go to Jerusalem. Then the missionaries travelled on to Ptolemais and to Caesarea, where they lodged with Philip the Evangelist. Philip had four unmarried daughters who had the gift of prophecy. While there, a prophet called Agabus (see also 11:28), "symbolically informs Paul of the fate that awaits him in Jerusalem". However, despite warnings from friends Paul is determined to go, "I am ready not only to be bound, but also to die in Jerusalem for the name of the Lord Jesus." The believers realised that Paul was not going to take their advice. Paul and his companions then got ready to go to Jerusalem, trusting in God's will.

Conclusion

This brings us to the end of Paul's missionary activity, although the story of Paul in Acts is far from over. The next sections of Acts, which you will study at A2 level, describe Paul's arrival in Jerusalem, transfer to Caesarea, and his journey to and stay in Rome. Paul dominates the rest of the story of Acts.

 TASKS

a) Comment on the claim that no matter how important Paul proves himself to be, he is *not* Luke's main character, but rather is one of a number of people who spread the gospel of Christ.

b) Describe what you regard to be the most significant struggles and successes during Paul's third missionary journey.
- Struggles: leaving synagogue for hall of Tyrannus; revolt of the silversmiths
- Successes: Baptism of John's followers; miracles; Sceva's sons; burning of books of magic; foiled a Jewish plot in Greece; Eutychus raised to life in Troas; Preaching to Elders of Ephesus

c) Describe the events in Ephesus during Paul's third missionary journey.
- Apollos
- Baptism of John the Baptist's followers
- Teaching in synagogue, then move to hall of Tyrannus
- Miracles of healing
- Sceva's sons
- Books of magic
- Revolt of the silversmiths

OTHER ASPECTS OF HUMAN EXPERIENCE

'Open Doors'

Open Doors' is a Christian Persecution Charity that has been providing Bibles, Christian literature, training and practical support to the Persecuted Church worldwide since 1955. You can access up-to-date information on the work of Open Doors from their website: www.opendoorsuk.org

Fernando[98] comments that there are many similarities between the way people opposed the gospel and its proclaimers at the time of Paul and the way they do so now. Below are some of the stories of Christians who have been persecuted throughout different parts of the world. As you read through them, take note of any similarities or differences you find with Paul's missionary activity in Acts. Focus in particular on similar types of persecution and the response to persecution.

1. Persecuted Christians in the Middle East

Christians in the Middle East are often discriminated against because of their faith in Christ. By providing training, counselling and Scripture resources, Open Doors' teams are helping to strengthen believers across the region.

> In June 2000, **Shaiboub from Egypt** was framed and convicted of murdering his cousin, also a Christian, and another young Christian in a village in Egypt. He was made the scapegoat in a blatant police cover-up, and was sentenced to 15 years' hard labour – the maximum penalty for manslaughter under Egyptian law. His wife and children were left bereft.
>
> Shaiboub is imprisoned in a high-security prison in Cairo. His family live 330 miles away and are allowed to visit him only once a month, for just 30 minutes.

2. Persecuted Christians in South East Asia

Four of the world's five remaining communist states are located in East Asia. In these countries, and across the region, Christians are suffering for their faith. Open Doors' teams support believers through delivering Bibles, Scripture resources and training.

> **Sister Mei from China** pastors a house church of over 300 people. Her story is one of faithfulness and resilience. Now over 80 years old, Mei is as determined as ever to serve God in any way she can. The desire of Mei's heart is to see the Chinese Church grow in size and maturity, despite the pressures and opposition it faces from the authorities.
>
> **'Pilot' Jemy from the Philippines** is often threatened with death by his Islamic

neighbours. He travels far across seas, which are often stormy, to attend Christian training courses. Living in the Muslim-dominated region of Mindanao, southern Philippines, Jemy's life is often threatened because of his faith in the Lord Jesus. Having enrolled in Open Doors' lay leader training programme, his enthusiasm to learn more about God is unquenchable. Jemy loves to serve the Lord through serving his people. He often pilots a small *'ëbanca'* (boat), bringing believers from remote islands together for fellowship.

Pastor Victor from Vietnam was pressured by his parents who object to his faith. He spent time in prison, shackled and tormented, for his active ministry. Since Victor decided to follow Jesus, his life has been very hard. His parents are staunch Communists, and they violently object to Victor's allegiance to Christ.

The same is true for Theresa. When Victor asked her to marry him, he knew their wedding would be bitter-sweet. Although they shared the joy of knowing the Lord, they had to come to terms with the fact that neither set of parents would attend their wedding.

Pastor SK Daniel from India is a convert from Hinduism and along with his wife runs an orphanage for 'untouchable' caste children. He has been threatened, assaulted, arrested and his house attacked. Along with their own four children, they care for 20 Dalit ('untouchable') children, their ministry motivated by the love of Christ.

He has experienced severe persecution from fundamentalist groups opposed to his Christian activities. Since 1995, he has been severely beaten and left for dead, and his house stoned by violent mobs who once beseiged his home for 15 days. To date, the police have failed to arrest those responsible and in fact arrested Pastor Daniel once, on trumped-up charges. Hindu extremists have ordered him to leave the region or they will burn him alive.

Santosh from India was beaten and threatened by extremists who attacked an evangelistic meeting that he was leading.

Along with six other evangelists, Brother Santosh had travelled to Tasra in Gujarat state to show the Jesus film to a large group of villagers. Suddenly, in the middle of the film, a mob of Hindu extremists descended on the gathering. They smashed the film projector and then turned their wrath on Santosh and his friends. When Santosh refused to pledge allegiance to the Hindu deity Ram, the assailants began to boil water to pour over him. Santosh was thankfully released without serious injury.

"I thought I was going to die," admits Santosh. "I was terrified. But I am glad to suffer for the Lord."

TASKS

General questions on journeys

a) 'Acts is very concerned with the opposition which surrounds the spread of the gospel'. Explore this claim with reference to the attitude of both the Jewish and Roman authorities.

As preparation for this question it would be useful to complete the following table, highlighting any incidents which reveal the attitude of the Jews or Romans towards the Christians. Look out for opposition in some of the following forms:
- opposition to Paul on economic grounds
- confrontation with evil
- jealousy

Journey	Attitude of Jews	Attitude of Romans
1st		
2nd		
3rd		

b) Describe the contribution made by the Holy Spirit during Paul's missionary activity.

To help you with this it might be useful to go through your notes with either a coloured sticker or drawing of a dove in the margin to indicate a mention of the Holy Spirit. Then try to collate the material to answer the question.

c) Evaluate the claim that Paul was worthy of the title 'Apostle to the Gentiles'.
- Compare the success that Paul had with the Gentiles compared to the Jews.
- Evaluate Paul's attitude to both groups.
- Compare with other preachers, eg Peter.

d) Comment on the claim that Paul was the most important evangelist in Acts.
- You need to make some comparison with other evangelists, eg Peter and Philip and argue your point of view.

e) Comment on the claim that the church today has much to learn from how Paul dealt with difficulties during his journeys.
- Go through the journeys, making note of how Paul dealt with setbacks and opposition. Try to come up with some suggestions of how the church today could learn from him.

Endnotes

[1] Drane, *op cit*, p247

[2] Willimon, *op cit*, p74

[3] Johnson, *op cit*, 166

[4] *ibid*, 166

[5] Marshall, *op cit*, p167

[6] Some scholars regard the events on the Damascus road as a calling rather than a conversion. Stendahl claims it was a call to be a missionary to the Gentiles, not a conversion, and Johnson regards it as the call of a prophet (Johnson, *op cit*, p167)

[7] Lewis, *op cit*, p43

[8] Calvin, J, *The Acts of the Apostles, an exposition in 2 volumes*: vol.1, Ch1–13, ed. DW & TF Torrance, Oliver and Boyd, originally 1552, translated into English, 1966, p256

[9] Stott, *op cit*, p169

[10] Marshall, *op cit*, p168

[11] From Josephus, antiquities 20; cited in Sanders, EP, Jesus and Judaism, London: SCM, 1985

[12] Fernando, *op cit*, p295

[13] Haenchen, E, *The Acts of the Apostles: A Commentary*, Philadelphia: Westminster, 1971, p320

[14] Marshall, *op cit*, p169

[15] Conzelmann, H, *Die Apostelgeschichte,* Handbuch zum neuen Testament, Tubingen, 1963. The Theology of Luke, London: Conzelmann Theology, 1960, p66

[16] Saul's conversion has been given physical and psychological explanations that seek to downplay the idea that a revelation of Jesus caused this huge turnaround – was it an epileptic fit?

[17] "Kyrios can mean both 'lord' and 'Sir' , but considering the circumstances of the light from heaven and the calling of his name, Saul must have realised that he was in the presence of the Lord God."

[18] Bruce, *op cit*, p182

[19] Fernando, *op cit*, p297

[20] Stott, *op cit*, p170

[21] Dillon, *op cit*, p744

[22] Bruce, *op cit*, p185

[23] Barclay, *op cit*, p74

[24] Marshall, *op cit*, p171

[25] Dillon, *op cit*, p744

[26] The title the 'Righteous One' referred to the Messiah.

[27] Boer, H, *A Short History of the Early Church*, Michigan: William B Eerdmans Publishing company, 1976, p22

[28] Marshall, *op cit*, p172

[29] Bruce, *op cit*, p188

[30] Cruz, N, *Run Baby Run*, Hodder and Stoughton, 1969

[31] Guy, *op cit*, p51

[32] Marshall, *op cit*, p214

[33] Longenecker, *op cit*, p240

[34] But this does not necessarily mean he became a Christian. Simon the magician also "believed" (8:13) and was even baptised but was hardly a Christian.

[35] Hanson, *op cit*, p141

[36] Fernando, *op cit*, p385

[37] Hewitt, *op cit*, p113

[38] Guy, *op cit*, pp53–54

[39] Marshall, *op cit*, p231

[40] Hanson, *op cit*, p147

[41] Fernando, *op cit*, p398

[42] *ibid*, p398

[43] Guy, *op cit*, p55

[44] Bruce, *op cit*, p279

[45] *ibid*, p279

[46] Bruce, p279

[47] Marshall, *op cit*, p240

[48] *ibid*, p241

[49] Bruce, *op cit*, p251

[50] Marshall, *op cit*, p257

[51] Fernando, p431

[52] Marshall, *op cit*, p263

[53] So Lydia was the first European Christian.

[54] *ibid*, p268

55 Evil spirits can recognise Christ and his servants, compare with Mark (1:23–26).

56 Marshall, *op cit*, p269

57 *ibid*, p269

58 A Roman citizen should not have been beaten but at this stage the authorities were unaware of Paul's Roman citizenship.

59 Bruce, *op cit*, p317

60 *ibid*, p315

61 May mean that these women were upper class.

62 Marshall, *op cit*, p278

63 or 'politarchs'

64 Williams, *op cit*, p198

65 Longenecker, *op cit*, p475

66 Marshall, *op cit*, p292

67 Bruce, *op cit*, p346

68 Romans Ch16

69 *ibid*, p350

70 Hanson, *op cit*, p186

71 Marshall, *op cit*, p299

72 Bruce, *op cit*, p354

73 Marhsall, *op cit*, p300

74 Marshall, *op cit*, p308

75 Apollos was to be a central figure in the church at Corinth.

76 Bruce, *op cit*, p364

77 Marshall, *op cit*, p304

78 Hanson, *op cit*, p189

79 Marshall, *op cit*, p308

80 *ibid*, p309

81 *ibid*, p310

82 Hewitt, *op cit*, p160

83 Marshall, *op cit*, p312

84 One drachma was the same value as a day's pay for an ordinary working man. So 50,000 drachmas would be a huge amount.

85 taken from Wikipedia, the free encyclopedia, http://en.wikipedia.org/wiki/Relic last accessed on 27.9.07

86 taken from BBC News, Northern Ireland, http://news.bbc.co.uk/1/low/northern_ireland/1353526.stm

87 Hanson, *op cit*, p194

88 Fernando, *op cit*, p518

89 Hewitt, *op cit*, p161

90 Marshall, *op cit*, p318

91 Marshall, *op cit*, p318

92 Fernando, *op cit*, p519

93 Marshall, *op cit*, p320

94 Bruce, *op cit*, p370

95 This is the first time it is mentioned in Acts that the believers met on a Sunday rather than a Saturday.

96 Marshall, *op cit*, p326

97 Guy, *op cit*, p94

98 Fernando, *op cit*, p401

Chapter 5

Faith, work and witness in Acts

THE ROLE OF THE HOLY SPIRIT IN ACTS

THE BOOK OF ACTS is saturated by the presence and power of the Holy Spirit. The Spirit is repeatedly mentioned, "on average just over twice in each chapter",[1] prompting a number of scholars to comment that it should have been called "The Gospel of the Holy Spirit"[2]; or "The Acts of the Holy Spirit".[3] "For Luke, everything that happens in the life of the Church from the beginning to the end of his story is in one way or another controlled, inspired and furthered by the Holy Spirit."[4] The Spirit's previous activity in Jesus is replicated on a wider scale through the believers. Luke gives us a practical demonstration of this through the lives of key people such as Peter, Philip, Stephen and Paul. However, he never loses sight of the fact that the Holy Spirit is the true centre of the story.

The Coming of the Spirit at Pentecost

Between Jesus' resurrection and ascension, Jesus taught his disciples more about the kingdom of God, telling them to wait in Jerusalem for the gift of the Holy Spirit. Clearly the Spirit's coming, which happened on the Day of Pentecost, did not come to them unprepared.[5]

As you will recall, in Peter's speech at Pentecost he reminded his audience that in the Old Testament scriptures God had promised he would "pour out" his Spirit on all people and all nations in the last days (2:17–18, 33; 10:45). This promise "of the Father" (Acts 1:4) reveals God to be the primary giver of the Spirit. It was accompanied by unusual physical phenomena: a sound like a "mighty wind" and "tongues like fire" (Acts 2:2–3), reminiscent of the wind and fire which, in John the Baptist's preaching, were to be the instruments of the Coming One's purifying ministry (Luke 3:16–17).

The Pentecost event was unique because it signified the beginning of the age of the church. God's people, described by Neil[6] as "ordinary men and women", became the spirit-filled body of Christ. The extraordinary signs of wind and fire were unique to this initial experience, since they are not repeated in Acts. Although the Holy Spirit would continue to be given, the outpouring would never again signify the inauguration of a new era.

A word on 'Glossolalia' (speaking in tongues)

The filling of the Spirit enabled the apostles to speak in other tongues. Speaking in tongues is a form of ecstatic speech, a sign of the activity and presence of the Holy Spirit. However, it was not the glossolalia that amazed the people, but the fact that they heard Galileans speaking in their own language (Acts 2:6). As discussed in Chapter 2 of this book, it is not clear if the miracle was one of speaking, or hearing, or both; what is clear is that the Spirit was active and responsible for the phenomena.

REPENTANCE AND BAPTISM

On the Day of Pentecost Peter was able to proclaim the Gospel with a new understanding: "Repent and be baptised, every one of you, in the name of Jesus Christ for the forgiveness of your sins. And you will receive the gift of the Holy Spirit" (Acts 2:38). The Spirit convicts and leads people to repentance of sin and faith in Jesus Christ. Bruce[7] describes such repentance as "a complete change of heart". The Spirit comes on all people, who repent and believe, not just on some individuals for certain purposes, as happened in the Old Testament (2:17). By the end of the day of Pentecost, receiving the Spirit was not confined to the apostles and their companions; many more enjoyed the heavenly gift. The Jews initially thought this meant all Jewish people, but they eventually realised it meant all people, regardless of religious background, race, age, sex or social standing (2:38–39; 15:8–9; 19:5–6).

Repentance was linked to baptism. On the Day of Pentecost about three thousand people repented of their sins, were baptised, and received the Spirit, making them members of a new community. John, who baptised with water claimed to be the forerunner of one greater than himself, who would baptise with the Holy Spirit. It might have been expected therefore that baptism in water would now become obsolete. This did not happen and believers in Jesus continued to be baptised in water. Bruce[8] explains: "Baptism in the spirit is an internal work; baptism in water now becomes an external token". Their water baptism was a sign that they belonged to God, and was accompanied (not replaced) by the baptism in the Spirit.

When was the Holy Spirit received?

1. At Baptism

From the events of the Day of Pentecost, we can see that a convert receives the gift of the Spirit at baptism (2:28). Lampe[9] believes that this was the normal practice.

2. After baptism, through the laying on of apostolic hands

Those who became believers on the Day of Pentecost clearly received the Spirit as soon as they were baptised in Jesus' name. However, when Philip baptised the Samaritan converts, including Simon Magus, they did not receive the Spirit there and then (Acts 8:12–13). On hearing the news of Philip's evangelism in Samaria, the leaders of the mother church sent Peter and John to see what was going on. They were pleased with what they found, but they discovered that something was missing. The Samaritan converts had not received the Spirit, so they prayed for them, laid their hands on them, and then the Samaritans received the Holy Spirit (Acts 8:14–17).

Luke does not explain the time lapse on this occasion between the Samaritans believing in Jesus and their receiving the Spirit. The most natural explanation of the interval is that when at last the Spirit fell on the Samaritan believers, they received assurance from the authoritative leaders of the church that they were no longer outcasts, but were full members of the people of God in the new age. It is obvious that the Samaritans' reception of the Spirit was accompanied by the same audible signs (speaking in tongues) that the believers had manifested at Pentecost.

It should be noted that there are three occasions when the Spirit is imparted by the laying on of hands:

1. The conversion of the Samaritans as described above (8:12–17). Bruce[10] comments that there is no suggestion here that the believers' reception of the Spirit was conditional on their having apostolic hands laid upon them.

2. The conversion of Saul of Tarsus (9:17–19). It was Ananias who laid hands on Paul, and he was not an apostle.

3. The disciples whom Paul found at Ephesus (19:1–7). Paul was not an original apostle.

Lampe[11] believes that these three exceptions have special importance and so are different.

3. Before Baptism

Shortly after the events at Samaria, under the unmistakable guidance of the Holy Spirit, Peter went to visit Cornelius, the Roman centurion, in Caesarea, taking six believers along as witnesses. On his arrival he explained to Cornelius that he had never entered a Gentile house before or taken food at a Gentile table, but that God had taught him not to look on anyone as "common or unclean." Then he related the gospel story to Cornelius, from John the Baptist's ministry to Jesus' death and resurrection, concluding that through Jesus – crucified and risen – forgiveness of sins was available to every believer (Acts 10:34–43).

Peter had barely finished speaking when the Holy Spirit fell on those present, the experience being accompanied by the same outward signs as at Pentecost. Both Peter and the six men he had taken along with him were stunned at what they saw and heard. Here were Gentiles, "speaking in tongues and praising God"! God had clearly shown his approval by sending his Spirit on them. Peter had no option but to go along with this act of God; "Can anyone keep these people from being baptised with water? They have received the Holy Spirit just as we have." So he ordered them to be baptised in the name of Jesus Christ (Acts 10:44–48).

Summary

In Acts the reception of the Spirit could take place:

- immediately after the confessing faith in Christ and submitting to baptism in his name, eg on the Day of Pentecost the believers in Jerusalem received the Spirit immediately after they were baptised.

- with the laying on of apostolic hands, a considerable time after the exercise of faith and submission to baptism, eg the believers in Samaria, although 'baptised into the name of the Lord Jesus', did not receive the Spirit until apostles laid hands on them.

- before baptism and without the laying on of hands. At Caesarea the Gentiles received the Spirit as they listened to Peter preaching. Peter realised their conversion was genuine and then they were baptised.

- after baptism, in the name of Jesus with the laying on of hands, in the experience of some who had to a certain extent become disciples of Jesus already.

Clearly there was no set pattern to how the Spirit was received. What is important is not the sequence of these stages in becoming a Christian, but their presence.

How was the Spirit active in the Christian community?

1. In individual lives

The first Christians thought of the Holy Spirit in terms of an invisible, but divine power, clearly marked by its effect on the life of the recipient. The impact of the Spirit left the individual (or onlooker) in no doubt that a significant change had taken place in him by a divine power. In Acts the most mentioned manifestations of the Spirit are inspired speech, speaking in tongues, prophecy, and praise. The Spirit encouraged, strengthened, and even comforted individual believers (9:31). Although the term 'comforted' is not directly used in Acts, it is surely implied that the Holy Spirit comforted Stephen (7:55) and Paul (23:11, 27:23). Neil[12] also points out that more often than not it was the "uncomfortable" comfort that the Spirit provided, pushing the believers "forward into uncharted and intimidating waters with only their faith to sustain them", turning them into missionaries and proclaimers of the good news (Acts 1:8).[13]

2. In Christian Fellowship

Becoming a Christian was not a solitary experience. Drane[14] comments that they "were bound together as a group not by the fact that they all belonged to the same organisation but because they were all inspired by the same Holy Spirit". The Spirit united them into a fellowship that could not be paralleled in any other group. "Acts presents a vibrant community that was passionate about mission, with members caring for each other, pursuing holiness, and dealing with matters that affected its unity."[15] The invisible fruit of the Spirit's activity is the 'koinonia', the unity and fellowship of Christians, manifested in a number of ways, not least in their sharing of goods. According to Hewitt,[16] both Paul and Luke obviously believed fellowship to be the creation of the Holy Spirit. It was a two-way sharing; together they shared Christ and through Christ they shared with each other.

3. As a Guide/ instructor

Through the Spirit, Jesus exercised his authority over his followers. One of Luke's purposes in writing Acts is to show that the Holy Spirit initiated and guided the activities of the church, especially concerning mission. This theme is regularly repeated in Acts, where we read of instances where the Church or individuals follow a certain course or adopt a certain policy through the guidance of the Spirit.

TASK

In Acts, Luke shows us how each of the key apostolic leaders depended on the Holy Spirit for guidance or instructions. Complete the following table of examples (some of it has been done for you):

The Holy Spirit as a Guide	
Enables Jesus to give instructions to the apostles	
1:2	
1:7–8	
Directs new developments in the church regarding the spread of the gospel	
8:26, 29	Willimon[17] comments that in being obedient to the Spirit, preachers like Philip find themselves in the oddest of situations with the most surprising sorts of people: Following the conversion of the Ethiopian, Philip was sped northward by the Spirit on another mission, the manner of which can be compared with the experiences of Elijah and Ezekiel (Ezek 3:14 & 8:3).[18]
9:17–18	
10:19–20	
13:1–3	Drane[19] believes that this sense of dependence on the Spirit's guidance is perhaps the main characteristic of Paul's work, both in the stories of the Acts and in his own writings. What do these verses tell us? When the Church at Antioch in Syria sent Paul and Barnabas off as missionaries, it was acting on the instructions of the Holy Spirit, who spoke directly to the congregation through certain Spirit-filled individuals within it.
Gives wisdom about problems within the Church	
6:1–6	

Leads and guides the decisions and actions of the Christian leaders	
15:28	One of the occasions in Acts when the Christian community exhibits a strong awareness of the Spirit's centrality in its life comes to light in the letter sent to the Christians in Syria and Cilicia by the Council of Jerusalem. As you will not study the proceedings of the Council of Jerusalem until A2 level, some explanation might be useful at this point. The decision made by the Council of Jerusalem was introduced in the letter with the words, "It seemed good to the Holy Spirit and to us"; that is, "The Holy Spirit has decided, and so have we" (Acts 15:28). The spontaneity and matter-of-factness of this declaration stresses the church's role as "the vehicle of the Spirit".[20] The apostles and elders do not try to explain why the decision was primarily the Holy Spirit's and only secondarily theirs. They were so conscious "of being possessed and controlled by the Spirit that he was given prior mention as chief author of their decision."[21]
16:6–7	
19:2–7	
20:22–23	
Prohibits, compels and warns, often by visions	
16:6	
16:6–10	He directs the course of Paul and his companions, as he had previously done for Philip (Acts 8:29) and Peter (Acts 10:19–20), indicating which routes they must avoid and which they must follow (Acts 16:6–10).
20:22–23	

4. Prophecy

The Spirit who spoke through the Old Testament prophets continued to speak in the church, through prophets of the new age. Prophecy could be a form of ecstatic speech of the Spirit, which differed from glossolalia in that it was intelligible to the hearer. Prediction of coming events formed part of the prophet's function but a prophet's greatest contribution in the early church was preaching, which was inspired by the Holy Spirit.[22]

For example, through the prophet Agabus, for example, the Spirit foretold the great famine of Claudius' day, enabling the church of Antioch to take steps to provide for their fellow believers in Jerusalem (Acts 11:27–30). And it was probably through one of the prophets in the church of Antioch that the Spirit gave directions for the release of Barnabas and Saul for the special work for which he had called them (Acts 13:1–2).

TASK

Copy and complete the mind-map below. Draw lines from each of the four circles to explain the relevant information about prophecy from each of the references.

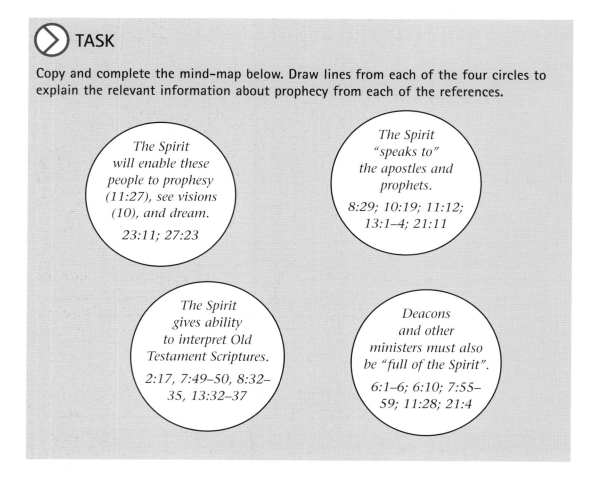

The Spirit
will enable these
people to prophesy
(11:27), see visions
(10), and dream.

23:11; 27:23

The Spirit
"speaks to"
the apostles and
prophets.

8:29; 10:19; 11:12;
13:1–4; 21:11

The Spirit
gives ability
to interpret Old
Testament Scriptures.

2:17, 7:49–50, 8:32–
35, 13:32–37

Deacons
and other
ministers must also
be "full of the Spirit".

6:1–6; 6:10; 7:55–
59; 11:28; 21:4

5. To Discipline/purify the church

The power of the Holy Spirit in the early church is underlined in another way in the incidents involving Ananias and Sapphira (Acts 5:1–11) and Elymas (13:9–11). Ananias and Sapphira tried to deceive the church by acquiring credit for being more generous than they actually were. The Christian community was so closely identified with the Spirit that a lie told to the church was a lie told to the Spirit.

The Holy Spirit gave Peter insight as to what Ananias and Sapphira had done and gave him authority to deal with them. When Ananias and Sapphira realised the enormity of their actions, that they were guilty of such a serious offence against the Holy Spirit, they were so appalled that one after another they fell down dead.

When the sorcerer Elymas opposed the missionaries (13:9–11) on the first missionary journey, Paul was forced to rebuke him because of his negative influence upon the proconsul. Note how Luke points out that Paul was "filled with the Holy Spirit" for this task (v 9),[23] evidence that the Holy Spirit acted as a purifying agent, stamping out corruption.

Resisting the Spirit

God's bestowal of his Spirit is his response to genuine faith. The withholding of faith, especially on the part of those who have heard his voice, is seen as resistance to the Spirit, and there is no deadlier sin than this. In the Old Testament those did not pay heed to the prophets were in effect resisting the Spirit who spoke through them, and the consequences for them were disastrous. Similarly in the early church, those who continually refused to accept Jesus had no hope of repentance or salvation. This is the point of Stephen's charge: "You are just like your fathers: You always resist the Holy Spirit!" (Acts 7:51). The same point is made by Paul at Pisidian Antioch: "Look, you scoffers, wonder and perish, for I am going to do something in your days that you would never believe, even if someone told you" (Acts 13:41). Paul makes this point again at the end of Acts when he applies the warning of Isaiah 6:9–10 about "unhearing ears and unseeing eyes" to the leaders of the Roman Jews: "The Holy Spirit spoke the truth to your forefathers when he said through Isaiah the prophet: 'Go to this people…'"(Acts 28:25–28).

6. In Mission

Bruner[24] observes that in Acts the Holy Spirit is Jesus at work "in continuation of his ministry". The main emphasis of the work of the Spirit was mission. The apostles were to play a full part in this mission, and they would be empowered to do so when the Spirit came upon them: "you shall be my witnesses … to the end of the earth" (Acts 1:8). Boer[25] describes how the Spirit restlessly drives the Church to witness. The gospel would be heard in Jerusalem, in Judea and Samaria, and to the end of the earth, revealing the Holy Spirit as the principal actor in the drama of the expanding Church.[26]

TASKS

Copy and complete the table below which highlights the methods used by the Spirit to spread the gospel:

The Spirit used various means to carry out the church's mission

Testimony, story and the proclaimed word	Acts 2:14, 36; 3:12–26; 5:32; 7:2–53; 8:4; 13:16–41; 18:5; 19:10	
Trances	Acts 10:19	
Prophets	Acts 11:28	
Worship services	Acts 13:2	The Holy Spirit sent this message, probably through one of the prophets.
Church councils	Acts 15:28	
Inner constraint	Acts 16:7	

Through these means the Spirit was active in making the mission of Jesus universal.[27] In other words, salvation was available for Jews and Gentiles alike. For example, after Peter's preaching at Caesarea, Gentile evangelisation was approved and promoted. Not only that but it was marked by the spontaneous outpouring of the Spirit, as spontaneous as the initial outpouring on the Day of Pentecost.

The Holy Spirit told the apostles what to say in their preaching (1:8; 2:4; 4:8, 31; 11:24; 13:9, 52) and gave them the boldness to say it. During his ministry, Jesus had told his disciples not to be concerned about the form of words they should use when called to account in a court of law – the Holy Spirit would tell them what to say (Luke 21:15). Just as the Spirit had spoken through David and the prophets in ancient Israel (1:16; 4:25; 28:25), so he now gave power, courage and boldness to preach and witness (2:14, 4:8, 6:10, 7:1–53, 8:4–5).

The apostles experienced the significance of this assurance the first time that they were challenged by the Jewish authorities in Jerusalem. Fernando[28] comments that "this is one of several instances in Acts where God's servants are filled with the Holy Spirit in order to face a special challenge" (see 4:31; 7:55 and 13:9). You will have read in Chapter 3 of this book how the healing of a lame man in the temple precincts led to the arrest of Peter and John. When they were brought before the chief priests they were asked on whose authority had they acted? Peter then, "filled with the Holy Spirit" replied that the lame man had been healed by the power of the crucified and risen Jesus.

Another example of a courageous speaker is Stephen, who is described as "a man full of faith and the Holy Spirit". It was the Spirit who enabled him to speak before the Synagogue of the Freedmen, giving him such "inspired wisdom"[29] that when he spoke "they could not refute him" (Acts 6:10).

7. Giving Power to perform miracles

Miracles were impossible without the work of the Holy Spirit. Through the Spirit's power Peter performed miracles to such an extent that many hoped his shadow would fall on them so that they would be healed.

Similarly, throughout Paul's journeys the Holy Spirit's presence and activity are evident in Paul's acts of healing and exorcism. Paul, too, was held in such high regard that handkerchiefs and aprons that touched him were taken to the sick (19:12). However, it is important to bear in mind that God was the one who carried out these miracles through the power of the Holy Spirit, not Peter's shadow, or belongings that had come in contact with Paul.

8. Appointed for a task

Seven men were appointed to take charge of the common fund to needy members of the community. The qualifications laid down for them were that they should be "of good repute, full of the Spirit and of wisdom" (Acts 6:3). One of them, Stephen, is especially singled out as "a man full of faith and of the Holy Spirit." He showed these qualities when he was challenged by his opponents who "could not withstand the wisdom and the Spirit with which he spoke." When they accused him of blasphemy before the Sanhedrin, his defence speech filled them with such rage that his execution inevitably followed. Luke describes how, full of the Holy Spirit, he gazed into heaven and said, "Behold, I see the heavens opened, and the Son of man standing at the right hand of God" (Acts 7:55–56).

Guthrie[30] adds that in Acts 20:28 in Paul's address to the Ephesian elders, he reminds them that the Holy Spirit has made them guardians of the flock, to feed it. "This suggests that Paul accepts as a matter of course that elders were appointed by the Holy Spirit." Church offices will be explored further in the section entitled "Church organisation" (p166).

Conclusion

Acts leaves us in no doubt that the church was essentially a community of the Spirit. It was controlled and directed by the Spirit and this had an important bearing on the function of the ministry[31] and on the spread of the gospel to Rome. Throughout Acts the Spirit is shown to be as important a character as Stephen, Peter and even Paul, giving support for the idea that the book could have been called 'The Gospel of the Holy Spirit'.

 OTHER ASPECTS OF HUMAN EXPERIENCE

The role of the Holy Spirit in churches today

Does the Holy Spirit still play a vital role in churches today?

In your answer research some of the following areas:
- The Pentecostal movement
- The Toronto Blessing
- Attitudes to gifts of the Spirit in churches today

 TASKS

a) Describe the ways in which the Holy Spirit is presented in Acts.

- How the Spirit is received
- The Spirit in individual lives and in the community
- How the Spirit guides, disciplines, inspires and motivates

b) Explain the importance of the Holy Spirit in the outreach of the early church. Give examples from Acts.

- As a motivator
- Boldness to preach
- Encourages through opposition
- Guides

c) Comment on the claim that 'The Gospel of the Holy Spirit' is a more appropriate title for the book of Acts.

- Do you think the Spirit is as important a character as Peter and Paul etc? Could the mission have happened without the Spirit? Discuss using examples from Acts.

THE ROLE OF MIRACLES IN AIDING THE SPREAD OF THE GOSPEL

What is a miracle?

From Wikipedia, the free encyclopaedia[32]:

> "The word miracle, comes from the old Latin word miraculum meaning 'something wonderful'. It describes divine intervention by God in the world by which the ordinary course of nature is overruled, suspended, or changed. Although many religious texts and people confirm witnessing or prophesying various events which they refer to as 'miraculous', it is disputed whether miracles are scientifically confirmed. People in different faiths have varying definitions of the word 'miracle'. In everyday usage, 'miracle' may also refer to any statistically unlikely but beneficial event (such as the survival of a natural disaster) or even to anything which is regarded as 'wonderful' regardless of its likelihood, such as birth."

Miracles in Acts (the references to be studied for AS examination are in bold)		
Peter's miracles	**3:1–9**	**Healing of the lame man at Beautiful Gate ***
	5:12–16	**General miracles – Peter's shadow ***
	9:33–34	Healing of Aeneas at Lydda
	9:40	Raising of Tabitha to life at Joppa
Paul's miracles	13:11	Striking of Elymas the sorcerer blind at Paphos
	14:10	Healing of lame man at Lystra
	16:16–37	**Casting out evil spirit from girl at Philippi/escapes prison ***
	19:12	Many healed through contact with aprons and handkerchiefs
	20:9–10	Raising Eutychus to life at Troas
	28:5	Not being affected by snake bite in Malta
	28:8	Healing of Publius' father
Other	2:43	Apostles performing miracles
	4:23–31	**Prayer for miracles (overleaf)**
	6:8	Stephen performing miracles
	8:6	Philip performing miracles

* A detailed commentary on three out of the four references has already been covered in this book on pages: 63, 72 and 122–123

Luke records the miracles in Acts as a natural succession to those of the Gospels.[33] They are a key part of the ministry and mission of the church in Acts. Like the gift of powerful speech we see how miracles had an effect on those who witnessed them. A miraculous event can be described as a time when something happened that challenged what was natural in the eyes of the people. For example, it was not natural that a man who had been lame from birth could suddenly walk or that people could be healed through the contact of an apron that had touched Paul. Such events were accompanied by a verbal explanation of God's power working through the Holy Spirit. Note how Peter explains (Acts 3:11–26) that it was through the power of Jesus' name that the lame man was healed, not through Peter himself. The effect of this healing was "all the people were astonished and came running to them" (3:11). Then Peter seized the opportunity to declare the gospel. Clearly the miracle helped to attract the crowd. This had a knock-on effect, for the subsequent arrest of Peter and John then led to their witness before the Sanhedrin.

 TASK

Read the material In Ch 5:12–16 and Ch 16:16–37. Using your study of the Book of Acts so far, explain how the miraculous events recorded helped to spread the Gospel.

Faith played a vital part in miracles both in the gospels and Acts. In the gospels on three occasions Jesus said, "Your faith has made you well" and an absence of faith would have prevented a miracle from taking place. Similarly in Acts, faith also played a key role in miracles. Such faith would have been a witness to unbelievers and may have prompted them to think more about the truth of the gospel message.

Prayer for miracles (Ch 4:23–31)

This prayer comes after the release of Peter and John from prison, following their arrest by the Sanhedrin after the healing of the lame man in Acts Ch 3. Peter and John returned to where the other believers were and told them of their experience before the Sanhedrin. Bruce[34] explains how "the whole company resorted to prayer". They specifically prayed for courage to speak boldly and to proclaim the gospel without fear. There is a clear understanding of a connection between the power of miracles alongside preaching the gospel (v 29–30). They asked for God to give his approval of their witness by "granting further mighty works of healing and similar signs and wonders through the same name which had cured the lame man".[35]

"Once again the Spirit came to the company with shattering power."[36] The place shook as if there was an earthquake, showing God's approval and assurance that their prayer would be answered. Marshall[37] regards this as "indicating a divine response to prayer". It was God's way of saying that he was present and would answer the prayer.[38] Bruce[39] comments how "the Holy Spirit filled them all and sent them forth to proclaim the good news with renewed confidence".

 OTHER ASPECTS OF HUMAN EXPERIENCE

The healing of the sick has had renewed emphasis in recent years among Christians. For a long time many people believed that the power to heal had died out with the apostles but today some churches still have a healing ministry. Find out what you can about healing ministries in Christian churches today.

Read the following examples of healings that lie outside your course of study. You could use these examples in answering a part B question concerning other aspects of human experience.

1. Introduction to Lourdes

It is reported that in 1858 in the grotto of Massabielle, near Lourdes, France, the Blessed Virgin Mary appeared eighteen times to Bernadette Soubirous, a 14 year old peasant girl. She told Bernadette to: "Pray and do penance for the conversion of the world". The Church investigated Bernadette's claims for four years before approving devotion to 'Our Lady of Lourdes'. Lourdes has since become one of the most famous shrines, attracting more than a million pilgrims each year. There have been thousands of miraculous cures at this shrine.

A Medical Bureau was established in 1882 to test the authenticity of the cures. The doctors include unbelievers as well as believers, and any doctor is welcome to take part in the examination of the alleged cures. As many as 500 medical men of all faiths or no faith have taken advantage of the invitation each year. Many books and movies tell the story of Lourdes. In the 1940s, a film called 'The Song of Bernadette', which won six academy awards, was made in Hollywood depicting the remarkable event. Many believe that moral and spiritual cures are more amazing than physical cures. Those who are not cured of bodily pain receive an increase of faith and resignation – true peace of soul.

The story of two outstanding miracles that occurred at Lourdes are the stories of Gabriel Gargam and John Traynor. Find out what you can about their experiences.

2. Lourdes 'miracle' is official [40] (14/11/2005)

The Roman Catholic Church has recognised as 'miraculous' the case of an Italian woman who recovered from a serious illness after a pilgrimage to Lourdes in 1952, the sanctuary said on Monday.

Anna Santaniello's recovery has become the 67th 'miracle cure' officially attributed to the sanctuary in south-western France. Lourdes is Christianity's most-visited place of pilgrimage after Rome. Now aged 94, Santaniello had Bouillaud's disease, a rheumatic condition that causes trouble with speaking and walking, as well as acute asthma attacks, cyanosis of the face and lips, and swelling of the legs. She has returned several times to Lourdes as a nurse. In 1961, the international medical committee at the sanctuary described her case as "extraordinary".

Every year, about six million pilgrims flock to the small town at the foothills of the Pyrenees, where the Virgin Mary is claimed to have appeared to a miller's daughter, Bernadette Soubirous, inside a cave in 1858.

Among the pilgrims are hundreds of thousands of sick and handicapped, fervently praying for a cure from the holy power of the site's spring water.

3. Miracle baby comes back from the dead [41]

by Chris Brooke, *The Daily Mail*, 28th February 2007 *(names have been changed)*

After trying for 30 minutes to bring two-week-old Kevin Thompson back to life, doctors decided there was nothing more they could do and called in his parents to say their tearful farewells. A nurse passed Kevin to his heartbroken father and gently pulled a tube from his mouth so they could kiss him goodbye.

It was then that the miracle happened. The lifeless baby suddenly coughed and moved. Nurses immediately grabbed Kevin back, re-attached the tubes and lifesaving equipment and he came back to life in front of his astonished parents. No one has been able to explain why Kevin, who had suffered a massive heart attack, was able to return from the brink. And despite being starved of oxygen for so long, he appears to have suffered no permanent brain damage. Now 14 months old, Kevin is a happy-go-lucky youngster who should be able to lead a normal life. His parents Bill, 34, and Kate Thompson, 32, still can't believe what they went through.

They had been shopping in a supermarket near their home in York in December 2005 when they noticed Kevin looked ashen and felt cold. They rang the NHS Direct emergency line from their car and an ambulance was sent to take them to hospital. Soon after arrival, he suffered a heart attack and stopped breathing. Mr Thompson and his wife, an administration worker, were taken to a room to see Kevin on a bed and a doctor giving him heart massage. They were taken to another room to wait for news.

Mr Thompson, a civil servant, recalled: "It was awful, those 30 minutes seemed to last forever. After what seemed like an eternity the doctor came out and said, 'I think we have done all we can'. They had reached the cut-off point for resuscitation.

"We were taken back to see him and Kevin was handed to us to say goodbye. We were just in bits. We didn't know what to say or do. They started taking his tubes out and that's when he started twitching. They took him straight back off us. They managed to get his heart going again and he came back to life in front of us. It was amazing. We still don't know how he managed to come round – we just know he's a little miracle. He's growing up into a happy and healthy little boy."

Two weeks before the drama, Kevin, the couple's first child, had been born naturally at the hospital, weighing 7lb 11oz. After the heart attack, doctors discovered he had a blocked aorta which was restricting blood flow to his heart. He underwent a major operation to repair it and was allowed home three weeks later. Mr Thompson added: "The doctors said they had never heard of anyone coming round after 30 minutes of apparent lifelessness, let alone a baby. But the people at the hospital were unbelievable. They made the miracle happen. There must have been 100 people gathered round him."

 TASKS

a) Using examples, describe the different types of miracles in Acts.

- Direct healing miracles – Peter and the lame man
- Indirect healing miracles – Peter's shadow; Paul's contact with aprons and handkerchiefs
- Nature miracles – earthquake at Philippi
- Exorcisms
- Raising from the dead – Tabitha

b) Give an account of how miracles in Acts aided the spread of the gospel.

- Usually followed by preaching
- Attracted large crowds
- Led to conversions

Give examples from Acts to support these.

c) Comment on the claim that 'the author of Acts records miracles as a central part of the ministry of the Church.'

- Number of miracles scattered throughout Acts
- Various believers carried out miracles, not just Twelve
- A sign of the Holy Spirit

Give examples from Acts to support these.

d) Evaluate the view that miracles belong exclusively to the period of the early church.

- Explore the view that some people feel that miracles do not happen today versus those who believe that there is still a place for them.
- Argument that routine operations carried out by doctors today would have been regarded as miraculous in New Testament times.
- Use examples from other aspects of human experience eg Lourdes or healing rallies.
- Discuss the validity of miracles today.

CHURCH LIFE AND ORGANISATION

The references concerning Church life and organisation required to be explored for the purpose of the AS level examination are:

- The fellowship of the believers 2:43–47
- The believers share their possessions 4:32–47
- The choosing of the seven 6:1–7

In this section, for your own interest, reference may be made to other parts of Acts which give further insight into the nature of church life and organisation.

Who belonged to the Church?

The members of the first group of believers, who waited in Jerusalem for the coming of the Holy Spirit at Pentecost, consisted of the apostles (1:13) and many others including women and relatives of Jesus. Guthrie believes that[42] "there is significance in the special mention of women in the company of believers. This at once shows the Christian company to be distinct from their environment, since few in the ancient world assigned value to women for their own sake". The early church clearly held the same attitude towards women that Jesus had shown, recognising that men and women are on an equal footing through the gospel.

Entry into the church was through repentance of sin, faith in Christ, baptism and receiving the Holy Spirit. Infant baptism was not a feature in the book of Acts. Instead baptism was performed on "consenting adults who had confessed their sins and acknowledged Jesus as Lord".[43] The bestowal of the gift of the Holy Spirit *usually* followed through the laying on of hands. In Jerusalem on the Day of Pentecost 3,000 people became Christians. Luke tells us how the Lord continued to add to that number daily.

Two events changed the locality (originally Jerusalem) of membership of the Church.

1. The martyrdom of Stephen and James, the son of Zebedee, led to the dispersion of the early Christians throughout other parts of Judea, into nearby Syria,

and further, perhaps even to Rome (eg Priscilla and Aquila).

2. The conversion of Saul, the main persecutor of the church. Paul began his ministry in Antioch, preaching not only to Jews in the synagogues but also to Gentiles. More often than not, the Gentiles were more receptive to Paul's preaching than the Jews (Acts 13:47–48, 15:3, 16:13, 17:12). After the Council of Jerusalem, Gentiles soon outnumbered Jews as Christians.

Church Life

The Fellowship of the Believers 2:43–47

In Acts 2:43–47 Luke presents "an ideal picture of this new community, rejoicing in the forgiveness of sins and the gift of the Spirit".[44] Bruce[45] comments that "the apostolic fellowship found expression in a number of practical ways."

Four ways are specifically mentioned: the apostles' teaching, the fellowship, the breaking of bread, and the prayers, paint a picture of an aspect of early church life.

1. The Apostles' teaching

"They devoted themselves to the Apostles teaching"

The Christian community relied on apostolic teaching, realising that just because they had received the Spirit, he was not the only teacher they needed. Barclay[46] insists that the word used for 'teaching' or 'doctrine' in verse 42 is not passive; it is active. This conjures up a picture of the believers actively seeking guidance and instruction in their new Christian lives. One of the methods of teaching used by the apostles with the new community may have been the exposition of Old Testament prophecies.[47]

2. The fellowship

"They devoted themselves to the fellowship"

The Greek word for 'fellowship' is '*koinonia*'; it comes from '*koinos*' which means 'common'. It shows that the first Christians shared together and this fellowship was in God – Father, Son and Holy Spirit. As they were also Jews they continued to meet and worship in the Temple in Jerusalem (Acts, 2: 46; 3:1; 21: 20–26), and the synagogues.

3. The breaking of bread

"They devoted themselves … to the breaking of bread …"

The fellowship of the early Christians was expressed not only in caring for each other, but in corporate worship too. Guthrie[48] explains that this was carried out through "worship in the Temple and common meals in the Christians' homes". The worship of the early Church was both formal and informal, for it took place both in the Temple Courts and in their homes. The worship of the early Church was joyful and reverent.

Worship included times for the breaking of bread (Acts 2:42–47). Acts gives no indication of how the Lord's Supper was observed, but there is no doubt that the earliest Christians saw at once the need to observe it.[49] In a closely knit community it may have been a daily celebration at the main meal of the day. In the early days the breaking of bread does seem to have taken place before, during, or at the end of an ordinary meal (the agape). The practice of eating together as a group was common and was clearly motivated by concern for the physical needs of each believer.[50]

Further insight into the celebration of the Lord's Supper is given in Acts 20, where Luke describes events at Troas. A farewell meeting was held on the first day of the week (20:7), suggesting that the Christians were already regarding Sunday as the day for worship.

4. Prayer

"… and to prayer"

The early Christians knew that they could not meet life in their own strength and that they did not need to do so.[51] Prayer was very important both for the individual believer and for the Christian community as a whole. Bruce[52] comments that while the community's prayers would follow Jewish models,[53] "the content would be enriched because of the Christ-event."

 ## OTHER ASPECTS OF HUMAN EXPERIENCE

The Mass

Synagogue worship began with prayers in praise to God, and the Shema (confession of faith), followed by readings from the books of the Law, the singing of a psalm, and a reading from the books of the Prophets, which was explained by the rabbi. The service ended with a collection for the poor, a prayer, and a closing psalm. In the Catholic Church this Jewish form of worship can still be recognised in the 'Liturgy of the Word' that forms the first part of the Mass. The first Christians continued to use the Jewish structure for prayer after being excluded from the Synagogue. Jewish Christians came to meet early on the day after the Sabbath (Sunday) in one of their homes for the 'Breaking of Bread'. This worship has become known as the Eucharist, the second part of the Mass. So the structure of the Mass has its roots in the earliest days of Christianity.

TASK

Hewitt[54] provides a summary of prayer in Acts. Look up the references and complete the table:

Prayer in Acts	Reference	Examples
In corporate worship	1:14 2:42 16:13	
During hours of Jewish prayer	3:1 10:9 10:30 22:17	
Special occasions	1:24 6:6 8:15 9:40 13:3 14:23 20:36	
Times of trial and suffering	4:23–31 7:59 9:11 16:25 28:8	
For intercession	7:60 12:5, 12 21:5	

5. Sharing

"Selling their possessions and goods, they gave to anyone as he had need"

The Believers Share Their Possessions (Ch 4:32–37)

Bruce[55] points out that one of the chief means of linking the Christian groups planted all over the Eastern Mediterranean world was the practice of mutual aid. This practice was based on the example at the start of Acts where Luke describes the believers sharing their possessions. Barclay[56] explains how the early Christians had an intense feeling of responsibility for each other, resulting in the sharing of possessions. "They never forgot that someone was hungry, that someone had not enough and that all must help ... it seemed to be unthinkable that anyone of them could have too much whilst another had too little. This awoke a real desire to share all that they had."[57]

Hewitt[58] describes this as an "experiment in communism" and believes it arose out of the belief that Jesus was going to return very soon (the Parousia). However, it must be pointed out that it was a voluntary communism of goods in which all shared and none went short.

In practical terms it seems that there was a common fund set up for individual needs. Believers could voluntarily sell their property to contribute to the fund. It was not something imposed by the leaders of the church. For example, when Peter rebuked Ananias he told him that it was his own decision whether he contributed his money or not (5:4).

Even more important was the strong social concern which the believers had for each other. Special provision was made for widows (6:1) which, as we read in Chapter 3 of this book, caused some dispute between the Hebrews and the Hellenists and led to the appointment of the seven. Clearly there was a sense of responsibility among the believers towards those of their members who were socially deprived. After all, a large number of the first believers were drawn from the lower levels of society, "which would have imposed on the Christians a common need to take some sort of concerted action".[59]

 ## OTHER ASPECTS OF HUMAN EXPERIENCE

Liberation theology

Liberation theology is a movement which originated in Latin America in the 1960s. It has been adopted by some churches in countries where there is a lot of poverty or where oppressive regimes exist. It is very critical of European theology, particularly for being mainly concerned with intellectual rather than practical problems.

Find out more about 'Liberation Theology' and compare it with the attitude of the early Christian Church.

This will be useful for you in answering a Part B question on other aspects of human experience.

 TASK

Look at the list of terms below which describe different aspects of life in the early church. As a class revision activity, divide into two teams.
Ask for a volunteer to start by talking for 30–60 seconds about one of the aspects mentioned. Someone must take over at the end of the time in order to complete the task. The team who can keep going through all nine aspects wins!

Many being saved
A good reputation
Praise
Glad and sincere hearts
Breaking of Bread
Generosity
All things in common
Unity
Signs and wonders
The life of the early church

Church Organisation

The word 'Church' (*ekklesia*), which literally means 'an assembly', appears for the first time in Acts 5:11. Unlike the use of the word today, 'church' does not refer to a building anywhere in the New Testament.[60] Instead it is associated with the group of believers in Christ, ie the people.

When the church began its life in Jerusalem it was led by a group of apostles, who guided it in the power and wisdom of the Holy Spirit. "That was the government with which the church was born. There were no elders, no deacons, no bishops .... Governmental structure and administrative organisation developed as the need for these arose".[61] As there were no buildings, the structure of the church was based on the house-church. Christians met in the home, often that of women, such as Lydia (Acts 16:14–15 and 40) in Philippi and Chloe in Corinth (1 Cor 1:11). Here they prayed and shared in the breaking of bread.

For a long time Christianity was considered to be just another Jewish sect and so it existed as a group within Judaism. Therefore the Christian community continued its Jewish connections, and continued Jewish practices, such as worshipping in the Temple.[62] There is also evidence that Christianity was influenced by some of the Jewish models of organisation. However, Acts gives us little insight into the 'offices' of the church such as the role of apostle, or elder, or deacon. As a result it is necessary to read between the lines to try to come up with a picture of what their organisation was like.

Apostle

The office of apostle was obviously of great importance, probably because Jesus himself had appointed the twelve. The qualifications for an apostle (1:21–22) were that he must have been with Jesus since his baptism by John and been a witness of the resurrection. The term 'apostle' is derived from a Greek verb meaning 'send forth' and means a messenger.[63] In the early church an apostle was a special kind of disciple or follower.

Kirk[64] however, believes that while the twelve were apostles, this does not exhaust the term which could also be applied to others. He argues that the New Testament idea of apostle is a person who is sent by Jesus to proclaim the gospel and to plant churches. Guy[65] agrees, pointing out that later in Acts we find others are named as apostles, "so the designation was not confined to the twelve." For example, in Acts Paul and Barnabas are twice referred to as apostles (14:4; 14), although Luke does seem to draw a distinction between them and the Jerusalem apostles (15:2).

Deacon

The Choosing of the Seven (Ch 6:1–7)

"As the church grew it began to encounter all the problems of an organisation and an institution."[66] Acts 6:1–7, which is explored in more detail in Chapter 3 of this book, describes how a second group within the Christian community was installed when trouble arose over the daily distribution to widows. "The seven men chosen for this task were to be men of good repute and full of the Holy Spirit and wisdom, although their task was essentially practical".[67] Bruce[68] elaborates that they were to be "competent in administration".

Bruce[69] points out, however, that "their activity was by no means confined to this". Two of the men chosen, Stephen and Philip, were also very involved in the preaching ministry. "The choice was made after prayer, and confirmed by the usual method employed amongst Jews and in ordinations ever since, namely by the laying on of hands".[70] While the seven are not specifically described in Acts as 'deacons', their function seems to be similar to the later office of deacons. They were appointed to serve a particular need which was tedious, but nevertheless, important. Lewis[71] argues that as the word 'deacon' itself comes from a Greek word meaning 'to serve, or minister to', it remains a suitable title in view of the task given to the first seven elected to the office.

Elder

A third office, that of elder came into being in the early church and has remained until the present day. However, there is no record of its origin in the New Testament. Later offices, such as that of the bishop, grew out of the office of elder. The earliest reference to elders in Acts (11:30) speaks of the poor brethren in Jerusalem, and how aid was sent to the elders there by Barnabas and Saul. This reference assumes the existence of elders as a known and established fact. Boer[72] suggests that it is possible that the separate meetings for worship that the believers in Jerusalem began to hold after Pentecost were patterned on the Jewish synagogue. In the synagogue the elder, who was next to the rulers in authority, occupied a prominent place. It may also be that the older members of the Christian community were automatically looked upon as the leaders, and after that the office of elder was either elective or appointive. Neil[73] suggests that they would have been charged with the oversight of worship, discipline, administration and instruction, more or less along the lines of the "rulers of the synagogue."

There are various references to elders in the church in the rest of Acts. In Acts 14, Luke describes how at the end of the first missionary journey Paul and Barnabas backtracked through each of the towns they had visited, to strengthen the disciples and encourage them to remain true to the faith (14:22). Paul and Barnabas are also reported to have appointed elders in churches they had established. These elders "would be local leaders among the Christians, responsible for the church during the absence of the missionaries."[74] Later in Acts, mention is made of elders in the Ephesian church (20:17). Elsewhere in the New Testament (1 Timothy 5:17; Titus 1:5; James 5:14; 1 Peter 5:1, 5) there is further evidence of the existence of elders.

Other Offices

Acts 13:1–2 speaks of two further groups, "prophets" and "teachers" (1 Cor 12:28). They had different functions. Prophets (Acts 11:27–28; 13:1) were not attached to any one local church so they wandered from place to place, "listening for the word of God then taking that word to their fellow men."[75] They shared with the apostle "the place of pre-eminence in the church."[76] Teachers (Acts 18.26) on the other hand, were placed in local churches and it was their duty to instruct those who joined the church, and to explain and reinforce the truth that was already possessed.

Other groups mentioned in Acts are miracle workers, healers, helpers and administrators and evangelists. An evangelist was one who held no office but possessed a gift for proclaiming the gospel, and like the prophet, they moved from place to place (21:8).

Why does the Book of Acts tell us so little about church organisation?

Christians in the early days believed that the end of the world was imminent (1 Thes 1:10, 2:19, 3:13, 4:17) and so they were urged by Paul to live in such a way that they be ready for the end (1 Thes 5:6–22). It appears that clerical functions were to a large degree fulfilled by men who had been specially endowed for this purpose by the Holy Spirit (6:1–7).

 OTHER ASPECTS OF HUMAN EXPERIENCE

Church organisation in the first two centuries

References:
- 'A short History of the Early Church', *Boer, H, Michigan: William B. Eerdmans Publishing Company, 1976*
- 'The Early Church: the Christian Church to 325AD', *Banks, R., Newtownards: Colourpoint, 2003*

Thirty years after Christ's death, both Peter and Paul were dead (martyred AD64 in Rome). A further thirty years on, the Parousia was no longer thought of as being imminent (1 and 2 Timothy; Titus). Towards the end of the first century a more structured ministry emerged in some of the churches: presbyters/bishops (including one regarded as the 'first among equals') and deacons.

Acts, the letters of Paul, Clement's letter to the Corinthians, (AD96) and Ignatius of Antioch's letters to the seven churches written on his way to Rome (AD107), enable us to discover a reasonably accurate account of how church life developed in the New Testament and beyond.

Using the suggesting reading, explore how church organisation developed in the first three centuries, making comparisons with the early days.

The Role of Women in 'Montanism'

Montanism arose in Phrygia (modern central Turkey) in AD156. It was a movement that emphasised the work of the Holy Spirit. It was called after Montanus, who had previously been a pagan priest before becoming a Christian. He was joined by two women, Maximilla and Priscilla, who had left their husbands to help him. Initially they worked within the umbrella of the Catholic Church but soon their teachings were regarded as heretical and they were forced to set themselves up as a separate organisation.

Banks[77] describes it as a "charismatic movement in the sense that it encouraged the involvement of all believers, including females, and the use of spiritual gifts in church life." Find out why the church was opposed to Montanism (Refer to Banks, R, *The Early Church*, Newtownards: Colourpoint Books, 2003, pp177–173).

In your opinion, was there anything of value in Montanism that the church lost for being so opposed to it?

 DISCUSSION

'No branch of the Christian Church today can claim to reproduce in its present practice or structures the church that Luke describes in Acts'.

 TASKS

a) Describe the main features of church life and organisation in the early church in Acts.

- Church life includes an exploration of fellowship, teaching, breaking of bread, prayer and sharing.
- Organisation includes the roles of Apostle, Deacon and Elder.

b) Comment on the claim that as the church developed it has lost its sense of spontaneity.

- This answer requires a look at other aspects of human experience. You might find it helpful to look at how the church developed during the first three centuries (Banks, 'The Early Church', pp137–149). Compare how the role of the Holy Spirit took a step into the shadows as the Church reacted against movements such as Montanism. Look at the role that the Holy Spirit has on guiding the church today. Have positions of authority taken over from spontaneity?

LEARNING INTENTIONS CHECKLIST/TARGET SETTING

By the end of this unit I will be able to:	Yes	No	To be achieved
• explain the importance of the Pentecost event for the spread of the gospel			
• understand the relationship between repentance, baptism and reception of the Holy Spirit			
• describe the different sequences of receiving the Holy Spirit, using examples from Acts			
• describe the signs of the Holy Spirit in a person's life in the early church			
• explain what is meant by 'uncomfortable comfort'			
• explain the meaning of the term 'koinonia'			
• use examples to show how the Holy Spirit acts as a guide and instructor for the first Christians			
• explain the difference between 'prophecy' and 'inspired preaching', using examples			
• relate one occasion when the Holy Spirit acted in a disciplinary role			
• describe the different means that the Holy Spirit used to carry out the church's mission			
• explain the relevance of the Holy Spirit to at least one other aspect of human experience			
• explain the meaning of the term 'miracle'			
• describe the different types of miracles in Acts, using examples			
• give an opinion on whether or not I believe miracles still happen			
• describe the four key aspects of church life from Acts 2:43–47			
• understand the importance of sharing of possessions for the early church			
• explain the meaning of the terms 'apostle', 'deacon' and 'elder'			

• understand why Acts tells us so little about church organisation			
• compare the church in Acts with how the church had developed by the end of the third century			
• discuss how churches today have changed from that described in Acts			

Endnotes

1 Hull, JHE, *The Holy Spirit in the Acts of the Apostles*, London: Lutterworth, 1967, p11

2 Ehrhardt, A, *The Acts of the Apostles* (Manchester: Manchester University Press, 1969) 129; Barclay, *op cit*, p46

3 Bengel, JA, *Gnoman Nom Testamenti* (3rd ed.; Tubingen: n.p., 1742; repr.London: Williams and Norgate, 1862) p389

4 Neil, *op cit*, p70

5 Marshall, *op cit*, pp347–369

6 Neil, *op cit*, p71

7 Bruce, *op cit*, p69

8 Bruce, *op cit*, p70

9 Lampe, GWH, *The Seal of the Spirit*, London: Longmans, Green, 1951

10 Bruce, *op cit*, p169

11 Lampe, *op cit*, p76

12 Neil, *op cit*, p89

13 Stott, JRW, *The Spirit, the Church, and the World* (Downers Grove, IL: InterVarsity, 1990), pp29–45

14 Drane, *op cit*, p393

15 Fernando, *op cit*, p123

16 Hewitt, *op cit*, p232

17 Willimon, *op cit*, p72

18 Bruce, *op cit*, p178, n74

19 Drane, *op cit*, p392

20 Bruce, *op cit*, p298

21 *ibid*, p298

22 An example of a prophet in Acts is Agabus.

23 Fernando, *op cit*, p376

24 Bruner, FD, *A Theology of the Holy Spirit*, London: Hodder, 1970, pp156–157

25 Boer, HR, *A Short History of the Early Church*, Michigan: William B Eerdmans Publishing Company, 1976, p71

26 Barclay, *op cit*, p13

27 Green, M, *I Believe in the Holy Spirit*, Grand Rapids: Eerdmans, 1975

28 Fernando, *op cit*, p152

29 *ibid*, p245

30 Guthrie, *op cit*, p740

31 *ibid*, p733

32 http://en.wikipedia.org/wiki/Miracles

33 Hewitt, *op cit*, pp255–256

34 Bruce, *op cit*, p98

35 *ibid*, p99

36 Guy, *op cit*, p31

37 Marshall, *op cit*, p107

38 Fernando, *op cit*, p170

39 Bruce, *op cit*, p160

40 http://www.news24.com/News24/World/News/0,,2-10-1462_1834134,00.html

41 http://www.dailymail.co.uk/pages/live/articles/health/healthmain.html?in_article_id=438900&in_page_id=1774&ico=Homepage&icl=TabModule&icc=picbox&ct=5

42 Guthrie, *op cit*, p733, fn109

43 Hewitt, *op cit*, p201

44 Bruce, *op cit*, p73

45 *ibid*, p73

46 Barclay, *op cit*, p25

47 ie studying and explaining the meaning of the prophecies.

48 Guthrie, *op cit*, p735

49 *ibid*, p735

50 Breaking of bread and the agape later became carried out separately.

51 Barclay, *op cit*, p26

52 Bruce, *op cit*, p73

53 We know that the apostles also attended the Jewish prayer services in the temple; 3:1.

54 Hewitt, *op cit*, p199

55 Bruce, *op cit*, p188

56 Barclay, *op cit*, p26

57 Guthrie, *op cit*, p735

58 Hewitt, *op cit*, p56

59 Guthrie, *op cit*, p735

60 Guy, *op cit*, pp31–32

61 Boer, *op cit*, p27

62 Guthrie, *op cit*, p734

63 Guy, *op cit*, p22

64 Kirk, JA, *Apostleship since Rengstorf: Towards a Synthesis*, New Testament Studies, 21, 1975, pp249–264

65 Guy, *op cit*, p22

66 Barclay, *op cit*, p50

67 Guthrie, *op cit*, p740

68 Bruce, *op cit*, p121

69 *ibid*, p122

70 Lewis, *op cit*, p35

71 *ibid*, p35

72 Boer, *op cit*, p28

73 Neil, *op cit*, p102

74 Guy, *op cit*, p56

75 Barclay, *op cit*, p96

76 Hewitt, *op cit*, p206

77 Banks, *op cit*, p177

Chapter 6

Paul in Captivity

INTRODUCTION

THE FINAL SECTION OF ACTS (Chapters 21–28) deals with the account of Paul's imprisonment and trials, the circumstances that led to Paul being taken to Rome, the events that took place on his way there, and his stay in Rome. As a Roman citizen, Paul longed to visit Rome, the capital of the Empire. He probably wanted to have some part in the life of the Christian community flourishing there (Rom 1:8–13). This section occupies a quarter of the book which highlights the significance of these final events in the eyes of the author.[1] Luke does not tell us of Paul's death.

JERUSALEM (Ch 21:15–23:35)

Luke uses two chapters of his work to describe the final events that took place in Jerusalem. Ladd[2] argues that Luke devotes such space to the record of Paul's last visit to Jerusalem "not because the visit was important in itself, but because it showed the final rejection of the Gospel by Jerusalem". This supports the notion that the purpose of Acts was to show how the gospel was for the Gentiles.

Paul's Arrival at Jerusalem (Ch 21:17–26)

Paul's group was extended by people from Caesarea who wanted to go with him to Jerusalem for the celebration of Pentecost. Among them was Mnason, a Cypriot, who lived in Jerusalem and invited Paul to be a guest at his home. He may even have been converted by Paul and Barnabas on the first missionary journey or even on the Day of Pentecost.

On arrival, Paul was "warmly received by the believers"[3] and the next day he gave his report to James, the brother of Jesus, and the elders of the Jerusalem church. Marshall[4] points out that by this time James had fully taken over the leadership of the church in Jerusalem. They received the news of his missionary successes with joy and thankfulness, but they also told Paul of rumours that were circulating about him in Jerusalem: that Paul was going beyond his practice of not expecting Gentile converts to be circumcised by also telling Jewish converts not to practise circumcision or to observe the customs of Judaism. Obviously, there were still people around who were intensely suspicious of Paul.[5] So as a result, thousands of converted Jews in the city were furious. Therefore, Paul had to somehow show that these rumours were false and that he had only freed Gentile converts from circumcision and the Jewish law, but still insisted on Jewish Christians living up to the law.

Fernando[6] explains how James and the elders proposed that to show his support Paul should pay the Temple expenses of four men who had taken a Nazarite vow, go into the Temple with them, and join them in their ritualistic purification, which lasted seven days. Paul himself had taken such a vow before (18:18). At the end of the vow they would be required to bring an offering of two lambs, one ram, a basket of unleavened bread, a grain offering and a drink offering to the Temple (Num 6:13–15). Paul may no longer have been a Jew by religion but he was still racially a Jew and as such, observed Jewish practices. "If he were seen to take part publicly in one of the ancestral customs, it would be realised that he was, after all, an observant and practising Jew."[7] Paul began the ritualistic process the day after the suggestion had been made to him. Seven days later they would make their sacrifices together, and Paul would pay for all of them.

Some scholars[8] question whether this really happened, as such a sacrifice to please the Jewish Christians would be too great a compromise for Paul to make. After all, he was the apostle to the Gentiles. However, the same Paul confessed he could be all things to all people if by any means he might save some (1 Cor 9:22). He was willing to be a Jew to the Jews, that is, keep the law for the sake of those living under the law, and to be like a Gentile to the Gentiles. So it could be argued that Paul's readiness to perform the necessary purification rites was for the sake of others. He knew that he had been freed from the law and lived entirely by the grace of God in Christ, but he did not want to get in the way of the progress of the newly converted Jews in the Christian faith.

TASK

In pairs jot down what is meant by the following statement. Use examples to explain your answer:

"He [Paul] himself was happy to conform to Jewish customs when he found himself in Jewish society. Such conformity came easily to him, in view of his upbringing, but he had learned to be equally happy to conform to Gentile ways in Gentile company."[9]

Paul Arrested (Ch 21:27–36)

It could be argued that the advice given to Paul by James and the elders was unwise. It might have convinced the Jewish Christians in Jerusalem that Paul had not broken the Jewish law and was one of them; however, it placed Paul in the temple, exposing him to the unconverted Jews in the city. These hostile Jews from Asia saw Paul with Trophimus, one of his Gentile converts from Ephesus. Perhaps Trophimus followed him into the Court of the Gentiles in the Temple area. Bruce[10] explains that there was a sign in the doorway between this court and the Court of Women, stating that any foreigner who passed over from the Court of the Gentiles into the Temple area would be put to death. The Romans allowed the Jews to execute any Gentile, even a Roman citizen, for proceeding beyond the barrier.[11] These Asian Jews spread the false rumour through the crowd that Paul had brought Trophimus into the sacred precinct of the Temple. Hewitt[12] suggests that the Jews deliberately invented the lie about Trophimus in order to get their revenge on Paul for what he had achieved in Ephesus. However, the possibility that Trophimus might have wandered of his own accord into the forbidden area of the Temple is about as likely as a Protestant carrying a Union Jack up the Falls Road in Belfast.

When Paul had completed his sacrifice on the seventh day, the Asian Jews spotted him in the Temple, and shouted: *"Men of Israel, help us! This is the man who teaches all men everywhere against our people and our law and this place. And besides, he has brought Greeks into the temple area and defiled this holy place"* (21:28). The basis of the charge was feeble,[13] however, it was enough to anger many Jews in the Temple area, who turned on Paul and dragged him out of the inner courts, shutting the doors behind him. Jeremias[14] suggests they closed the doors to prevent the defiling of the inner courts by the uproar and bloodshed. However, Fitzmyer[15] regards it as a symbolic action deliberately added by Luke to show that from now on the Temple "would have no meaning for the Christian Church".

Fortunately for Paul, the 'Antonia', the Roman fortress, was right beside the Temple. It held a force of 760 infantry and 240 cavalry, which made up an auxiliary Roman cohort. The fortress was built above the Temple and higher than any other building in Jerusalem, so that the Romans could keep constant watch over the population. Flights of stairs led down from it into the Court of the Gentiles.[16]

When the Romans saw what was going on in the outer court of the Temple, the commander of the troops, Claudius Lysias (23:26), rushed down with troops to stop Paul being killed by the mob. Fernando[17] describes his intervention as timely. One thing Rome insisted on was civil order. "A riot was an unforgivable sin both for the populace who staged it and the commander who allowed it".[18] Marshall[19] explains how the arrival of the Romans was therefore enough to stop the crowd attacking Paul.

Paul was handcuffed to two soldiers, fulfilling the prophecy of Agabus (21:11).[20] The commander tried to find out what Paul had done to cause such uproar. But "so great was the din and so confused and conflicting the accusations that were being hurled at Paul"[21] that he could not get a straight answer. Most of those present did not know what Paul was supposed to have done.

 TASK

This is the sixth time that Paul's ministry caused a public disturbance. Compare this to the other occasions. Do you think Paul was a public nuisance?

- 14:19　　• 16:19–22　　• 17:5–8, 13　　• 19:25–34

(Ch 21:37–40)

Paul was arrested, bound with two chains and carried from the crowd up the stairs towards the entrance of the Antonia. The commander, who was very surprised when Paul addressed him in Greek, asked him, *"Do you speak Greek? Aren't you the Egyptian who started a revolt and led four thousand terrorists out into the desert some time ago?"*[22] (21:37–38). Perhaps Paul's appearance made him assume that he was a criminal. Instead Paul informed him that he was a Jew and a citizen of Tarsus. Fitzmyer[23] argues that in this incident Luke clearly makes his point: "Paul is not the one who causes political uprising (as did 'the Egyptian') or jeopardises the law and order of the Roman world." Paul's use of Greek and tone of voice were such that the commander let him speak, realising that he was more than just an ordinary man.

Paul Speaks to the Jewish Mob (22:1–21)

Paul spoke to the Jewish mob in Aramaic (Hebrew), which was "an effective way of commanding their attention".[24] Choosing the language familiar to the crowds would have helped them realise that he was one of them. He further secured their silence with a characteristic gesture of his hand which was "probably intended by Luke to bear witness to the power of his personality".[25] They became very quiet and listened to him immediately.

Fernando[26] points out that like Stephen (7:2), Paul addressed his audience as "brothers and fathers". He spoke of his experience of being led to accept Christ as his Saviour. It is similar to the account in Acts 9 with a few details added:

Early Life

- Paul describes his life before conversion, emphasising his orthodox background and education in Jerusalem under Gamaliel, the most respected Jewish teacher of his day. He goes into this detail to show his audience that he was as devout a Jew as any of them.

Saul the Persecutor

- Marshall[27] comments how Paul describes how he had gone further than his audience in religious zeal: he had persecuted Christians far and wide. This description of his activity as a persecutor of Christians "opened the way for him to describe his conversion".[28]

Conversion

- Paul recalls the events of his conversion, stressing the supernatural revelation God had given him. This account "focuses on his call rather than his conversion".[29] He explains that it was noon when the experience took place, and the heavenly light was strong enough to outshine the noonday sun.

- He refers to Jesus as "Jesus of Nazareth", so there would be no mistake on the part of his audience as to who had appeared to him.

- He adds that his companions also saw the light but did not hear the voice so they became afraid; "they were conscious of something unusual, but only Paul experienced the event as divine revelation."[30]

- Paul is careful to add detail that would have been especially significant to his audience. He describes that Ananias, "a devout and law-abiding Jew",[31] who was highly respected by the Jews, was the instrument of God in restoring his sight. Ananias also baptised him and told him to witness to Jesus Christ. Paul reports that he came back to Jerusalem and prayed in the Temple. Ananias had even called Paul his brother. Bruce[32] comments that it was important for Paul to stress before this Jewish mob that his commission was to a large extent communicated through the lips of this pious and believing Jew.

Jerusalem

- On his return to Jerusalem Paul had gone to the Temple to pray and in a vision God had told him to leave the city for his own safety. Paul hints that as he had persecuted Christians, and had done nothing when Stephen was being martyred, then surely his audience should listen to him of all people. "His point seems to have been that people who knew his former record would be more readily convinced that his change of attitude must be based on the most compelling grounds."[33] However, this did him no favours with crowd, for when he explained how he was told by God that he must go to witness to the

Gentiles, there was uproar. "The real crime of Paul was preaching to the Gentiles … Hence he defends himself by asserting his loyalty to Israel, and that his preaching was simply obedience to a divine command."[34]

 TASK

Pick out the words and phrases in this speech which supports the fact that Paul was addressing a Jewish audience.

Paul the Roman Citizen (22:22–29)

The crowd had listened to Paul without interruption up to this point. However, at the mention of the Gentiles, they broke into a rage; "the speech was now more than they could stand."[35] Paul was placing Gentiles on an equal footing before God as the Jews. "Luke's story is at its liveliest; he switches the crowd off for Paul's speech; now he switches it on to fever pitch."[36] Discarding their clothes and throwing dust in the air, they demanded Paul's death. The commander ordered Paul to be taken into the barracks to be questioned and to be flogged in order to get the truth out of him, as to what he had really done to cause such an outbreak. This meant being beaten with a whip weighted with pieces of sharp metal that ripped the body. If a man did not actually die under the scourge, he might well be crippled for life.[37]

At this point Paul revealed that he was a Roman citizen. Roman law protected Roman citizens from such a beating, even if they were guilty.[38] The centurion was stunned and he told his superior that they had more on their hands than they realised, for such punishment of a Roman was forbidden by law. The commander stopped his orders, pointing out to Paul that he had bought his Roman citizenship. Perhaps he was implying that it was no longer the honour it used to be, since anyone who could afford to, could pay a bribe in return for citizenship. However, Paul replied, *"But I was born a citizen"* (22:28). The commander would have completely accepted Paul's verbal claim to being a Roman citizen because a false claim to citizenship was a capital offence.[39] Bruce[40] explains how the commander "shuddered as he realised how near he had come to perpetrating a serious illegality".

Paul Before the Sanhedrin (22:30–23:11)

The commander summoned the members of the Sanhedrin to the Antonia to try to find out why Paul was being accused. He needed to know exactly because if Paul was being charged with a religious crime it would be the responsibility of the Sanhedrin to try him. However, if it was a civil crime, then he would be tried before the Romans.

- When Paul was brought before the Sanhedrin he addressed them with the term "brothers", which was a common formal address among Jews.

- And as his commitment to Judaism was questionable, he also identified himself as a Jew.

- In an attempt to point out that nothing he had done was against the will of God, Paul claimed *"I have fulfilled my duty to God in all good conscience to this day"*.

- The high priest at the time was Ananias (AD47–58), an undeserving and dishonourable man. He was known to have used bribery, violence and even murder to get his own way.[41] Guy suggests that he ordered those nearest to Paul to strike him in the mouth, "perhaps because he started to speak without permission".[42] Hewitt[43] agrees, adding that Paul's use of the term "brothers" may also have upset the high priest.

- Paul was outraged and responded "with a typically human reaction"[44] to this slap, proclaiming: *"God will strike you, you whitewashed wall! You sit there to judge me according to the law, yet you yourself violate the law by commanding that I be struck!"* (23:3). A whitewashed wall is often weak on the inside but looks good on the outside.[45]

- The Jewish leaders were shocked by Paul's remark and told him that he had violated the law which forbade anyone to speak evil of God's high priest (Exod 22:28).

- Paul admitted he had broken the law, but added he had not realised this man was the High Priest.

Why would Paul not have recognised the High Priest?

- Longenecker[46] suggests that Ananias may not have been wearing his high priestly robes or been in his usual seat, as it was not a regular meeting of the Sanhedrin.

- Paul had visited Jerusalem on and off over the previous twenty years so Paul may not have known Ananias to see.

- McGee[47] points to Paul's poor eyesight, perhaps because of the blinding that took place on the road to Damascus. In Galatians 4:13–15 Paul comments that the Galatians would have given their eyes to him.

- Perhaps Paul was being ironic[48] or even sarcastic.[49] He must have known who Ananias was due to his leadership role in the interrogation. Rackham[50] suggests Paul meant that he had not sufficiently reflected that the man who uttered the objectionable words was the high priest. Hewitt[51] agrees suggesting that what Paul actually meant was: "One would never guess from his behaviour that he was a High Priest." Maybe Paul could hardly believe that God's high priest would behave in such a violent way, which was clearly contrary to the law (Lev 19:15).

- Marshall[52] argues that theories that Paul had bad eyesight or that he did not recognise the High Priest lack foundation.

- At this point Paul probably realised that he was not going to get a fair trial, so he cleverly divided his audience, which was made up of Sadducees, who denied the resurrection of the dead,[53] and Pharisees who believed in resurrection. When he announced that he was a Pharisee, he strategically added that he was being accused of preaching the hope in the resurrection of the dead. Fernando[54] asks if this was simply a crafty ploy used by Paul to divide the Sanhedrin.

Aftermath of Paul's Appearance before Sanhedrin

There was immediate uproar as the statement "set the Sanhedrin at each other's throats".[55] The less powerful members, the scribes (who were Pharisees), supported Paul against the chief priests, (who were Sadducees). The Pharisees found no fault with Paul and some even said that they should not fight against God as it was possible an angel had spoken to Paul. Bruce[56] comments that they were "immediately inclined to concede that a man who was so sound on a central Pharisaic doctrine could not be so bad at heart after all". Because Paul is vindicated by the Pharisees in his audience, Fitzmyer[57] regards this as "the most important defence scene in Acts".

The Pharisees and Sadducees began to fight with each other and their argument became so violent that the commander had to have Paul removed. That night the Lord appeared to Paul, as he had done at critical times before (cf 18:9; 22:17),[58] and encouraged him by commending him on his witness in Jerusalem. The Lord also promised Paul that he would testify about him in Rome. "This assurance meant much to Paul during the delays and anxieties of the next two years, and goes far to account for the calm and dignified bearing which seemed to mark him out as a master of events rather than their victim."[59]

The Plot to Kill Paul (23:12–22)

Disappointed that Paul had so far escaped death, a group of more than forty Jews agreed together that they would neither eat nor drink until they had killed him. They appealed to the chief priests for a second hearing from Paul, even though it was against the law for the Sanhedrin to be associated with a plot of this type. The plan was to kill him somewhere "along the narrow streets"[60] between the fortress of Antonia and the council chamber. Paul's sister lived in Jerusalem, and when her son heard about the plot he warned Paul, who was able to receive visitors due to his Roman citizenship. Paul sent his nephew with a centurion to tell the commander about the plot.

Paul Transferred to Caesarea (23:23–35)

Believing the boy's report, the commander decided to get Paul out of Jerusalem immediately, and refer his case to the Roman procurator of Judea who lived in

Caesarea. Bruce[61] explains that the commander could not afford to be responsible for the assassination of a Roman citizen. He wrote a letter to the procurator, giving him an account of what had happened, but insisting that he had rescued Paul because he was a Roman citizen. Guy[62] explains that the letter was something between a personal letter and an official report. Stott[63] points out how he "manipulated the facts in order to portray himself in the most favourable light". He did not mention the beating, for example. Another important thing to note is that the commander did not think Paul was guilty of any crime, and that his dispute with the Jews was a theological one.[64]

The commander sent Paul by night to Caesarea, with a military escort of two hundred foot soldiers, two hundred spearmen, and seventy cavalrymen. They reached the town of Antipatris, thirty-seven miles away, at which point the spearmen and the infantry returned to their barracks; the cavalry took Paul the remaining miles to Caesarea where the governor received him and placed him in Herod's palace. Kent[65] comments that the delivery of Paul to Caesarea marks the beginning of a two-year imprisonment there.

 TASK

Outline the events that led to Paul's arrest in Jerusalem and his transfer to Caesarea.

- The charge against Paul in relation to Trophimus
- How Paul was rescued from the mob by the commander
- Paul's speech to the mob; second conversion account
- His escape from scourging on the grounds of his Roman citizenship
- His hearing before the Sanhedrin
- The plot against his life and his removal for safe custody to Caesarea

CAESAREA: ACTS 24:1–26:32

The Trial Before Felix 24:1–21

Three writers of the first century, Josephus, Tacitus and Suetonius, write about Felix the Roman governor and "all agree that he was bad".[66] For example, Tacitus[67] describes him as practising "every kind of cruelty and lust, wielding the power of [a] king with all the instincts of a slave". Felix was an unusual character, who had a reputation for ruling with "notorious cruelty and corruptibility".[68] He had been a slave and had not only achieved freedom and Roman citizenship, but had climbed the ranks to this high position in the government of the empire. Felix was married to the Jewish princess, Drusilla, the daughter of Herod Agrippa I, who had jailed Peter (12:22–23). Drusilla was Felix's third wife.

Felix heard Paul's case at a formal trial five days after his arrival in Caesarea.

Fernando[69] comments how the seriousness with which the Jewish leaders took this case is apparent in that "the high priest [Ananias] himself made the sixty-five mile journey to Caesarea along with the elders and the lawyer Tertullus". Ananias and the elders presented their charges against Paul through Tertullus, a lawyer, who was probably a Roman practising law in Judea.

Flattery of officials in formal speeches was a common approach in Paul's day, and Tertullus' introduction was phrased "to win favour and goodwill"[70]; although Barclay[71] considers it no more than "nauseating flattery". For example, the title "most excellent" was usually applied to those of a higher social rank than Felix. Tertullus also praised Felix for being a peacemaker, which was far from the truth. He probably was paving the way for his charge that Paul was a disturber of the peace (v 5–6).

Charges against Paul

There were **four charges** against Paul. Hanson[72] describes how many commentators have complained of the vagueness of these charges. Fernando[73] comments that each statement in Paul's defence makes a telling point that convinces Felix of Paul's innocence:

	Charges against Paul	Paul's Defence
1.	Paul was a public nuisance, "a troublemaker" (24:5).	Felix can verify when Paul arrived in Jerusalem (v 11). He had been in Jerusalem for only twelve days and had not the time to be a troublemaker. He had gone to Jerusalem to worship. His accusers did not find him doing anything to cause trouble (v 12);
2	He agitated the Jews and caused riots wherever he went in the Empire.	Paul's accusers have no proof to back up their charges (v 13).
3	Paul was a ringleader of the Nazarene sect (24:5), which was regarded as a cult that was not part of Judaism.	He was not the leader of a cult; he was a member of the Way, a sect which had similar beliefs to the Jews. The real issue in the case was that he believed and taught the resurrection both of the righteous and of the unrighteous.[74]
4	Paul had tried to desecrate the Temple (by bringing a Gentile into the inner courts).	Rather than desecrating the Temple, Paul had actually come to Jerusalem to give money to the Jewish Christians and to present offerings in the Temple (v 17).
		Paul's original accusers were not there, and his present accusers could not say that the Sanhedrin had found him guilty. Bruce[75] argues that this was a strong point in Paul's defence.

"This is the only place in Acts where speeches take the form of a debate."[76] Winter[77] comments that in this debate "Paul conducted his defence in an able manner against a professional orator". Tannehill[78] agrees, praising Paul's superior skill of "making use of Tertullus' words to build his own case".

When the debate was over it was clear that Felix should have released Paul, but he was reluctant to displease the Jews.[79] He postponed his decision on the grounds that he needed to talk directly with Lysias, the commander. Meanwhile Paul was put in the custody of a centurion but was able to have a considerable amount of freedom and visitors.

Felix and the Gospel 24:24–27

Something seemed to draw Felix to Paul for he met with him privately many times to talk. On one occasion he brought Drusilla, his wife with him. Hewitt[80] argues that Paul obviously "touched their consciences in his private interviews with them". However, his words about sin, righteousness and the judgement to come made Felix so uneasy that he was afraid. Perhaps he did not want to consider the moral implications an acceptance of the gospel would have on his life. Fernando[81] thinks this accounts for his "couldn't care less attitude", in saying that he would only send for Paul again when it was convenient.

Marshall,[82] however, comments that Felix had no intention of repenting. Perhaps what was really at the forefront of Felix's mind was money. Bruce[83] suggests that Felix seemed to think Paul was in a position to pay a handsome bribe for his release. Neil[84] tells us that "although provincial governors were prohibited by law from taking bribes from prisoners, the practice was common and, in the case of Felix, quite in character". Maybe he thought that as Paul had just brought a substantial gift for the poor then he must have access to great wealth.[85] So Felix put off making a decision on Paul's case and let it drag on until the end of his rule, two years later.

 OTHER ASPECTS OF HUMAN EXPERIENCE

Terry Waite's imprisonment [86]

Church envoy Terry Waite went to Beirut in January 1987 to negotiate the release of several hostages being held there. But he ended up a hostage himself and was held captive for 1,760 days before being released on 18 November 1991.

"I remember saying three things to myself after I was taken hostage which somehow stood me in good stead:

- No regrets – you haven't done everything correctly, you're bound to have made mistakes, but stick by what you've done.

- No self pity – don't begin to feel sorry for yourself, there are loads of people who are in worse situations than yourself.

- And no over-sentimentality – don't look back and say, "If only I'd spent more time with the family and had longer holidays – life has been lived, you cannot relive it.

Solitary confinement

But I had no contact at all with my family for five years – they didn't know that I was alive or dead for about four years when the news got to them from the Irish hostage Brian Keenan. Brian knew I had been in the next cell and of course when he was released he went and told my wife. I was in solitary confinement and I used to communicate with hostages in the cell next door by tapping on the wall in code. You can't use Morse code on a wall because you can't differentiate between a dot and a dash, but you can use the laborious code of one for A, two for B, three for C. It was then that I regretted my name was Terry Waite, because it's a long way down the alphabet when you want to communicate your name. However, I communicated with them. They had a radio and for about nine months I depended on the news being tapped through the wall.

In the last six months my captors relented and I was given a small radio. I listened to the BBC World Service constantly and I was enormously grateful, particularly for the fact that at the time they were broadcasting virtually 24 hours-a-day to the Middle East. I heard my cousin John broadcasting on Outlook and that meant a great deal to me because John, in a subtle way, got me news from my family.

Depression

He also broadcast on my birthday and played a piece of Bach's organ music for me as a gift from the family. It was a great source of hope and comfort to me, that something was getting through to me from my family. Because although I had to put my family and friends out of my mind – to dwell on them would have made me unnecessarily depressed – I was always concerned about them. And particularly about my children – the eldest of whom were in university, and I thought perhaps my actions had wrecked their family life. That wasn't true because I underestimated the enormous resilience of children and the enormous strength of my wife to deal with this very complex situation.

Final journey

We were gradually aware of the fact that we would be set free. When it did happen it was really rather a low key event. They simply came into the room and said, "You're going to be released", and threw in some clothes, which were all far too small – I looked ridiculous. I was taken out, blindfolded again, put into the boot of a car, then another car, and when they took the blindfold off I was with a Syrian intelligence operative, who drove me to the Syrian intelligence headquarters.

When I was on the plane coming from Cyprus to RAF Lyneham a former colleague of mine, Richard Chartres, who is now Bishop of London, came out to meet me – and I'm very glad he did. Richard said it would be very appropriate if, before meeting my family, I made a statement and deliver it to the press – to satisfy them and they could then go their own ways. I also regarded myself as being still on duty until such time as I could sign-off by making that statement, so I quickly jotted a few notes down on the back of a bit of paper. I went into the hangar and made this impromptu speech, when I said what I had to say about hostages and hostage-taking and what I'd attempted to do.

Emotion

Then I left the hangar and thought, "That's it, it's over". And I met my family for the first time and it was quite emotional. My son who was a teenager when I'd been captured had now grown up and I didn't recognise him – he'd changed so much. I remember my youngest daughter simply saying to me, "Daddy, take all the help that they're going to give you here." That I did, and I'm enormously grateful for the supportive help the RAF medical staff gave both to me and my family during those first days of release."

 TASKS

1. Can you make any comparisons between the experiences/attitudes of the apostle Paul and Terry Waite?

2. What lessons can be drawn from both the apostle Paul and Terry Waite's experiences of trial/imprisonment?

3. Find out about other similar cases, eg John McCarthy.

The Trial Before Festus (Ch 25:1–12)

Felix was replaced by Festus, who ruled from AD59–61. He was a more honourable leader who tried to be fair in the cases tried. When he made his first visit to the Jewish leaders in Jerusalem, the chief priests brought Paul's case to his attention and asked for the trial to take place back in Jerusalem. It seems they had realised that their hopes of getting rid of Paul through the Roman courts were wearing thin. So they intended to have Paul killed on his return to Jerusalem. Hewitt[87] comments that it is to Festus' credit that he did not agree immediately to the Jews' request to have Paul brought to Jerusalem. Instead it seems he was too astute to be taken in by them and refused to grant them their request. As he had not heard of the case before, he invited them to come to Caesarea for the trial.

The Jews produced the same complaints against Paul that Tertullus had presented (24:5–6), but they could not produce any evidence to support what they said. Paul declared that he had not broken Jewish law or profaned the Temple; neither had he done anything harmful to the reign of Caesar. However, the fact that they were so heated in their attack on Paul may have made Festus wonder if there was more to the case than met the eye. Festus may also have been nervous of getting on the wrong side of the Jews. Therefore he asked Paul if he would be willing to have his trial moved to Jerusalem after all.

Paul refused. He probably realised that the chances of a fair trial were slim. Luke hints at this in his use of the word 'favour' in v 3 and v 9. Jerusalem was the last place he could expect to receive a fair trial. Therefore he took advantage of his rights as a Roman citizen[88] and appealed his case to Caesar. He may have regarded this as the only way to reach Rome. Bruce[89] comments that Festus was probably relieved by Paul's decision for it enabled him to escape from a responsibility with which he felt unable to cope. There was nothing more Festus could do but grant Paul his request: *"You have appealed to Caesar. To Caesar you will go!" (25:12).*

Festus Consults King Agrippa (Ch 25:13–22)

Shortly after, Festus received a state visit from King Agrippa and his sister, Bernice, rumoured to be his mistress. Agrippa ruled territory north of Judea and lived in Caesarea Philippi. He was a Jew and had a reputation for being an expert in the Jewish religion. Festus was pleased to have the opportunity to consult Agrippa about Paul for he had no idea what to write in his report to Caesar. "If it was to be coherent and intelligible he would require a better grasp of the matters at issue than he possessed at present".[90] He had been surprised that the charges which the Jews brought against Paul were matters to do with the Jewish religion; in fact he saw the resurrection of Jesus as a pivotal point in this case (25:19 –20).[91] "There is no more mention of the desecration of the Temple; the discourse concentrates on the central issues of the continuity of Christianity with Judaism …".[92] Marshall[93] agrees, pointing out how by this stage the question of Paul's alleged desecration of the temple seems to have disappeared.

The case evidently interested Agrippa for he asked to hear Paul in person and a gathering was arranged for the next day. Agrippa and Bernice arrived in great pomp and splendour, as did their host Festus.

Paul Before Agrippa (Ch 25:23–26:23)

Paul's trial before Agrippa has been described as "the longest and most elaborate of the five".[94] Festus used it as an opportunity to honour Agrippa and Bernice before the high ranking officers and the leading men of the city. The grandeur of their arrival to the hearing "reminds us of the prediction God made to Ananias that Paul would appear before the kings of the Gentiles (9:15)".[95] Festus admitted to the gathering that in his opinion Paul had done nothing that deserved the death sentence,[96] but that Paul had appealed to Caesar and would have to be sent to Rome.

McGee[97] regards Paul's testimony in this trial not a defence of himself but a declaration of the gospel, with the purpose of winning Agrippa and the others present to Christ. Bruce[98] agrees, adding that it is also a defence of how Paul's life has changed in conformity with the gospel. The style of the speech is more literary and the grammar used more classical, which suited the distinguished audience.[99] It is perhaps regarded as Paul's fullest testimony in Acts because it describes his pre-Christian activity, his conversion, his calling and his mission.[100]

Speech before Agrippa:

- Paul began with a customary introduction by complementing the king sincerely and urging him to listen patiently.

- Paul admitted that he had done all in his power to persecute and destroy Christians. He was so zealous in his persecution that he even pursued them to foreign cities. Crowe[101] comments that "The picture of Paul's activity as persecutor is painted in blacker colours than before".

- Paul related the remarkable experience he had on the Damascus road, and the commission God gave him to go to the Gentiles. Paul's commission from Jesus himself is unique to this account (26:16–18).

- He insisted that his case rested entirely on the resurrection hope, which should have been the hope of the Jews too.

- It was Paul's belief that the Gentiles could obtain salvation simply by faith in Christ which infuriated the Jews and led to Paul's arrest.

- However, God had helped Paul and stood by him.

- The Old Testament prophets had claimed that the Christ would suffer, be the first to rise from the dead, and would proclaim light to his own people and to the Gentiles.

Festus and Agrippa's Response (Ch 26:24–32)

Festus had no understanding of what Paul was saying. His comment: *"You are out of your mind, Paul. Your great learning is driving you insane"*, sounds like an interruption, but in fact the speech has reached its conclusion.[102] Festus acknowledged that Paul was an educated man, but thought perhaps he was too educated for his own good.

- However Paul noticed that Agrippa was listening to his words carefully. What Festus called madness, Paul asserted, was true. Using the Old Testament prophecies of the coming Messiah, Paul tried to convince Agrippa that Jesus had fulfilled them, that it was necessary for him to suffer, and as a result to be the first person to rise from the dead. If Agrippa believed the Old Testament prophets, it followed that he should realise that Jesus fulfilled what they predicted.

- The speech ends with a missionary appeal to Agrippa.[103] Paul said confidently that Agrippa knew what he was talking about. Agrippa replied light-heartedly,[104] *"Do you think that in such a short time you can persuade me to be a Christian?"* (26:28). His calm manner "stands in contrast to the governor's emotional outburst".[105] However, Agrippa was backed into a corner. Guy[106] suggests that Paul had embarrassed him and that he "resented this reminder that he was a Jew, with a peculiar religion". Bruce[107] explains that if Agrippa agreed with Paul he would have made Festus look foolish. However, if he said he did not believe the prophets, then he would have lost the respect of his Jewish listeners.

- Paul's defence concludes with a courteous but firm reply that he hoped that all his listeners, not just Agrippa, would become Christians.

Differences with Acts 21

There is no contradiction in the two accounts. Paul probably used what he thought was relevant to his audiences. Ultimately he stressed the divine commission given to him by Jesus, to go to the Gentiles. In this account before Agrippa there are a few differences in detail from what Paul said to the Jewish crowd in Jerusalem:

- He related how he and his companions were struck to the ground by the heavenly light, but he did not mention his blindness and/or his sight being restored.

- He supplied no factual details about himself and his work except that Jesus was sending him to free people from the power of Satan to God, so that they would have a place among the saints.

- He also recalled that Jesus said to him: "It is hard for you to kick against the goads" (26:14), which he had not mentioned to the Jews in Jerusalem. A goad was a sharp stick that was used to drive cattle. Kicking against the goads was a Greek metaphor which means trying to oppose the inevitable or trying to resist fate. Festus and Agrippa would have been familiar with this saying, but it would have meant nothing to the crowd at Jerusalem.

When Festus and Agrippa left the chamber to discuss Paul's case privately, Agrippa assured Festus that Paul had done nothing wrong. Both men realised Paul was completely innocent. "When measured by Roman law, Paul's behaviour appeared to be free from any guilt; mad he might appear to be, but not a criminal."[108] They shook their heads and said that Paul could have been set free if he had not made an appeal to Caesar. Festus had no choice but to send Paul to Rome since his appeal was a matter of public record.

What kind of a speech is this?

1. An evangelistic speech – the speech focuses on an evangelist appeal rather than on the charges against Paul

2. An apology – it shows how Paul's relations with the Romans in Judea ended with an acknowledgement that he was innocent of any crime against the state.

 TASKS

1. **Discuss Paul's appearances before Felix, Festus, and Agrippa.**
   - Comment on how this section allows Paul to make an extended apologia for his faith through the different speeches
   - Felix: Tertullus' accusations, Paul's response, Felix's delay, Drusilla, Paul's innocence, two year imprisonment, Felix's character
   - Festus: Jewish desires, Festus inherits Paul, Caesarean court, Paul's defence, appeal to Caesar
   - Agrippa: Festus consults Agrippa, Festus introduces Paul, lack of charge to present to Emperor, Paul defends himself, strict Jew, Messianic hopes, persecution of Christians, Paul's third conversion account, commission to the Gentiles, challenge to Agrippa
   - Agreement about Paul's innocence
   - Significance of his appeal to Caesar

2. **Comment on the claim that this section of Acts would be of particular interest to Roman officials who had to make up their minds about what attitude they were to take to the new religion.**
   - The generally good light in which Luke has presented the Roman authorities so far in Acts (Sergius Paulus, Acts 13; Magistrates, Acts 16; Gallio, Acts 18)
   - Paul's 'rescue' by the commander in Acts 21
   - The Roman authorities' reluctance to get involved in religious dispute between Paul and the Jewish people
   - The main concern of the Roman authorities is if Paul is causing a disturbance and upsetting the peace
   - The reaction of Felix, Festus and Agrippa

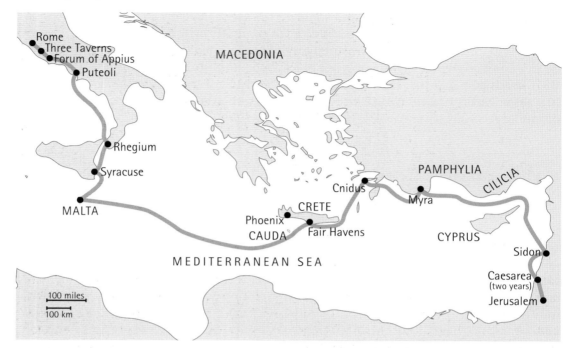

Above: A map of Paul's journey to Rome

THE VOYAGE TO ROME (Ch 27:1–28:13)

The last two chapters of Acts record the fulfilment of Paul's great ambition to go to Rome.[109] Ever since the purpose of going to Rome had been planted in Paul's mind by the Holy Spirit, his plans had been formulated with that goal in view (19:21).[110] He had been confronted with one crisis after another, but he had divine assurance that Rome would be reached (23:11). The final stage of this journey takes Paul on an eventful, dangerous and exciting sea journey.

Marshall[111] points out that in proportion to the book as a whole, the length of the narrative describing Paul's sea journey to Rome is remarkable. Bruce[112] regards the story as "a small classic in its own right". It reads like an exciting novel, urging the reader to turn the pages to see what is going to happen next. You are left wondering if Paul will in fact reach Rome at all.

As well as being an interesting story, Holtzmann[113] believes that the final chapters of Acts provide "one of the most instructive documents for the knowledge of ancient seamanship". Rackham[114] agrees, adding that the story is told with such a wealth of detail that "in all classical literature there is no passage which gives us so much information about the working of an ancient ship".

Paul's role in the voyage to Rome

27:1–11	Paul warns of danger and his advice is ignored, but eventually he is proved right
27:21–26	Paul's Speech
27:31	Paul's intervention stops the desertion of sailors
27:33–36	Paul urges everyone to eat
27:43	Paul saved by the Roman centurion
28:2b–6	Paul saved by the viper

From Caesarea to Crete (Ch 27:1–8)

Paul was sent to Rome along with other prisoners in the custody of a centurion called Julius. Like Cornelius in Acts 10, Julius was a centurion who exhibits mercy and fairness, which we will see as the story unfolds. He probably took enough troops with him to guard his prisoners, or even to kill them if necessary. As a Roman citizen Paul had greater privileges than the other prisoners. However, the narrative clearly implies that Paul enjoyed the respect during this voyage that a penniless traveller without a servant to attend on him would never receive.[115] It is also clear that Julius liked Paul and treated him with respect.

Aristarchus of Thessalonica is mentioned as a fellow passenger. He, too, was on his way to trial (Col 4:10). The narrative changes from the third person to the first person pronoun, indicating the presence of Luke himself, which may have added to the respect Paul received on board.[116] Some scholars suggest he may have signed up as the ship's doctor.

It was not a direct journey to Italy. Passengers could travel as far as a ship was going in their direction, disembark, and pick up another ship as soon as one was available. The first ship used sailed out of Adramyttium, a port on the northwest coast near Troas. It stopped at Sidon to unload and load cargo, and Julius graciously allowed Paul to visit Christian friends there, although he would have been accompanied by a soldier. Fernando[117] describes this as the first of Julius' many acts of kindness to Paul.

The ship sailed north up the east side of Cyprus, headed north to the coast of Cilicia and turned west past Pamphylia. Paul and company got off at Myra in Lycia and transferred to another ship which was destined for Italy. It was a grain ship, taking wheat from Egypt to Rome, with room for about 276 passengers (v 37).

After some difficulty reaching Cnidus, a wind forced Paul's ship southwest to the island of Crete. Sailing across the Mediterranean was usually safe from May to early September. However, from early November to early March it was so dangerous that sailings stopped altogether. The captain of the ship hoped to reach Italy before the bad weather had set in. Unfortunately winds were not favourable, and the ship had difficulty reaching Fair Havens, a harbour near Crete. As it was an open harbour, it was vulnerable to damage from storms and ships lacked the protection that land around them would provide.

The Storm at Sea (Ch 27:9–26)

Paul, who had been shipwrecked three times already (2 Cor 11:25) and so "could claim to be an experienced sailor",[118] recommended staying at Fair Havens for the winter, arguing that to attempt moving on would risk lives as well as the cargo. Fernando[119] comments that we do not know whether this advice was given through direct divine guidance or through Paul's human wisdom. There was another harbour, Phoenix, on the same southern coast of Crete which was on the direct route to Italy. In order to protect his cargo, the owner of the ship wanted to leave Fair Havens and spend the winter there. The captain of the vessel agreed that they could make it to Phoenix in relative safety.

Paul knew that the Day of the Atonement which fell on the tenth day of the seventh month had already past. In AD59, the most likely year of the voyage, the Day of Atonement, was as late as 5th October. In other words "they were now well into the dangerous season".[120] The weather had already deteriorated and the ship had difficulty going any further. However, the centurion had the final word, and the captain and the owner as "experts"[121] carried more influence with him than Paul did.

On the first fair day, they set out from port expecting to reach Phoenix safely. There was a gentle south wind but the weather seemed to be fine, and they took every precaution by staying as close to the shore as they could. However, the gentle wind was short-lived and was soon replaced by a violent northeasterly gale, formed by a meeting of winds from the north and the east. Marshall[122] points out that ancient ships could not face heavy seas. The winds were so strong that the crew could not keep control of the sails of the ship, so they had to let the ship drift with the winds. "Any chance of making Phoenix was now out of the question."[123]

As the ship drifted past the small island of Cauda, twenty-three miles south of where they had hoped to land, the crew had to pull in the little lifeboat attached to the larger ship to keep it from crashing into their ship by the winds. They also had to support the ship by passing ropes under the ship to reinforce the internal braces of the hull.

"Fearing that they would run aground on the sand-bars of Syrtis, they lowered the sea anchor and let the ship be driven along". The "sandbars of Syrtis" probably refers to the dreaded quicksands off the African coast west of Cyrene, towards which the ship was headed.[124] The ship must have been taking on too much water because the next day they lightened the ship and on the third day they threw the tackle overboard. However, the storm would not die down and for several days they sailed, not knowing where they were, because the storm prevented them from even knowing if it was day or night. Eventually they gave up all hope, became seasick and were too distressed even to eat.

Paul took the opportunity to reassure them. "Even though he was technically a prisoner, he is still Luke's hero."[125] He probably mentioned his former advice not in an 'I told you so' manner, but to encourage them to believe what he was about to tell them. What he had predicted had taken place, and what he was about to tell them would also happen. He told them that during the night an angel of God had stood by him and told him that he would stand before Caesar in Rome, and that all those on board the ship would be safe. There would be no loss of life among them but they would lose the ship. Barclay[126] comments how "the prisoner had become the captain" for he was the only man with any courage left. Fernando[127] agrees that from this point on, "Paul seems to have assumed a leadership role in the ship". The episode clearly presents Paul "as the man full of faith who dominates his fearful situation".[128]

The Shipwreck (Ch 27:27–44)

After a fortnight, the sailors saw signs that they were approaching land. They could have smelled the land, which is something experienced sailors sense, or they may have heard the waves breaking on the shore. They tied a weight to a line and threw it into the sea to determine the depth of the water. When the water got less deep, they stopped, casting out four anchors to stop the ship being smashed against the rocks. It was the middle of the night, and they waited anxiously for the morning (27:29). However, some of the crew became scared, and tried to leave the ship by escaping in the little lifeboat. They pretended they wanted to use the lifeboat to cast anchors out of the bow of the ship. Paul asserted his leadership and warned the centurion and the soldiers that unless the sailors stay with the ship no one would be saved. So the soldiers cut the ropes and set the lifeboat adrift before the sailors could use it.

The next morning the sight of land encouraged them. Paul again asserted his leadership by urging everyone to eat in order to gain strength for the work of getting ashore, and assured them that no one would be hurt (27:33–34). "He knew that hungry men are not efficient men; and so he gathered the ship's company around him and made them eat."[129] Guy[130] comments on Paul's presence of mind and calm confidence. Taking bread in his hands, Paul broke it and publicly gave thanks to God. "This may mean nothing more than that Paul, in Jewish fashion, says 'grace' before eating."[131] Some commentators[132] suggest that he was actually celebrating the Lord's Supper. Fitzmyer[133] points out that "the phraseology has a Eucharistic ring to it". Bruce[134] argues that it was probably a Eucharistic meal in a limited sense; ie meaningful only to those who were Christians. Others disagree, pointing out that apart from Paul, Luke and Aristarchus, there were no Christians among them; and that the circumstances and the terminology Luke used[135] were not appropriate for this to be the Lord's Supper. The rest of the passengers would not have known what the Lord's Supper was all about.

They saw a cove ahead, which they thought would make a good harbour for the ship. They had to throw out the rest of the wheat to help the ship sail towards the land. However, the ship struck a sandbar and got stuck in the mud and sand (27:39 –41). The soldiers realised that they would have to pay with their own lives if any of the prisoners escaped[136] so they planned to kill them, in case they tried to escape. However, the centurion ordered them to stop as he needed to keep Paul alive. He ordered all who could to swim to land, while those who could not were to take pieces of the ship and float in. Everyone reached the shore safely, as predicted by Paul (v 24).

Ashore on Malta (Ch 28:1–10)

The events in this dramatic and exciting chapter stress God's complete control over circumstances in order to ensure that Paul should minister in Rome. It begins with the kind hospitality of the natives of the island, who lit a fire and received Paul and the others. Luke calls them "barbarians" only because they could not speak Greek. Guy[137] explains that Luke was speaking from the standpoint of an educated Greek. They were actually very civilised and decent people. Their island was called Melita which means 'refuge' and is better known as modern day Malta.

Paul had an immediate influence on these people. When he was placing wood on the fire, a poisonous viper crawled from the wood onto his arm and bit his hand. Paul took no notice except to throw the snake in the fire. However, "these people thought that calamity was proof of guilt"[138] and took it as a sign that Paul had committed some crime. They figured that the gods had sent this viper to destroy Paul, but when his hand did not swell up, and he showed no signs of being poisoned, they changed their minds and decided he must be a god (28:6).

The ruler of the island, a man called Publius, provided lodgings for Paul and his fellow passengers for three days. His father was suffering from dysentery, and Paul healed him. News of this miracle spread around the island and many people came to Paul for physical and spiritual healing. Tannehill[139] compares the account of these healings with the account of Jesus' healings at Capernaum (Lk 4:38–40). In both cases the healing of an individual is followed by the healing of many in a region. This shows that "Jesus' healing ministry still continues through his witnesses, with benefit both to the host who receives the healer and to the whole community".

Paul stayed the three winter months on the island of Malta. When it was time to leave, the natives gave the shipwrecked passengers all they needed for their journey, honouring them, especially Paul, as best they could.

The centurion booked them onto another ship which had wintered in Malta and was to sail from Alexandria to Italy. On the way the ship stopped for three days at Syracuse, a busy and important port on the island of Sicily. They called at Rhegium which was at the toe of the Italian mainland and after one day in port there, the gentle south wind allowed them to arrive safely at Puteoli, where they got off the ship. Their long voyage was over.

 **TASKS**

1. Outline the main events of Paul's journey from Caesarea to Rome.

- Outline of events found in Acts 27–28:16 (Caesarea, Sidon, Myra, Fair Havens, the storm, the shipwreck, on Malta, Rome)
- Discussion of points of interest: amount of material, the sea voyage, 'we' passages, Paul's leadership, miracles connected with Paul/proof of apostleship, the arrival at Rome

2. Discuss in particular the storm at sea and the shipwreck on Malta.

- The storm at sea and Paul's interventions
- The call to keep up their courage
- The call to stay together
- The call to take food
- The shipwreck on Malta: escape from the sea, the bonfire on the beach, the healing on the island and aftermath

Example of Determination – Norman Kember [140]

In November 2005 four peace workers were kidnapped in Iraq. One American, Tom Fox; two Canadians, James Loney and Harmeet Singh Sooden; and one Briton, Norman Kember. They were acquaintances rather than friends, but they shared a passion for peace. All were in Iraq with 'Christian Peacemaker Teams', a pacifist organisation that works in trouble spots around the world to promote non-violent resolutions to armed conflict and carries out humanitarian work.

Norman Kember, a retired professor, was 74. He was held captive, appeared on TV, and was made to plead for his life. Part of his motivation in going to Iraq was that he believed pacifists should be willing to face the same dangers for their beliefs as armed soldiers. When he came back from Iraq he went to a Baptist assembly. "Everybody wanted to say, 'Oh, aren't you wonderful. You are a living example of answered prayer'… I had to remind them, rather gently, that Tom Fox died. If it worked for me, why didn't it work for him?

Did Kember, a lifelong Baptist, find his beliefs challenged by the circumstances in which he found himself? "No, that wasn't a problem for me." However, he admits that he experienced suicidal feelings, despite suicide being taboo in Christianity. He was in precarious health, and reached a point where he did wonder if he would be better off dead. He certainly didn't fear death. "I feared the process of dying, but not death itself." And yet, he acknowledges, if the method had been available perhaps something else would have stopped him, because he surprised himself with his own will to survive. "I think that's what kept me out of my depression, really –

that somewhere in me there was this survival instinct that I was going to get out at some point. When it was going to be, I didn't know. But in the end I came to the decision that if this was the way life was going to be for the next few months, so be it. I was going to have to sit it out." Once released Kember refused to be counselled, and said he would talk it through using a dictaphone rather than to a person. He hasn't dreamed about Iraq once since his return. He obviously has enormous spiritual strength.

'Hostage in Iraq', by Norman Kember, Darton, Longman and Todd

 TASKS

Other Examples of Determination

1. In groups of two or three find out how the people in the diagram below can be described as being determined.
2. Can you think of anyone to add to the diagram?
3. Explain to the rest of the class how the person you have chosen to research can be compared to Paul regarding his determination to fulfil his commission.

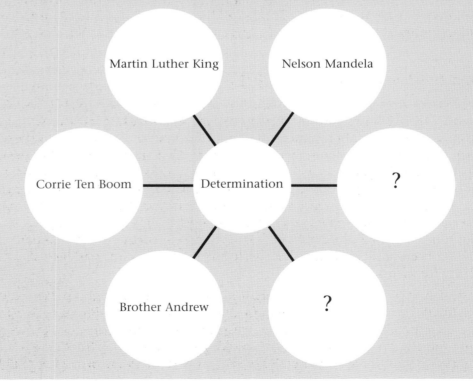

PAUL'S STAY IN ROME: ACTS CH 28:11–31
Arrival at Rome (Ch 28:11–16)

Paul's destination was Rome. However, before going there he was met by the Christians at Puteoli and stayed with them for a week. Bruce[141] comments that it is not surprising that Christians were found there as it was both an important seaport and had an important Jewish colony. Clearly the centurion was being very lenient with Paul to allow him to enjoy the company of the local church. He was not expected to arrive in Rome at a fixed time, so he adapted himself to Paul's wishes and let him do more or less what he wanted.

Paul's aim has been to spread Christianity to Rome but Bruce[142] points out that Luke is far from giving the impression that Paul was the first person to bring the gospel to Rome. When the Roman Christians heard of Paul's arrival in Italy, they came out to meet him and to escort him into Rome. He had written to them three years earlier (in AD57) from Corinth during his third missionary journey. Seeing them was a great encouragement to Paul and brought him great joy and courage. All in all, the journey from Caesarea to Rome had probably been about 2,250 miles.[143]

The centurion completed his duty by delivering his prisoners to the captain of the guard. Paul was allowed to live in a house with only one soldier to guard him. He was able to receive visitors and we know that these included Timothy, Tychicus, and Epaphroditus. "The environment was not ideal, but it was adequate for Paul to have a bold and unhindered witness in Rome for two years (Acts 28:30–31)."[144]

Paul and the Jews in Rome (Ch 28:17–31)

Crowe[145] comments how Luke's story is not complete with his arrival at "the ends of the earth". In fact "Luke ends the second volume of his writing with a telling and climatic episode about Paul's testimony in Rome".[146] After three days, Paul invited the Jewish leaders of Rome to visit him in his house. He may have wanted to preach the gospel, but he also saw it as a chance to explain to them why he was in Rome and to point out who was responsible for his predicament. The Jewish leaders in Rome however, had received no information from Jerusalem about Paul. In fact, they told Paul that people who had come from Judea to Rome had had nothing negative to say about him. They had heard about the Christian movement, but these reports had probably not been positive, so now they welcomed the opportunity to hear about Christianity for themselves.

They gave Paul time to prepare his apology, and came back as a group. Paul spent a day talking to them about the gospel, using both Moses and the prophets to try to convince them to believe in Christ. Luke says some were persuaded and some were not. Paul's mission can be compared to that of Isaiah whose preaching to the Jews was intended to light up the darkness. However, in both cases the preaching "finally blinded a people who would not understand their need for conversion".[147] As they left, Paul told them that since they refused to hear, he would preach the gospel to the Gentiles.

Therefore, as Paul had done everywhere else on his travels, so he did in Rome, by preaching first to his own people, the Jews, and then moving on to the Gentiles when the Jews would not listen to him. Paul received as many in to his house as he could and preached to them for the following two years (AD60–62). The Roman government appears to have put no restraint on him so long as he stayed in his own home.

The bridge from Jersualem to Rome had at last been completed, with Paul as one of the main builders. At this point the Acts of the Apostles ends.[148] If Paul arrived in Rome in the spring of AD60, based on the probable dating of the shipwreck in the winter of AD59, then Acts ends in the spring of AD62. Jesus' Commission in Acts 1:8 and Paul's hope of reaching Rome had been fulfilled. Paul now became an important influence in the development of the church at Rome and would give it drive by his martyrdom some years later.

 ## TASKS

1. Perhaps Luke devotes so much of his text to these few weeks at sea to highlight Paul's determination to reach Rome no matter what obstacles appear in his path. Draw a spidergram illustrating the events in the journey that show Paul's determination.

2. Comment on the claim that "much may be learned from Luke's portrayal of Paul's character and behaviour in circumstances in which the real man is most likely to be revealed".[149]

3. Evaluate the claim that Paul's mission was fulfilled when he reached Rome.
    - The significance of Rome within the Book of Acts
    - Jesus' commission to his followers (Acts 1:8)
    - The centrality of Paul within Acts
    - Controversy concerning the ending of Acts

4. Discuss the significance of Paul's stay in Rome.
    - Gospel has already reached Rome; church was already there
    - Paul under house arrest but with significant freedom
    - Reaction of the Roman Jews; invitation for Paul to speak about Christianity
    - Disappointment of final Jewish rejection of gospel

THE ENDING OF ACTS

"Paul's journey to Rome completes not only the programme of the apostle's career, but also the programme of Luke's second volume, the spread of the witness to Christ 'from Jerusalem to the ends of the earth' (1:8)".[150] However, for many scholars the ending of Acts seems abrupt and unresolved. Since Ch 25, readers are left waiting for Paul's appearance before Caesar (25:12), but Luke never records the trial of Paul. Instead he concludes Acts with Paul's last appearance in Rome: "And he stayed two full years in his own rented quarters and was welcoming all who came to him." There is no information on what happened to Paul when those two years were up.

Suggested Reasons for the 'abrupt' ending

1. *The lifespan of Luke*

Many scholars who think that Acts ends abruptly feel there must be some reason outside the text of Acts that can tell us why it seems to stop without a conclusion.

One opinion is that Luke died before he could finish writing the rest of Acts[151] or before he could undertake a third volume. However, even if the text does end abruptly it does not end all that abruptly. Fitzmyer[152] points out that the last few verses in Acts (28:28–30) is a planned summary similar to other summaries in Acts; "it seems clearly to be meant as the literary ending of Acts".

2. *A third volume*

Many scholars think that Luke was planning to write another book to Theophilus.[153] There have been various suggestions as to what or where that third volume might be. Some have said that it was merely lost over time, and others have said that it was planned to be written but never was.

3. *Luke's method in writing*

The compiler of the 'Muratorian Canon', which was a compilation of New Testament books put together in the late second century, explained that Luke did not tell of the martyrdom of Peter or Paul's subsequent journey to the West, because he wanted to relate only those things that had occurred in his presence.[154] However, this seems very unlikely because there were many other events in Acts where the author was not present, such as Jesus' Ascension and the Pentecost event.

4. *Luke's writing had caught up with events*

A view of Harnack's[155] is that Luke wrote up to his present time. In other words, Luke's writing had caught up with the events he was recording. Others suggest that Luke finished this volume at this stage just before Paul's case came to its conclusion. This was necessary because the book of Acts was to be used to present Paul's case. "We are not told the outcome of Paul's trial because it had not yet taken place."[156] This could be possible, but is unlikely since there are many inferences to Paul's death throughout Acts (20:29 and 38).

5. *Luke chose not to record Paul's death*

Luke ends his story with Paul preaching in Rome, and with the gospel being presented first to the Jew and then to the Gentile under the guidance of the Holy Spirit. Luke's emphasis is on the success of the Christian mission, not the death of Paul. Given the purposes of Luke, it is not surprising that he would leave out the unjust execution of Paul during Nero's persecution.

Some scholars argue that Luke has not left the reader wondering what happened to Paul because his death was already common knowledge so there was no reason to mention it.[157] There is good evidence within the book of Acts that implies that Paul was indeed executed in Rome. Conzelmann[158] points out how the farewell speech in Miletus (Acts 20:25–38) leaves no doubt as to what happened: Paul was executed. But Luke did not wish to tell about that. So based on prophecy the reader knows that Paul made his defence before Caesar (27:24), and knows further that Paul died as a witness to the gospel (20:24; 20:22–23, 29, 38; 21:10 –14). Outside the New Testament the historian Eusebius[159] records how Paul was beheaded by the Emperor Nero in Rome.

6. *Luke's purpose was not to record Paul's biography*

Acts was not written as a biography of the life of Paul, but rather a book of the spread of the gospel and the work of the Holy Spirit in the early church. Luke was selective and did not describe how the gospel was first preached in all regions. Acts describes how the gospel was originally proclaimed in Jerusalem, and then in Judea and Samaria, and throughout the Empire to the capital city of Rome, in fulfilment of Acts 1:8.

It is through reflecting upon Luke's overall purpose that we can best appreciate the ending of Acts. There is a presumption that Luke was most concerned with Paul's fate. However, as you will have read in Chapter 1 of this book, Luke's purpose in writing involves far more than the life of Paul. While Paul's importance to Luke is obvious, he remains only one of a number of people through whom the gospel was proclaimed.

7. *Luke's purpose was fulfilled*

There are some who believe that within the text there is a perfectly good explanation as to why Luke ended his book the way he did. The ending of Acts is part of Luke's narrative plan from the beginning. Everything that Luke wrote or even left out in his conclusion was for some purpose. There was not some awful historical situation that caused Luke to end abruptly: the ending that we have today is perfectly acceptable.

The ending of Acts with Paul in Rome fulfils the words of Jesus at the ascension in Acts 1:8: "But you will receive power when the Holy Spirit comes upon you, and you will be my witnesses in Jerusalem, throughout Judea and Samaria, and to the ends of the earth." The book of Acts portrays the fulfilment of Acts 1:8, the climax of which is the confident and unhindered preaching of Paul in Rome, the capital of the Empire. So the ending of Acts recalls the beginning of the book and shows how Luke has completed his work as intended.

8. *Luke ends Acts on a positive note*

It has been suggested that Luke deliberately ended Acts in this way because he had a particular purpose in mind. As we read in Chapter 1 of this book, Luke was not the sort of historian who was overly concerned with factual accuracy and completeness. Throughout the book of Acts he selected material to suit his own interests and concerns. The ending of Acts is no different.

Therefore, if Paul was executed at the end of the two-year period mentioned in 28:30, then there must be some reason why Luke left this detail out. One obvious reason is that Luke did not want to end Acts with the negative impression of Paul's martyrdom. Fitzmyer[160] comments: "it may seem strange that the reader is not told anything about the death of Paul, the hero of the second half of Acts". Yet the ending, such as it is, may not be as puzzling as some think, because it does record that Paul continued to preach the kingdom of God, even in Rome, "with all boldness and without hindrance" (28:31). That is the note of triumph on which Luke wanted his story to end.

Marshall however, finds it extremely difficult to understand how Luke could have painted such a generally favourable picture of the Roman authorities and their attitude to Paul, if he knew of Paul's martyrdom by the Roman Emperor Nero. Other scholars[161] suggest that at this time Paul was acquitted of his charges when he went before Caesar. Guy[162] describes how some traditions say that following release Paul went on further missionary journeys, even to Spain, but was later rearrested and brought to trial in Rome. If this is true then perhaps Luke did not report it in Acts because the "story of Paul's journey to Spain and of his martyrdom would have followed as a sequel to his two volume"'.[163]

Conclusion

The final verses of the book of Acts give us some clue as what Luke might have been trying to say to the reader. In Acts 28:30–31 it says: *"For two whole years Paul stayed there in his own rented house and welcomed all who came to see him. Boldly and without hindrance he preached the kingdom of God and taught about the Lord Jesus Christ".* It seems that Paul accepted everyone, even Jews with openness, and unhindered. Spencer[164] argues that this leads the reader into the hopeful future, which was particularly important to Christians at that time because the persecution of Christians by the Romans had begun. To end with the fact that Paul was "without hindrance" in his ministry brought hope to Christians who were indeed hindered in their own time.[165] By ending with these last two verses, Luke was attempting to focus on the positive side of Christianity.

Dillon[166] aptly concludes that, "as the reader closes Acts, Paul's personal fate is overshadowed by this open-ended triumph of the gospel over its powerful opposition". The gospel had reached the centre of the known world. The reader is left anticipating the further spread of the gospel.

 TASKS

1. Critically assess the view that the ending of Acts is disappointing.

- Disappointing: trial, release, death of Paul untold
- Disappointing because to the very end Paul preaches to the Jewish people who do not have ears to hear the gospel
- Questions about the success of the gospel in Rome unanswered
- Seems abrupt
- Not disappointing because salvation has been received by the Gentiles
- Appropriateness of ending, Luke's purposes have been fulfilled, the gospel has reached Rome, and is being preached without hindrance
- Acts ends with a positive and inspiring tone
- Acts is not a biography of Paul

2. Comment on the claim that Acts is an unfinished story.

- Make reference to the purpose of Acts, ie that the book was to give an accurate account of the birth, formation and development of the Christian Church
- The purpose of Acts was not to give an account of the lives of Peter and Paul, but rather to show how the commission to take the good news from Jerusalem to Rome was achieved
- Acts ends abruptly with Paul's stay in Rome and no account being given of the results of his appeal to Caesar
- Possibility that Luke was planning to write a third volume

Endnotes

1 Marshall, *op cit*, p350

2 Ladd, E, The Acts of the Apostles, In *The Wycliffe Bible Commentary*, pp1123–78. Edited by Charles F. Pfeiffer and Everett F. Harrison. Chicago: Moody Press, 1962, p1164

3 Fernando, *op cit*, p553

4 Marshall, *op cit*, p342

5 *ibid*, p343

6 Fernando, *op cit*, p553

7 Bruce, *op cit*, p406

8 Marshall, *op cit*, p346

9 Bruce, *op cit*, p406

10 *ibid*, p409

11 Josephus, F, *The Works of Flavius Josephus*, Translated by William Whiston; Antiquities of the Jews and The Wars of the Jews. London: T. Nelson and Sons, 1866, 6:2:4

12 Hewitt, *op cit*, p170

13 Marshall, *op cit*, p348

14 Jeremias, J, *Jerusalem in the time of Jesus*, Philadelphia: Fortress Preww, 1969, pp209–10

15 Fitzmyer, JA, *The Acts of the Apostles*, A New Translation with Introduction and Commentary, New York: the Anchor Bible, 1998, p697

16 Marshall, *op cit*, p348

17 Fernando, *op cit*, p554

18 Barclay, *op cit*, p172

19 Marshall, *op cit*, p349

20 *ibid*, p349

21 Bruce, *op cit*, p411

22 An alleged prophet of Egyptian origin led, according to Josephus, a mob of Zealots to the Mount of Olives and assailed the city of Jerusalem to rid it of the Romans. Most of the assailants were hunted down and killed by the Roman governor Felix, but the Egyptian leader had escaped.

23 Fitzmyer, *op cit*, p696

24 Marshall, *op cit*, p353

25 Bruce, *op cit*, p413

26 Fernando, *op cit*, p564

27 Marshall, *op cit*, p354

28 Fernando, *op cit*, p564

29 *ibid*, p564

30 Marshall, *op cit*, p355

31 Bruce, *op cit*, p417

32 *ibid*, p417

33 *ibid*, p419

34 Rackham, RB, *The Acts of the Apostles*. Westminster Commentaries series. 9th ed. London: Methuen and Co, 1922, p407

35 Marshall, *op cit*, p350

36 Crowe, J, *The Acts, New Testament Message 8*, Dublin: Veritas Publications, 1979, p170

37 Bruce, *op cit*, p420

38 Longenecker, *op cit*, p528

39 Suetonius, 'The Deified Claudius', in *The Lives of the Caesars*, 2:5:25

40 Bruce, *op cit*, p422

41 Josephus, The Wars...2:12:6; 2:17:6, 9; Antiquities of...20:5:2; 20:6:2; 20:9:2, 4

42 Guy, *op cit*, pp126–127

43 Hewitt, *op cit*, p173

44 Fernando, *op cit*, p566

45 Ezekiel 13:10–16; Matthew 23:27

46 Longenecker, *op cit*, p531

47 McGee, J Vernon. *Through the Bible with J. Vernon McGee*. 5 vols. Pasadena: Thru the Bible Radio, 1983, 4:614

48 Marshall, *op cit*, p364; Hewitt, *op cit*, p174

49 Guy, *op cit*, p127

50 Rackham, *op cit*, p433

51 Hewitt, *op cit*, p174

52 Marshall, *op cit*, pp363–364

53 Because it is not taught in the Pentateuch or the law of Moses.

54 Fernando, *op cit*, p567

55 Hewitt, *op cit*, p174

56 Bruce, *op cit*, p429

57 Fitzmyer, *op cit*, p714

58 Bruce, *op cit*, p430

59 *ibid*, p455

60 Stott, *op cit*, p354

61 Bruce, *op cit*, p433

62 Guy, *op cit*, p128

63 Stott, *op cit*, p356

64 As did Gallio in 18:14–15

65 Kent, HA, Jr, *Jerusalem to Rome*, New Testament Studies series, Brethren Missionary Herald, 1972; reprint ed., Grand Rapids: Baker Book House and BMH Books, 1985, p172

66 Hewitt, *op cit*, p178

67 Tacitus, *The Histories*, The Loeb Classical Library series, translated by Clifford H. Moore. London: William Heinemann Ltd., New York: G. P. Putnam's Sons, 1931, 5:9

68 Longenecker, *op cit*, p538

69 Fernando, *op cit*, p578

70 Gempf, C, *Acts*, NBCTCE, Ed DA Carson et al., Downers Grove, 111, IVP, 1994, p1102

71 Barclay, *op cit*, p184

72 Hanson, *op cit*, p226

73 Fernando, *op cit*, p579

74 This is the only place in the New Testament where we read that Paul believed in the resurrection of the unrighteous as well as the righteous.

75 Bruce, *op cit*, p446

76 Fitzmyer, *op cit*, p731

77 Winter, W, 'Official Proceedings and Forensic Speeches in Acts 24–26' in Winter, BW and Clarke, AD(eds), the *Book of Acts in its Ancient Literary Setting* (The Book of Acts in its First Century Setting, vol.1); Carlisle: Grand Rapids/Eerdmans/Paternoster, 1993, p327

78 Tannehill, RC. *The Narrative Unity of Luke – Acts: A Literary Interpretation*. Vol. 2: The Acts of the Apostles. Minneapolis: Fortress Press, 1990, p298

79 Fernando, *op cit*, p580

80 Hewitt, *op cit*, p180

81 Fernando, *op cit*, p580

82 Marshall, *op cit*, p381

83 Bruce, *op cit*, p448

84 Neil, *op cit*, p236

85 Fernando, *op cit*, p580

86 http://news.bbc.co.uk/onthisday/hi/witness/november/18/newsid_2903000/2903953.stm

87 Hewitt, *op cit*, p181

88 Longenecker, *op cit*, p545

89 Bruce, *op cit*, p454

90 *ibid*, p456

91 Fernando, *op cit*, p593

92 Crowe, *op cit*, p186

93 Marshall, *op cit*, p388

94 Stott, *op cit*, p368

95 Fernando, *op cit*, p594

96 This is another occasion where Christianity is deemed to be politically harmless.

97 McGee, *op cit*, p624

98 Bruce, *op cit*, p461

99 Blass, F, *The Philology of the Gospels*, London, 1898, p9

100 Fernando, *op cit*, p594

101 Crowe, *op cit*, p187

102 Marshall, *op cit*, p398

103 Tannehill, *op cit*, p316

104 Marshall, *op cit*, p407

105 Fiztmyer, *op cit*, p763

106 Guy, *op cit*, p131

107 Bruce, *op cit*, p471

108 Marshall, *op cit*, p386

109 Fernando, *op cit*, p609

110 Kent, *op cit*, p184

111 Marshall, *op cit*, p401

112 Bruce, *op cit*, p474

113 Holtzmann, HJ, *Handcommentar zum Neuen Testament*, Freiburg im Breisgau, 1889, p421

114 Rackham, *op cit*, p476

115 Ramsey, WM, *St Paul the Traveller and the Roman Citizen*, London: Hoddar and Stoughton, 1987; reprint ed., Grand Rapids: Baker Book House, 1960, p316

116 *ibid*, p316

117 Fernando, *op cit*, p610

118 Hewitt, *op cit*, p187

119 Fernando, *op cit*, p611

120 Bruce, *op cit*, p481

121 *ibid*, p482

122 Marshall, *op cit*, p408

123 Bruce, *op cit*, p485

124 Pliny, Natural History, 5:26

125 Fitzmyer, *op cit*, p775

126 Barclay, *op cit*, pp202–203

127 Fernando, *op cit*, p612

128 Fitzmyer, *op cit*, p775

129 Barclay, *op cit*, p204

130 Guy, *op cit*, p133

131 Fitzmyer, *op cit*, p779

132 Neil, *op cit*, p252

133 Fitzmyer, *op cit*, p779

134 Bruce, *op cit*, p492

135 Compare v 35 with Lk 24:30

136 Hemer, CJ, *The Book of Acts in the Setting of Hellenistic History*, Ed Gempf, C, Winona Lake: Eisenbrauns, 1990, p152

137 Guy, *op cit*, p134

138 Robertson, AT, *Words and Pictures in the New Testament, Vol.3, the Acts of the Apostles*, Grand Rapids: Baker, reprint of 1930 ed., p479

139 Tannehill, *op cit*, pp341–42

140 http://news.scotsman.com/topics.cfm?tid=1204&id=449952007

141 Bruce, *op cit*, p502

142 *ibid*, p503

143 Beitzel, Barry J. *The Moody Atlas of Bible Lands*, Chicago: Moody Press, 1985, p177

144 Fernando, *op cit*, p624

145 Crowe, *op cit*, p198

146 Fitzmyer, *op cit*, p790

147 Crowe, *op cit*, p199

148 A lot of scholarly debate surrounds the reasons for the abrupt ending of Acts.

149 Bruce, *op cit*, p475

150 Crowe, *op cit*, p192

151 Adolf von Harnack, *The Acts of the Apostles*, tr. J.R. Wilkinson, London: Williams and Norgate, 1909, 40.

152 Fitzmyer, *op cit*, p791

153 Guy, *op cit*, p135

154 Johnson, *op cit*, 474–476

155 Harnack, *op cit*, p101

156 Hanson, *op cit*, p29

157 Walaskay, PW, *'And so we came to Rome'*, The Political Perspectives of St Luke, Cambridge: Cambridge University Press, 1983, p19

158 Conzelmann, H, *Acts of the Apostles*, Translated by James Limburg, A. Thomas Kraabel, and Donald H. Juel. Hermeneia. Philadelphia: Fortress Press, 1987, pp227–228

159 Eusebius. *The Ecclesiastical History of Eusebius Pamphilus*. Twin Brooks series. Popular ed. Grand Rapids: Baker Book House, 1974, 2.25.5–8

160 Fitzmyer, *op cit*, pp791–792

161 Hanson, *op cit*, p31

162 Guy, *op cit*, p136

163 Fitzmyer, *op cit*, p791

164 Spencer, FS, *Acts, a New Biblical Commentary*, Sheffield: Academic, 1997 p241

165 Haenchen, E, *The Acts of the Apostles: A Commentary*, Oxford: Basil Blackwell, 1971, p98

166 Dillon, *op cit*, p766

Chapter 7

The Theology of Acts

INTRODUCTION

THE THEOLOGY OF ACTS is concerned with the beliefs of the early Christian church. While these beliefs are not directly stated in a creed or formula, they are evident through an examination of early Christian preaching and through important decisions made by the church.

THE JERUSALEM COUNCIL: ACTS CH 15:1–35

To be a real Christian you shouldn't drink alcohol or go to clubs.

Only people who belong to *our* denomination are Christians!

You can't be a Christian unless you go to church every Sunday.

Maybe I need to be baptised as an adult to be a true Christian?

What do you think?

The Jerusalem Council met to discuss issues a bit like those mentioned above. Even today some people attach 'conditions' to being a Christian. Discuss the conditions in the speech bubbles and see if you can come up with any others. What effects might these conditions have on the spread of the Christian faith today?

Introduction to the Jerusalem Council

The Council of Jerusalem "forms the centre of Acts both structurally and theologically".[1] There are two accounts of this meeting held at Jerusalem, in Acts and Galatians 2:1–10 and while they differ in places it does seem that they refer to the same meeting. It marks out an historical turning point for Christianity: transforming it from a small Jewish sect into an independent church.

Constable[2] highlights that the "doctrinal controversy" that led to the calling of the Council posed the fourth crisis in the history of the early church. He argues that it was the most serious problem so far, both in terms of the issue itself and its potential consequences. The other three crises were:

1. Selfishness (Ananias and Sapphira, Ch 5),
2. Murmuring (over the treatment of the Hellenistic widows, Ch 6),
3. Simony (Simon Magus, Ch 8)

What prompted the calling of the Jerusalem Council? (Ch 15:1–3)

At Antioch Gentiles who became believers were not expected to keep the Jewish Law. However, so many Gentiles were becoming Christians that it raised a problem within the church. Soon the number of Gentile Christians might outnumber the Jewish Christians. The Jewish Christians were probably a bit nervous at losing their Jewish identity. Therefore, some Jewish Christians from Judea came down to Antioch and claimed that a person could not become a Christian without first becoming a Jew, which included being circumcised. They may have based their theology on texts such as Genesis 17:14 and Exodus 12:48–49. It also seems that "they insinuated that the apostles and elders agreed with what they were saying"[3] (cf 15:24; Gal 2:12).

This situation led to heated debate among the believers. Paul and Barnabas opposed the visitors because they worried that such teaching would have a negative effect on their missionary work. People might not find Christianity so appealing if they had to be circumcised. In the end it was decided to move the discussion to Jerusalem and consult the apostles and elders there for a verdict.

On the way to Jerusalem Paul and Barnabas told the Christians in Phoenicia and Samaria everything God had done in Cyprus and Asia Minor. These believers rejoiced because it meant that "Gentiles were converted on a direct basis apart from any necessary commitment to Judaism".[4]

Who was the dispute between?

Lewis[5] makes the important point that "it was not a dispute between Christians and Jews but one between Christians themselves about the terms which, if any, Gentiles were to be admitted into the Church". Essentially the dispute was between two groups of people, Jewish Christians and Gentile Christians (Christians who had never been Jews).

1. Jewish Christians

On one hand there was a group of Christians who had been strictly orthodox Palestinian Jews. They would have continued to observe/keep many of the Jewish practices, such as the Sabbath, circumcision and food laws. Guy[6] suggests that "these men apparently considered that the Church was a Jewish sect and new members would therefore have to become Jewish proselytes before they could be accepted." They simply could not accept that Gentiles could be saved without "accepting the obligations of the Jewish law."[7] They could see no reason to consider that the law had been abolished.

It is not that they were being awkward just for the sake of it. They were genuine Christian believers but as devout Jews up to the point of conversion, they could not simply let go of all that had been important to them regarding their religion. Being Jewish was also part of their culture and identity. However, if their attitude was allowed to continue, Christianity would inevitably become nothing other than a sect of Judaism.[8]

A second problem, "the issue of table fellowship between Jewish and Gentile Christians was also included in this controversy".[9] It was concerned with table fellowship, which simply means eating with others. Fernando[10] explains that in the early church eating together was an important element of community life (2:46). However, Jewish Christians who still wanted to keep Jewish laws felt unable to sit at the same table as their Gentile friends who did not keep the law and were therefore regarded as ritually unclean.[11] Maintaining their purity was an extremely important aspect of their survival and identity.[12] The whole issue was also particularly sensitive when the Christians met to celebrate communion.

2. Gentile Christians

On the other hand were Christians who had never been Jews at all (Gentiles) or had been God-fearers. They would have respected Jewish moral and religious ideas but would have found circumcision and obedience to the Law of Moses difficult to take on board. Therefore, in terms of what was required of them, they had found that Christianity was much more appealing than Judaism.

Proceedings at the Jerusalem Council (Ch 15:4–11)

The two issues before the council were:

1. Did Gentiles need to be circumcised or not in order to become Christians?
2. Could Jewish Christians have table fellowship with Gentile Christians?

1. Initial discussion

When Paul's party reached Jerusalem, the leaders there listened to their story (15:4 15:5).

Some Christians, especially those who had been Pharisees and were more conservative, made the same demand as the Jewish Christians at Antioch, arguing that Gentile Christians needed to become Jewish proselytes, which involved being circumcised and obeying the Mosaic Law. Kent[13] points out that these Christians were not necessarily ex-Pharisees since a Pharisee could become a Christian without giving up his distinctive beliefs.

2. Peter's testimony

It has been suggested that Peter interrupted his missionary work to attend the Council.[14] "Peter referred to his own experience through which God had shown his readiness to accept uncircumcised Gentiles into the church on the basis of faith alone …".[15]

God had given the Holy Spirit to Cornelius and his friends as soon as they believed in Jesus, the same gift he had given to the Jews at Pentecost. All they did was believe and they received the Spirit as a sign of their acceptance by God. Peter explicitly stated "that God broke all barriers separating Jews and Gentiles; in purifying the Gentile's hearts by faith, God 'made no distinction between us and them'".[16]

Asking Gentiles to become Jews in order for God to save them, was testing God. It would question the rightness of God's action in giving the Holy Spirit to Cornelius (15:10). Peter referred to the law of Moses as a "yoke" that was both unbearable and unnecessary. "What Peter disputed was thus the need to obey the law in order to be saved; whether Jews kept it for other reasons was a secondary matter."[17]

Constable[18] argues that "By referring to the Jews being saved in the same manner as the Gentiles, instead of vise versa, Peter repudiated any thought of Jewish superiority". Salvation is by grace (v 11) through faith alone (v 9); nothing more is added.

3. Barnabas and Paul's testimony (Acts 15:12–21)

Barnabas, as a respected member of this church (4:36–37; 11:22), took the lead in describing the experiences he and Paul had gone through in ministering to Gentiles. Barnabas drew attention to the signs and wonders God had performed because these would have shown the Jews that God had been behind their ministry (cf 1 Cor 1:22). Williams[19] comments how such signs and wonders "showed that God's kingdom was breaking in even upon the Gentile world." The "implication was that by his acts God had revealed his will."[20]

4. James' testimony 15:13–21

James was Jesus' half brother and the leader in the Jerusalem church (12:17; Gal 1:19; 2:9, 12).[21] 'Simon' was Peter's older Jewish name. James may have used it to highlight Peter's Jewishness, and also to show affection for him. James reminded those present that the Old Testament prophets supported the salvation of Gentiles. He quoted Amos 9:11–12 as an example. Neither Amos nor any other prophet said Gentiles had to become Jews to be saved. Amos predicted that the Messiah would set up His kingdom on earth and restore the nation of Israel under which the Gentiles would seek the Lord.

Longenecker[22] explains that James is saying, 'God's people will consist of two groups: the restored Israel, with a group of Gentiles gathered around them, who will share in the messianic blessings but will remain as Gentiles without needing to become Jewish proselytes'.

5. The four prohibitions

James recommended that new Gentile converts should avoid four things, which involved ethical and moral issues and were not merely matters of ceremonial uncleanness.

1. The things associated with idolatry (food etc., cf 1 Cor 10:14–22)
2. Fornication (all kinds of sexual immorality)
3. Eating strangled animals rather than those with the blood drained out
4. Blood (the essence of life; cf Gen 9; Lev 17:11)

Why were the four conditions imposed?

In the synagogue, teachers of the Mosaic Law had always stressed Jewish morals regarding these matters. All Jews regarded them as extremely important. If Gentile Christians now disregarded what the Jews held dear, they would only alienate or drive away those Jews whom they were trying to save (cf 1 Cor 8:13). Therefore, "some kind of compromise was necessary in order not to offend the consciences of the strict Jewish Christians".[23]

Savelle[24] explains that the four conditions were associated to some degree with pagan religious practices and that this association was highly offensive to Jews. The purpose of asking the Gentiles to avoid the practices altogether was to promote unity among believing Jews and believing Gentiles. Constable[25] explains that James was not forcing the Gentile converts to obey the Mosaic Law asking them to accept these restrictions. He was urging them to limit their exercise of Christian freedom "to make their witness to unsaved Jews more effective and their fellowship with saved Jews more harmonious" (cf 1 Cor 9:19–23). By keeping these restrictions the gospel would have more effect among the unconverted Jews.

The official letter outlining the decision of the Council (Ch 15:22–29)

The official decision reached at the Jerusalem Council was important because false teachers continued to promote the view that Gentiles needed to be circumcised and keep the Law of Moses before they could enter the church. A formal letter was drawn up to announce the decision of the Jerusalem church and was sent back to Antioch by two messengers, Judas Barsabbas and Silas, both prophets, along with Paul and Barnabas. The formal letter contained the restriction of eating any food offered to idols – that is, meat put on the market by pagan priests after they had used it in their sacrifices. This could have been a further concession to the tender feelings of Jewish Christians, but it might well have been just as much a precaution to Gentile Christians against making any contacts with pagan worship in any form.

Constable[26] points out that "the destination of this letter throws light on extensive missionary activity that had taken place, which Luke did not record." Luke mentioned nothing about the evangelisation of Syria. Nor did he tell his readers any detail about the missionary work in Cilicia. Here we learn that there were churches in these regions already.

"It should be noted that the letter traced the unanimity of the decision to the action of the Holy Spirit (15:28), even though the Spirit was not mentioned previously as intervening in the proceedings. This is the way in which the Spirit usually works in the church. There need not be miraculous displays to indicate his direction. Spirit-filled people can detect his presence through the harmony which prevails when men are responsive to his will."[27]

Why was the decision made at the Council of Jerusalem so important? (Ch 15:30–35)

1. Two types of 'necessary' questions were addressed at the Jerusalem Council:

   • The first had to do with the theological necessity of circumcision and the Jewish law for salvation, and that was rejected.

   • The second had to do with the need for Gentile Christians to abstain from certain practices for the sake of Jewish-Gentile fellowship within the church and for the sake of the Jewish Christian mission throughout the Diaspora, and that was approved.[28]

2. Longenecker[29] argues that "when one considers the situation of the Jerusalem church in AD49, the decision reached by the Jerusalem Christians must be considered one of the boldest and most magnanimous in the annals of church history". The principle was significant for the future of the early church, and it remains significant for all time: "no national, racial or social requirements can ever be made conditions or salvation and membership of the church alongside the single and sole requirement of faith in Jesus Christ, through whom the grace of God is brought to sinners"[30] (15:11).

3. It is also commendable that "the theological controversy was not swept under the carpet and allowed to simmer".[31] Perhaps the church today could learn a lot from this. Can you think of any examples?

 TASKS

1. **Outline and discuss the context and proceedings of the Council of Jerusalem.**
   Your answer should include a discussion on the significance of:
   • Events at Antioch, which led to the decision to call the Council
   • Initial discussion; Peter's contribution; Paul and Barnabas' testimony; James' testimony
   • The four prohibitions
   • The letter

2. **Comment on the view that the Council can be seen as a turning point in the book of Acts.**
   Your answer may include some of the following points:
   • The fact that up until Acts 15 all roads led to Jerusalem (with examples); after Acts 15 all roads led to Rome (Paul's journeys).
   • Up to Acts 15 Peter dominates the book; after Acts 15 Paul is the key character (with examples).
   • After Acts 15 the focus is on the Gentile mission.

3. **Comment on the claim that the account of the Council contains lessons of permanent value for the Christian church.**
   • The decision was taken after a thorough investigation.
   • The church did not brush the problem under the carpet.
   • The decision made shows that everyone is accepted as equal by Christ; Christians should not impose any conditions on potential converts.

OTHER ASPECTS OF HUMAN EXPERIENCE

Religious controversy

1. Critically examine the contribution of some key people from Acts to the issue of religious controversy.

    Your answer may include some of the following:
    - Issues concerning money, eg Peter's role in the disciplining of Ananias and Sapphira
    - Complaining, eg the treatment of the Hellenistic widows and the role of Stephen and Philip as deacons
    - Simony, Philip, Peter and the incident involving Simon Magus
    - The issue of Gentiles entering the church; circumcision or not? The significance of the decision made at the Council of Jerusalem
    - Immorality in the church at Corinth

2. Critically examine the contribution of some key people from your other area of study to the issue of religious controversy.

    To prepare an answer you should discuss with your teacher and others in your class what might fall under 'religious controversy' in your other area of study.

    Look at what caused the controversy; the implications of the controversy; how the church or state approached the controversy; what was the outcome?

    Are there any significant comparisons that can be made with religious controversy in Acts?

3. Critically assess the view that any radical message can be the cause of controversy. You should refer to other aspects of human experience in your answer.

    - In this answer you should try to make a connection with the previous two answers. For example, if you have focused on how the controversies were dealt with in your two areas of study then compare this with how other or contemporary controversies have been dealt with. Some examples of controversies you might want to research are:
    - Heresy in the early church
    - The Paschal controversy
    - The Reformation
    - The Ecumenical movement
    - Hitler and Christianity
    - Danish Cartoon controversy throughout the Muslim world in 2006
    - Dan Brown's 'DaVinci Code' in 2006

- Martin Scorsese's film 'The Last Temptation of Christ'
- 'The Satanic Verses' by Salman Rushdie
- Controversy in Australia in 2007 over churches putting up signs declaring that 'Jesus Loves Osama'
- Uniforms and religious head coverings in schools

PAUL'S SPEECHES

About one third of Acts consists of speeches, debates and dialogues, while the remainder is a description of various events. Out of about twenty-four speeches in Acts, nine are given by Paul. In this chapter we will look at three of these in more detail; two of them illustrating Paul's messages to unbelievers (Pisidian Antioch, 13:16–41; Athens, 17:22–31); and an example of Paul's preaching to Christians (Miletus, 20:17–38).

The Audiences

Marshall[32] comments that the variety of speeches in Acts "is no doubt meant to illustrate the different ways in which the gospel was presented to different groups of people, Jews and Greeks, cultured and uncultured". Longenecker[33] explains that there is enough in each account to suggest that Paul preached the same gospel wherever he went, but that "he altered the form of his message according to the circumstances he encountered".

Were the speeches made up by Luke?

During the time when Luke was writing, speeches were often invented by the authors. So some scholars argue that the speeches in Acts do not give an exact report of what Peter, Paul, Stephen, James, and the others said. For example, Paul's speech at Pisidian Antioch, which is the longest of the three, probably lasted much longer than what is recorded. Luke was not present at this speech so he would have had to get his information about it from another source. Robertson[34] suggests that Paul may have written out notes of this sermon afterwards for Luke. Longenecker[35] points out that "each sermon as we have it is only a précis of what was said, for the longest in its present form would take no more than three minutes to deliver and the shortest can be read in thirty seconds or less". It seems, therefore, that when Luke records Paul's speeches, he provides a careful summary of what was actually said. For example, concerning Paul's speech to the Ephesian elders, Lewis[36] comments that "the speech is from the pen of Luke, but there is little doubt that he has accurately caught the tone and content of what Paul would need to have said to such an audience".

It is now widely accepted that early Christian preaching followed a common pattern that was based on the models or examples of Jewish rabbis. These models were familiar to Paul, and naturally he adopted this pattern himself.

Paul's synagogue sermon in Antioch of Pisidia (Ch 13:16–41)

Paul's speech at Pisidian Antioch was delivered during his first missionary journey. It is the only speech Paul gave in a synagogue, and the summary Luke gives us is the longest of the three. It provides an example of how Paul preached to people who knew the Hebrew Scriptures and has been compared to the speeches of Peter (especially 2:14–40), in both outline and content,[37] and also to the speech of Stephen (7:2–53), as both contain a summary of Israel's history.

The speech contains three parts:
1. Preparation for the coming of Messiah (v 16–25)
2. The rejection, crucifixion, and resurrection of Messiah (v 26–37)
3. The application and appeal (v 38–41)

1. Preparation for the coming of the Messiah (Ch 13:16–25)

Fitzmyer[38] describes this section as "a recital of salvation history". It a summary of selected incidents of Israel's history which provides an overview of God's unchanging faithfulness, from the election of Israel to the time of Jesus.

Even though teachers in the synagogue in Palestine normally sat to teach, here in Asia Minor, where there was a greater Greek influence, Paul stood up[39] and motioned with his hand to get the audience's attention. He showed immediate respect for his audience by addressing his Jewish hearers as "men of Israel", and the Gentile God-fearers or "Jewish sympathisers",[40] as "you who fear God".

This first section is clearly designed "to suit an audience with a background of knowledge about the Old Testament".[41] Paul begins with what Marshall[42] describes as "a survey of Jewish history", highlighting "God's mighty acts in the election of Israel."[43] Moyes[44] points out that Paul clearly understood their pride in their history and their knowledge of Scriptures.

- God was the God of the Israelites (v 17). He chose the patriarchs out of all the nations on earth.
- God had worked with the Jews and made them great while they were in Egypt. God rescued them out of Egypt, led them through the wilderness, put up with their failings in the desert and brought them to the Promised Land (v 7–18).
- God demonstrated his power by driving out seven nations from this Promised Land so that his people could inherit the promise given to Abraham and the nation (Deut 7:1). God then raised up judges to help them in their rebelliousness, until the time of Samuel the prophet.

- The mention of Saul highlighted another point in the history of Israel's failure. God showed them mercy by removing[45] him and raising up a new and faithful king, David (v 20–22). In particular God regarded David as a man after his own heart.

- David's qualities were also evident in Jesus, his successor. Just as David was raised up at a particular time in Israel's history, so Jesus also came to take his part in history, by rising from the dead. This Jesus was the promised Messiah. (Isaiah 11:1–16 speaks of the Messiah coming from David's descendants.)

- Paul then speaks about John the Baptist's ministry,[46] which would have been familiar to most of the Jews of the dispersion (13:24–25). Bock[47] regards John the Baptist as a "bridge figure", which means he provided a connection. The connection is that John had announced and prepared for Jesus' coming (cf Mark 1:2–8), making it clear that he was the Messiah's forerunner (Luke 3:15–18).

2. The rejection, crucifixion, and resurrection of the Messiah (Ch 13:26–37)

The second part of the speech begins at verse 26. Before moving on, Paul paused again to personally address his hearers (cf v 16). By calling the Jews "brothers" Paul is bracing himself to talk about the recent events in Jerusalem, and to point to the Old Testament proof that Jesus was the promised Messiah. He wants to try to get his audience on side as much as possible before dealing with these issues.

- Jesus was rejected and crucified by the Jews of Jerusalem (13:27–28).

- These events fulfilled Old Testament prophecies. Most of the Jews living in Jerusalem did not realise this at the time (v 27, 29). It was ironic that the very scriptures which were read in their synagogues each week, and pointed to the death of the Messiah, were fulfilled in their rejection of Jesus. As Marshall[48] comments, "they themselves had unwittingly fulfilled those very prophecies by rejecting Jesus".

- Jesus was innocent of the charges brought against him (v 28).

- Fitzmyer[49] points to the contrast between what human beings did to Jesus and "what God has done". Jesus' resurrection shows how God vindicated him (v 30), and prepared him to rule.

- The apostles' personal witness of Jesus' resurrection is highlighted (v 31).

- The promise made to David in 2 Samuel 7:12–16, (and referred to by Peter in Acts 13:23[50]), was that seed from David's own body would succeed him and that his kingdom would be established forever. David's promised heir, the Messiah, had come in Jesus (v 33).

- Three Old Testament passages support the fulfillment of this promise: Psalm 2:7 (v 33), Isaiah 55:3 (v 34), and Psalm 16:10 (v 35).

Psalm 2:7 – Refers to God raising up David as Israel's king and is clearly interpreted in terms of the resurrection of Christ.[51]

Isaiah 55:3 –   Dupont[52] argues that the use of Isaiah 55:3 in Paul's argument is difficult to work out. Williams[53] agrees, referring to it as an "obscure phrase". The simplest way of attempting an explanation is that since Jesus rose from the dead, God can give people the blessings that he promised would come through David. The blessings mentioned in this Old Testament passage are those of the New Covenant.

Psalm 16:10 – Marshall[54] explains that Psalm 16:10 cannot be applied to David himself because he died an ordinary death which led to corruption (his body rotted). Psalm 16:10 implies that the "holy one" would not die. The fact that Jesus rose from the dead and his body did not decay in the tomb proves that he is the Holy One whom David spoke about.

3. The application and appeal (Ch 13:38–41)

"Having brought Scripture and history together ... Paul comes to his appeal."[55] He again refers to all those listening as "brothers" and emphasises that "through Christ come forgiveness of sins and justification, a message not to be spurned".[56] He also claims that it is for everyone who believes, with the implication that salvation is not for the Jews alone. Jews and Gentiles are on the same level.

This is the only place in Acts where Paul's teaching about justification by faith is mentioned. This issue dominates Paul's letter to the Galatians.

Paul appeals to Habakkuk 1:5, where Israel was warned not to be surprised that God was going to use Babylon (a Gentile nation) to discipline his own people for their disobedience. Paul evidently regards his own generation of Jews as being under a similar disciplinary judgement. So he now warns them to be careful not to reject God's work in Christ, even if it was very different to what they had expected.[57] The challenge is "to accept or refuse the Gospel message".[58]

The result seems to be favourable as both Jews and Gentiles wanted to speak further about the matters raised by Paul. You can refer back to Chapter 4 of this book for a more detailed account of what happened.

TASK

1. Discuss the theology and significance of Paul's speech at Pisidian Antioch.

- God has revealed his purpose through the saving acts (from Egypt, guiding through the wilderness, in Canaan, gave judges and kings)
- Culmination in a Saviour from the line of David, who has come, was proclaimed by John the Baptist; Jewish rulers rejected him and condemned him to death.
- Jesus rose from the dead, fulfilled prophecy, proved his Messiahship; David was not the messiah but died and his body decayed.
- Salvation is offered; sin forgiven; justified by faith and a warning was given.
- Salvation is not just for the Jews but also the Gentiles.

Paul's speech at Athens (Ch 17:22–34)

Background (Ch 17:16–21)

Although Athens had once been the cultural and intellectual centre of the ancient world, at the time of Paul's visit it was in a period of decline.[59]

It has been said 'that there were more statues of the gods in Athens than in all the rest of Greece put together, and that in Athens it was easier to meet a god than a man'.[60] Paul certainly would have seen many temples, statues and shrines, some of which are still found in Athens today. However, as a Christian who had experienced a strict Jewish upbringing, all Paul could see was idolatry[61] and he was very disturbed.

Paul continued his preaching to Jews and God-fearing Greeks in the synagogue but also took part in discussions about the gospel with various people in "the Agora, the market-place used for meetings and discussion".[62] The Agora lay to the west of the Acropolis, and was the centre of community life in Athens. Many philosophers, such as the influential Epicureans and Stoics,[63] would gather there to discuss religious and philosophical views.

Epicureans

Epicureans were followers of Epicurus (341–270BC) who sought pleasure, believing that it was the most worthy pursuit of man. Guy[64] explains that some Epicureans interpreted this as promoting the attitude: "Let us eat, drink and be merry for tomorrow we die"; but Epicurus viewed pleasure in a different way than it might be portrayed today. He did not mean sensual pleasures but those of the mind, such as freedom from pain and fears, especially the fear of death.

The Epicureans' attitude towards the gods was that they were not interested in man and would not punish sinners in the afterlife. Therefore there was no sense in organised religion such as the church as we know it today.

Epicureans also believed that everything happens by chance and that death is final. This philosophy is still popular today.

Rackham[65] suggests that "Epicureanism is most fairly described as the ancient representative of modern utilitarianism".

Stoicism

Stoicism was "the most popular form of Greek philosophy in Paul's day".[66] The word 'stoic' comes from 'stoa', a porch where Zeno (340–265BC) taught when he lived in Athens. He placed great importance on living in harmony with nature, and stressed the importance of being rational and self-sufficient.

Stoics were idealists[67] and had a reputation for being quite arrogant. They "scorned pain and pleasure alike; nothing could make any difference to the upright man". Stoics were pantheists, believing that God is in everything, and everything is God. They were also fatalists, meaning that they accepted everything as it came, without complaint and without enthusiasm.[68]

Their teaching is also common today. Henley, a modern poet who followed this philosophy of life, wrote in his poem Invictus, "I am the master of my fate; I am the captain of my soul".[69]

These philosophers called Paul a 'babbler', which refers to someone who picks up odds and ends of knowledge, as a bird picks up seeds.[70] They were implying that Paul had put together his own philosophy by picking up scraps of ideas from various sources.

What was the 'Areopagus'?

There are two suggested meanings for the term 'Areopagus' at the time of the writing of Acts.[71] It could refer to a location on Mars Hill, which was the place where the Council of the Areopagus met. Or it could mean a group of about thirty people who formed the Council of the Areopagus, and who met in the Royal Portico of the Agora. It is difficult to tell from Luke's description if the 'Areopagus' refers to the people or the place.

The Areopagus had a lot of authority over religion, education and morality in Athens. For example, Socrates had earlier been poisoned for teaching strange ideas in Athens. The members of the Areopagus heard that Paul was teaching strange things which they were not familiar with and wanted to know what exactly he was promoting. They were always interested in new ideas, and when Paul was brought before them it provided him with an opportunity to preach the gospel. This would have been an informal appearance because as Marshall[72] points out, "there is no hint of any legal proceedings".

Paul's speech (Ch 17:22–31)

This speech is an example of Paul's preaching to intellectual pagans.[73] It is clear to see how he again adapts and uses his message to suit his audience. Paul begins by calling his audience "very religious", although some scholars argue that he was not praising his audience at this point. Fernando[74] certainly argues that "it was probably not a compliment", for according to an ancient writer, Lucian, "complimentary exordia [beginnings] to secure the goodwill of the Areopagus court were discouraged". Fitzmyer[75] explains that the original translation means 'rather demon fearing' which could mean superstitious, although Grayston[76] argues that "it is most likely that Paul meant it in a good sense, to provide a way in to his address that would engage the attention of the audience". Morgan[77] agrees, commenting that "Paul really began with the note of conciliation, and from beginning to end there was nothing calculated to offend, or drive away the men whom he desired to gain".

Paul began with the Athenians' ignorance about at least one god and proceeded to explain what Yahweh had revealed about himself. Blaiklock[78] comments that "such altars had no special deity in view. The dedication was designed to ensure that no god was overlooked to the possible harm of the city".[79]

Some scholars feel that Paul probably intended to tell his audience more about a god whom they worshipped, but did not know much about. However, Marshall[80] argues that "Paul hardly meant that his audience were unconscious worshippers of the true God". Rather he may have intended to inform them of the existence of a God whom they did not know.

17:24

- Paul's message does not contain direct quotations or appeals to the Old Testament as he talks to the Jews and God-fearers. Fernando[81] comments that "such appeals would have meant nothing to hearers who did not accept the authority of the Scriptures". However, Marshall[82] points out that his language is based on the Old Testament description of God. The true God is Lord of heaven and earth who created all things. He is everywhere and human temples cannot contain him.[83] Some Greek philosophers agreed that temples did not really house their pagan gods, and it has been said that Paul was only repeating what the Stoic philosopher Zeno taught, that one should not build Temples of the Gods.[84]

17:25

- "Such a God has no need of men to supply him with anything."[85] Rather he sustains all life, human, animal and plant and participates in human existence. This contradicts the Epicurean belief that God was not interested in human life and the Stoic belief of man being self-sufficient.

17:26–27

- As Greeks, the Athenians would have considered themselves as racially superior to other people. However, Paul proclaimed that the Athenians, like all other people, had descended from one man, Adam. The Greeks also liked to think that they had control over their own destiny. Paul taught that God is ruler over the political world and determines the times, seasons and boundaries of nations.
- God kept this control so that people would seek Him. Fitzmyer[86] comments that this seeking may mean a philosophical search or it may involve something less intellectual, a more emotional effort. Marshall[87] explains that "the main point is that seeking should not be difficult since God is not far from each one of us".

17:28–29

- Paul referred to man's need of God, supporting his arguments by quotations from Greek poets.[88] He recited lines from two Greek poets whose ideas were similar to what Paul was preaching. Epimenides (600BC) had written, "For in thee we live and move and have our being"[89]; and Aratus (315–240BC), and Cleanthes (331–233BC) had written, "We are also his offspring."[90] Paul used these quotations to try to convince his audience that he was speaking the truth. He concluded that there is no logic in idolatry. God was divine and could not be an image or an idol.

17:30

- Until God revealed himself in Christianity, men lived in ignorance of him and God had been prepared to overlook their ignorance. But now the proclamation of the Christian message had brought this time to an end; they no longer had any excuse for their ignorance and God was calling on men everywhere to repent.[91]

17:31

- Paul stressed that true knowledge of God leads to repentance. It was the audience's responsibility to respond to his message. "The urgency of Paul's appeal for repentance is underlined by his claim that God has appointed a day of judgment of the world".[92] McGee[93] explains how Paul "has presented God as the Creator in His past work. He shows God as the Redeemer in His present work. Now he shows God as the Judge in His future work".

The response to Paul's preaching (Ch 17:32–34)

Jesus was qualified to judge humanity because of His resurrection. Jesus' resurrection vindicated His claim to be the Judge of all humankind (John 5:22, 25–29).

Lewis[94] points out that it is only here at the end of his speech that Paul "comes out boldly with distinctively Christian claims, speaking of Jesus and of the resurrection". Most Greeks rejected the possibility of physical resurrection,[95] since the body was increasingly regarded as earthly and evil in comparison with the soul,[96] although many of them, for example Platonists, did believe that after death the soul would finally be free of the body.

Nevertheless, Crowe[97] (p136) describes how this cultured Hellenistic audience dissolved at the mention of the resurrection of the dead. They responded to it in a predictable manner: some mocked, others refused to think about it, and a few believed (eg Dionysius, a member of the Council of the Areopagus and Damaris). Fitzmyer[98] sums up the response as a "polite but firm rejection of Paul's message".

 ## TASKS

1. 'Paul realised here that mere academic argument seldom really convinces anyone.'[99]
   - Do you agree or disagree?
   - How valuable is academic argument in convincing someone of the validity of a religious faith?
   - Find out about Justin Martyrs' dialogue with Trypho. Can you see any similarities between it and Paul's preaching regarding content and outcome?

2. **Outline and examine Paul's speech at Athens as recorded in Acts.**

   An examination may include some of the following, eg:
   - Paul's comments on the religious Athenians; the 'unknown god'
   - Describes this God as creator; does not require a man-made temple; controls the fate of mankind who are his creation
   - Repentance is necessary because God will judge the world, the judge is the one who rose from the dead

3. **Critically evaluate the claim that Paul became all things to all people that he might save some.**

A critical examination might include, eg:
- Paul can be seen in various different roles in his attempt to spread the gospel
- Paul as a preacher, adapting his message to suit his audience, eg Pisidian Antioch, Lystra, Athens
- Paul as a pastor, eg Miletus
- Paul as an apologist or defender of the faith, eg Jerusalem, Felix and Agrippa

Paul's Speech at Miletus

Fitzmyer[100] describes Paul's address to the Ephesian elders as "the third important Pauline speech in Acts". As the synagogue speech at Pisidian Antioch (13:16–41) is intended to be a sample of Paul's approach to Jewish audiences, and the speeches at Lystra (14:15–17) and Athens (17:22–31) samples of his approach to pagan audiences, so it might be said that this speech is a sample of his ministry to Christian audiences.[101] Fitzmyer[102] explains it as pastoral in that Paul reflects on his own work, ministry, and testimony, and urges the elders to imitate his example. It has also been described as a farewell speech, as Paul suggests he will never see these elders again.[103]

You will be familiar with what is meant by the 'we' passages. This speech falls into such a passage and is probably one of the few speeches in Acts that Luke heard with his own ears.[104] Neil[105] suggests that Luke may have made notes at the time, which would help him in his writing.

The speech is divided into three parts:
1. Paul looks back
2. Paul reviews the present
3. Paul looks forward

1. Paul looks back (Ch 20:17–21)

- In this first section of the speech Paul looks back over his own work as a missionary among these elders.[106] He defends his teaching and general behaviour by appealing to their personal knowledge of him[107] (cf 1 Cor 6:11; Gal 3:2–5). He appeals to the way he had lived among them, urging them to remain faithful in the future. He particularly highlights his humility, his sorrows, and the opposition to the gospel. He also reminds them of "the frankness of his preaching and teaching".[108] Paul had told them what they needed to hear (cf 19:8–10).

- Hanson[109] comments how it is not like Paul "to point out his own virtues". But his enemies may have been bad-mouthing him to his converts in his absence, as they did elsewhere. Stott[110] explains how "a vicious smear campaign had been launched against Paul in Thessalonica. Because he had had to be smuggled out of the city by night and had not returned, his critics accused him of insincerity.

Something similar seems to have happened in Ephesus during the year or so since he left the city. So he needed to defend the sincerity of his motives".

2. Paul reviews the present (20:22–27)

- Next Paul talks about his current circumstances, described by Fitzmyer[111] as "the path to suffering". He is determined to visit Jerusalem since he is sure this was what God wants him to do, even though he knows that trouble lies ahead.

- It seems Paul had been given a message from God warning him that the Jews would arrest him there. Bruce[112] explains that "the Holy Spirit, speaking presumably through the lips of prophets … showed him that imprisonment and other hardships would be his lot when he reached Jerusalem". Crowe[113] suggests that in this section, "Paul speaks as if he already considers himself a prisoner". Marshall[114] agrees, pointing out that while Paul did not know whether his sufferings would lead to his death, "he emphasises that he was prepared for that possibility". We certainly are given the strong impression in these verses that Luke knew of Paul's death.[115]

3. Paul looks forward (20:28–38)

- Paul continues by outlining his plans for the future. He is certain that these elders will never see him again. He can say his conscience is clear because he has carried out the mission that God had given him, of preaching to the Gentiles. The Christians remaining in Asia could continue this work. Furthermore he has been completely honest with the elders and "has not shrank back from proclaiming to them God's whole purpose of salvation".[116]

- Marshall[117] explains that Paul now instructs the church leaders for the future when he will no longer be with them. He gives them a challenge to guard their own lives from the attacks of the enemy and also the lives of those under their care. Stott[118] stresses the importance of this arguing that "they cannot care adequately for others if they neglect the care and culture of their own souls". Marshall[119] agrees describing the need "to pay attention to their own spiritual condition".

- Like Jesus, Paul describes his followers as a flock of sheep (John 10:27; 21:15). "The sheep will have to be guarded with unceasing vigilance, for ferocious wolves will try to force their way among them and ravage them".[120] Williams[121] argues that Luke could be writing with the knowledge that the church in Ephesus after Paul's day had troubles with false teachers. Paul may have suspected where future trouble would come from because of his contacts with the church at Ephesus, by revelation from God, or through common sense and experience. All in all "the prospects for the Ephesian church are not wholly promising."[122] Packer[123] explains that "the precise dangers Paul has in mind are false teaching and division". The false teachers, "described as wolves because of the havoc they cause",[124] would come "even from within the church and distort the truth".[125] Hanson[126] comments that this is the only place in Acts where Christians are warned against false teaching.

- Being on their guard was vital for these elders or 'shepherds'. Barclay[127] suggests that there was "a constant warfare ahead to keep the faith intact and the Church pure". Being a shepherd would involve "tending, caring for, feeding, protecting, and leading".[128]

Elder/Presbyter/Overseer/Bishop

The speech is addressed to "elders", a title already given to leaders in Jewish communities and to groups of churches founded by Paul.[129] Stott[130] explains that the elders are also referred to as "pastors" and "overseers" (bishops) but it is evident that these terms describe the same role in the church. Hanson[131] explains that it is not until the second century that the 'bishop' emerges as a separate leader in charge of the elders.

- Paul refers to his tears for these elders, showing he was emotionally involved with this church. Since he was no longer going to be able to build up these men, he commits them to God who would. He urges them to follow his example of selfless giving. He had been content to work with his own hands to support himself.[132] Fitzmyer[133] reminds us that Acts 18:3 tells how Paul worked at the tent maker trade. They too were to serve without concern for material reward.

- Hanson[134] comments that the precise saying of Jesus which Paul refers to in v 35 is not in the gospels. Paul may have been summarising Jesus' teaching (eg Luke 6:38) or the saying may have been passed on to Paul by word of mouth. Guy[135] suggests that Paul may have had a copy of a written collection of some of the teaching of Jesus.

- Paul kneels to pray even though the normal position for praying seems to have been standing (cf Mark 11:25). Hanson[136] explains that prayer on the knees was prayer of a "peculiarly solemn sort" in the early church. Lewis[137] describes how the chapter movingly ends, with tears which "reveal the deep affection in which Paul was held." For Paul the scene certainly stands in contrast to the hatred of the Jews that he was about to face in Jerusalem.

▷ TASKS

1. **Outline and examine Paul's farewell speech to the Ephesian elders at Miletus.**

   Your answer may include some of the following:
   - Looking back: Paul was a humble servant, a messenger of Christ.• For the future: for himself; compelled to go to Jerusalem; suffering; desire to complete the task; would not see him again
   - For the church: to be pastors; feed and protect the sheep
   - Commendation: to himself; to his example of self-sufficiency and hard work; to generosity
   - Stylistic parallels with Paul's letters
   - Paul's pastoral concerns
   - The audience
   - Reliability of Luke's account

2. **Critically evaluate the claim that Paul was passionate about preaching the gospel.**

   A critical evaluation of the claim may include:
   - Passion expressed in his commitment and perseverance, in personal suffering; in his speeches; in missionary journeys
   - Passion expressed in his letters to churches
   - Passionate about preserving the gospel
   - Passion was directed in other ways: Gentile inclusion; split with Barnabas; church morality; church unity; church leaders

Endnotes

1 Marshall, *op cit*, p242

2 *op cit*, p197

3 Fernando, *op cit*, p415

4 Longenecker, p443

5 Lewis, *op cit*, pp59–60

6 Guy, *op cit*, p57

7 Marshall, *op cit*, p242

8 Barclay, *op cit*, p122

9 *op cit*, p414

10 *ibid*, p419

11 While this issue is not highlighted in Acts 15 it is clear from Galatians 2:11–14 that it was an important issue.

12 Fernando, *op cit*, p419

13 Kent, HA, Jr, Jerusalem to Rome, New Testament Studies Series, Brethren Missionary Herald, 1972; reprinted, Grand Rapids: Baker Book House and BMH Books, 1985, p122, n3

14 Cullman, O, Peter: Disciple-Apostle-Martyr, trans. Floyd V Filson, New York: Living Age Books, 1958 [reprint of 1953 ed], pp49–50

15 Marshall, *op cit*, p243

16 Fernando, *op cit*, p416

17 Marshall, *op cit*, p250

18 Constable, *op cit*, p199

19 Williams, *op cit*, p181

20 Longenecker, *op cit*, p445

21 See Richard Bauckham, 'James and the Jerusalem Church,' in *The Book of Acts in Its First Century Setting*; Vol. 4: The Book of Acts in Its Palestinian Setting, pp415–480.

22 Longenecker, *op cit*, p446; Fernando, *op cit*, p418

23 Marshall, *op cit*, p243

24 Charles H. Savelle, 'A Reexamination of the Prohibitions in Acts 15,' *Bibliotheca Sacra* 161:644 (October–December 2004):468.

25 Constable, *op cit*, p203

26 Constable, *op cit*, p204

27 Kent, *op cit*, p128

28 Longenecker, *op cit*, p448

29 *ibid*, p450

30 Marshall, *op cit*, p247

31 Fernando, *op cit*, p415

32 Marshall, *op cit*, p33

33 Longenecker, *op cit*, p424

34 Robertson, *op cit*, p187

35 Longenecker, *op cit*, p424

36 Lewis, *op cit*, p72

37 Williams, *op cit*, p229

38 Fitzmyer, *op cit*, p507

39 See Conzelmann, *Acts*, 103, who says: "according to Luke, Paul opens his speech with the appropriate rhetorical gesture."

40 Fitzmyer, *op cit*, p510

41 Fernando, *op cit*, p386

42 Marshall, *op cit*, p223

43 Fitzmyer, *op cit*, p510

44 Moyes, G, *Discovering Paul*, Australia: Albatross Books Pty Ltd, 1986, p45

45 This could refer to Saul's deposition or to his death.

46 Although John the Baptist is never mentioned in any of Paul's letters.

47 Darrell L. Bock, "A Theology of Luke – Acts," in *A Biblical Theology of the New Testament*, ed. Darrell L. Bock and Roy B. Zuck (Chicago: Moody Press, 1994), 93.

48 Marshall, *op cit*, p225

49 Fitzmyer, *op cit*, p515

50 Williams, *op cit*, p164

51 Fitzmyer, *op cit*, p517

52 See Jacques Dupont, *Etudes sur les actes des apotres*, Lectio Divina 45 (Paris: Les Editions du Cerf, 1967), who says, "Il est beaucoup plus difficile de se rendre compte du rôle que la citation d'Isaïe joue dans la raisonnement et du sens qu'il faut attribuer aux termes qu'elle emploie."

53 Williams, *op cit*, p164

54 Marshall, *op cit*, p227

55 Stott, *op cit*, p225

56 Fitzmyer, *op cit*, p508

57 Williams, *op cit*, p237

58 Neil, *op cit*, p160

59 Marshall, *op cit*, p283

60 Barclay, *op cit*, p141

61 Toussaint, SD, *Acts*, *In the Bible Knowledge Commentary: New Testament*, Ed. Walvoord, J.F., and Zuck, R.B., Wheaton: Scripture Press Publications, 1983

62 Guy, *op cit*, p77

63 Hanson, *op cit*, p176

64 Guy, *op cit*, p77

65 Rackham, *op cit*, p304

66 Keener, CS, *The IVP Bible Background Commentary: New Testament*, Downer's Grove: IVP, 1993, p831

67 See David A deSilva, "Paul and the Stoa: A Comparison," *Journal of the Evangelical Theological Society* 38:4 (December 1995): pp549–64, for a comparison of Paul's teaching and the Stoics'.

68 Guy, *op cit*, p77

69 Henley, WE, cited in *Modern British Poetry*, ed., Untermeyer, L, 1920

70 Guy, *op cit*, p77

71 Barclay, *op cit*, pp141–142

72 Marshall, *op cit*, p285

73 Dean W. Zweck, "The Areopagus Speech of Acts 17," *Lutheran Theological Journal* 21:3 (December 1987): pp11–22.

74 Fernando, *op cit*, p474

75 Fitzmyer, *op cit*, p606

76 Grayston, K, *Theology as Exploration*, London: Epworth P., 1966, pp3–6

77 Morgan, GC, *The Acts of the Apostles*, New York: Fleming H. Revell Co. 1924; reprint ed., London: Pickering and Inglis, 1965, p327

78 Blaiklock, EM, *The Acts of the Apostles*, Tyndale New Testament Commentaries Series, London: Tyndale Press, 1959; reprint ed., Grand Rapids: WB Eerdmans Publishing Co., 1979, p140

79 Fitzmyer points out that no such altar at Athens has yet been discovered with this precise inscription.

80 Marshall, *op cit*, p286

81 Fernando, *op cit*, p476

82 Marshall, *op cit*, p286

83 This would have appealed to the Epicureans, who held the idea of God as above the world.

84 Fitzmyer, *op cit*, p608

85 Marshall, *op cit*, p287

86 Fitzmyer, *op cit*, p609

87 Marshall, *op cit*, p288

88 Guy, *op cit*, p78

89 From his poem *Cretica*, cited by Longenecker, *op cit*, p476.

90 From Aratus' *Phaenomena* 5, and Cleanthes' *Hymn to Zeus*, also cited *ibid*.

91 Marshall, *op cit*, p290

92 *ibid*, 290

93 McGee, *op cit*, p591

94 Lewis, *op cit*, p72

95 Croy, NC, Hellenistic Philosophies and the Preaching of the Resurrection (Acts 17:18, 32), *Novum Testamentum* 39:1 (1997): pp21–39.

96 Marshall, *op cit*, p291

97 Crowe, *op cit*, p136

98 Fitzmyer, *op cit*, p612

99 Lewis, *op cit*, p72

100 Fitzmyer, *op cit*, p674

101 Bruce, *op cit*, p388

102 Fitzmyer, *op cit*, p674

103 Bruce, *op cit*, p388

104 Robertson, *op cit*, pp346–347

105 Neil, *op cit*, p213

106 Marshall, *op cit*, p329

107 Bruce, *op cit*, p388

108 Fitzmyer, *op cit*, p676

109 Hanson, *op cit*, p202

110 Stott, *op cit*, p325

111 Fitzmyer, *op cit*, p677

112 Bruce, *op cit*, p390

113 Crowe, *op cit*, p156

114 Marshall, *op cit*, p332

115 Hanson, *op cit*, pp203–204

116 Marshall, *op cit*, p326

117 Marshall, *ibid*, p329

118 Stott, *op cit*, p326

119 Marshall, *op cit*, p333

120 Bruce, *op cit*, p393

121 Williams, *op cit*, pp234–235

122 Bruce, *op cit*, p393

123 Packer, *op cit*, p173

124 Bruce, *op cit*, p393

125 Fernando, *op cit*, p533

126 Hanson, *op cit*, p205

127 Barclay, *op cit*, p166

128 Akin, DL, Overseer, EDBT, p586, cited in
Fernando, *op cit*, p534

129 Crowe, *op cit*, p156

130 Stott, *op cit*, p323

131 Hanson, *op cit*, p204

132 Marshall, *op cit*, p336

133 Fitzmyer, *op cit*, p681

134 Hanson, *op cit*, p206

135 Guy, *op cit*, p94

136 Hanson, *op cit*, p206

137 Lewis, *op cit*, p85

Paul's letter to the Galatians

Chapter **8**

INTRODUCTION

ON PAUL'S THREE MISSIONARY journeys he preached the gospel and set up churches in the provinces of Galatia, Asia, Macedonia and Achaia. Following this, Paul wrote letters to these churches to provide the new Christians with support and encouragement.

One of these letters is the letter to the Galatians. Many scholars believe this letter to be one of the earliest letters that Paul wrote (around AD48 or 49).

PURPOSE AND MAIN THEMES

Why did Paul write to the Galatians? Stott[1] explains that since Paul's visit to Galatia the churches that he founded had been troubled by false teachers who had launched an attack both on Paul's authority and on his gospel. They argued against Paul's message that people could be saved through faith in Christ alone, arguing that circumcision and obedience to the Law of Moses were also necessary. In other words, anyone wishing to join the ranks of the people of God from the outside must conform to the normal procedure prescribed for proselytes – circumcision and commitment to Israel's Law.[2]

Paul immediately saw the threat that their message would have to the churches he had established and on the spread of the gospel, so he wrote his letter to the Galatians. Russell[3] explains that the general purpose of the letter was to persuade the

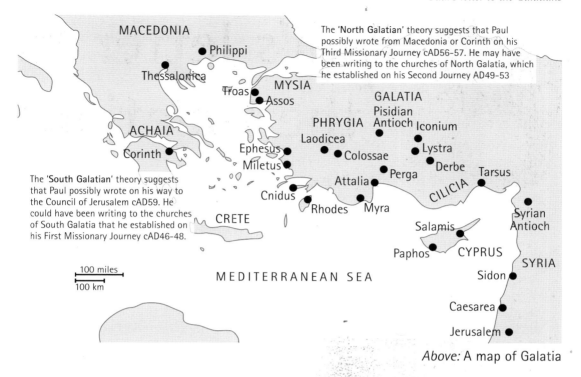

The 'North Galatian' theory suggests that Paul possibly wrote from Macedonia or Corinth on his Third Missionary Journey cAD56-57. He may have been writing to the churches of North Galatia, which he established on his Second Journey AD49-53

The 'South Galatian' theory suggests that Paul possibly wrote on his way to the Council of Jerusalem cAD59. He could have been writing to the churches of South Galatia that he established on his First Missionary Journey cAD46-48.

Above: A map of Galatia

Galatians to reject the Judaisers' non-gospel and to continue in the true gospel Paul had preached to them.

In particular, the purpose of the letter to the Galatians can be divided into three main themes:

1. to defend Paul's authority
2. to defend Paul's message of justification by faith
3. to explain the meaning of Christian freedom

These three themes are covered in detail in the rest of this chapter. In the A2 examination, for a question asking for the purpose of Galatians, a summary of these issues is all that is required.

Characteristics

Dispute over the destination of the letter

There has been dispute among scholars over what is meant by the term 'Galatia'. In the main view, referred to as the 'North Galatian' theory, Galatia covers the land in the central parts of Asia, which Paul visited during his second missionary journey, after the Council of Jerusalem. The other view is known as the 'South Galatian' theory. This theory holds that Galatians was written for the Roman province of

Galatia, which included towns such as Pisidian Antioch, Iconium, Lystra and Derbe. Paul visited these towns during his first missionary journey, which took place before the Council of Jerusalem. Most scholars agree that the North Galatian theory is the more likely.[4] It is not necessary to go into detail of the arguments of these theories for the A2 examination.

Tone of the Letter

Drane[5] explains how the letter to the Galatians "was written hastily in the middle of a raging controversy". Longenecker[6] describes the opening of the letter as "fiery", "like a lion turned loose in the arena of Christianity". Paul's message "is personal and polemic, direct and defensive".[7] Paul was so angry because of the seriousness of the issue at stake. Boice[8] explains that when the gospel was being preached mainly to Jews by Jews, the development of the church progressed smoothly. But as the missionaries pushed out into largely Gentile communities and the gospel began to take root there, questions arose regarding a Christian's relationship to the Law of Moses and to Judaism as a system. Was the church to open her doors wide to everyone, regardless of their relationship to the traditions of Judaism? Were her boundaries to be as wide as the human race? Or was she to be only an extension of Judaism to the Gentiles, as was being promoted by the Judaisers? Paul realised that "the future of Christianity was at stake: was it to become a sect of Judaism or a world-wide movement, embracing all peoples and races?"[9]

 TASKS

1. Why did Paul write the letter to the Galatians?

The discussion may include some of the following:
- Response to the threat of the Judaisers
- Preservation of the Galatian churches
- Defence of the gospel
- Defence of Paul's apostleship
- The inadequacy of the law
- The adequacy of faith in Christ
- Explanation of Christian freedom, life in the Spirit, the rule of love

2. Comment on the claim that we meet many of the weightiest themes in Paul's letter to the Galatians.

A critical evaluation may include, eg:
- An assessment of the importance of Paul's defence of his apostleship; of his doctrine of justification by faith; and of Christian freedom.

3. Comment on the claim that the message of Galatians is not out of date.

A critical evaluation may include, eg:
- Issues of religious authority
- Legalism, false teaching, influence of trends
- Christian living, freedom, fellowship
- Different contexts
- Circumcision

THE DEFENCE OF PAUL'S AUTHORITY

Overview of Chapters 1–2

The Galatians were a group of Christians who had previously been Gentiles. They were converted following Paul's preaching in his first missionary journey that all that was needed was faith in Christ.

However, it seems that "certain persons had been working against Paul after he had visited them".[10] Not long after Paul left Galatia a group of Jewish Christians, called 'Judaisers', arrived in Galatia and began to teach that for these Gentiles to be really saved they needed to be circumcised and keep the law of Moses. Much has been written on the identity of these men and their theology. Freed[11] argues that they were probably fellow Jewish believers from Jerusalem. Fitzmyer[12] agrees, adding that they were "of an even stricter Jewish background than Peter, Paul or James". And Cwiekowski[13] describes them as "Jewish converts to Christianity who sought to harmonise their former faith with belief in Jesus". Whoever they were, it is clear that they regarded themselves as Jewish Christians.

The main thrust of the Judaisers' message was a critique of Paul. Drane[14] explains that "the first thing the Judaisers had said was that Paul was not a proper apostle ... he had no right to give directions to new Christians, nor ought they to pay attention to what he said". They argued that Paul was inferior to the original apostles of Jesus and that his message had not come from God. Gorman[15] explains that they "seem to have found his apostleship dubious, his message deficient, and his ministry dangerous". They likely claimed that his message and ministry originated in himself and had the sanction of neither Jerusalem nor heaven. In other words, they were arguing that Paul had no authority to promote his message, a message in which he was "watering down the requirements of the gospel for the sake of Gentile converts".[16]

In Chapters 1–2 of Galatians, Paul defends both his apostleship and his message. The two chapters can be split into four sections:

1. Paul's gospel had been revealed to him by Christ himself (1:11–17).
2. Paul only met the original apostles three years after his conversion (1:18–24).
3. Fourteen years later they endorsed his message (2:1–10).

4. Paul was not inferior to the other apostles; in fact he had once had to rebuke Peter (2:11–21).

Greetings to the Galatians (Ch 1:1-5)

Letters in ancient times opened in a particular way, with the sender's name, the name of the recipients and greetings. Paul's letter to the Galatians opens in a similar way (v 1–3), however it differs from his other letters in two distinct ways:

1. Paul has no praise for the Galatians. Guthrie[17] comments that "in place of the usual thanksgiving, which is entirely lacking, Paul denounces the perverters of the gospel who are, in fact, preaching another gospel".

2. Paul adds some comments, which hint at the issues he plans to deal with in the rest of the letter. These comments are related to Paul's authority as an apostle of Jesus.

The Trouble in Galatia (Ch 1:6-10)

"Instead of the usual thanksgiving, Paul expresses his indignant astonishment that the Galatians are so quickly forsaking their original teaching for another gospel."[18] The Greek word used for 'astonished' is *thaumazo* which translates as 'I am amazed'. This was a conventional expression in Greek letters that signalled astonishment, rebuke, disapproval, and disappointment.[19] Fitzmyer[20] describes the action of the Galatians as "fickleness", which means they were inconsistent or easily persuaded. Ryken[21] argues that Paul "practically splutters with indignation. And rightly so … As far as Paul was able to tell, the Galatians were guilty of sheer spiritual stupidity".

MacArthur[22] explains that their stupidity "refers not to lack of intelligence, but to lack of obedience". The Judaisers had arrived in Galatia, preaching a message that was different to the message Paul had preached and the Galatians immediately agreed with them. Freed[23] comments that the different message was "a demand that Gentiles be circumcised and obey the Jewish law". Paul regarded this message as a perversion of the true gospel. It was not a true gospel. Not only was he stunned at how quickly the Galatians were accepting this other gospel but he was so outraged that he proclaims the Judaisers are now under a curse (v 8–9). Stott[24] explains that this means that Paul hopes God's judgement will fall upon them.

Paul shows that he is not trying to win favour for himself by placing himself under such a curse (v 10). The Judaisers accused Paul of being a man-pleaser. They intended to undermine Paul's authority to give support to their 'different gospel'. However, they could not attack Paul's gospel without first attacking him. They alleged that Paul's message was motivated by a desire to win man's approval, rather than God's (v 10).

Some might argue that there is an element of truth in the accusation of the Judaisers against Paul. Paul admits to changing his behaviour depending upon the cultural preferences of his audience. He did this to avoid undue offence to the gospel. Freed[25] describes how Paul "found it convenient to become all things to all persons that he might win some. To the Jew he became a Jew to win Jews. Although not himself under the law, he became as one under the law to win those observing the law. To those without the law, he became like one of them to win some of them, though not himself without law toward God yet under the law of Christ" (1 Cor 9:19–23). In other words, while Paul was willing to make cultural concessions, he stood firm with regard to the gospel that he preached.

Paul was certainly not a man-pleaser. The charge that Paul had changed his message in order to please men implied that those he most wanted to please were the other apostles. However, Paul was rarely in Jerusalem and when he did go there he did not seek the approval of the apostles, but rather sought the advancement of the gospel. The expression "those who were of reputation" (2:2 and 6) is not meant to be disrespectful to the other apostles, but to show that Paul had no undue sense of awe, since he also was an apostle.

 ## OTHER ASPECTS OF HUMAN EXPERIENCE

Exploring other aspects of human experience:

Morris[26] argues that "there have always been preachers who have sought popular acclaim above all else and there are some still. It is part of fallen human nature that even those charged with the responsibility of proclaiming the gospel can fall into the trap of trying to be popular rather than faithful."

a) Explain what is meant by this statement.

b) In groups try to think of some examples of the truth of the statement in contemporary society.

The Origin of Paul's Message (Ch 1:11–24)

Paul delves into detail of his own past as a fanatical supporter of the same views as the Judaisers. He wants to stress how his call to be an apostle was a dramatic change in his life, which can only be attributed to God himself (v 13–14). Paul was an unusually promising young man in Judaism before his conversion, exceeding his peers. Morris[27] explains that "this probably does not mean that he became more pious than they, but rather that he was more highly esteemed by those in positions of influence, which would have resulted in his being entrusted with more important assignments, such as the trip to Damascus during which he was converted".

Drane[28] stresses that Paul "had a face-to-face encounter with Jesus". As well his call to be an apostle, Paul also received his gospel message from God. After his conversion he went straight to Arabia and had no contact with other Christians (v 15–17). It was not until three years after his conversion that Paul met Peter and James, two of the original apostles (ie those who Jesus had appointed). Fitzmyer[29] comments that when Paul writes *"to see those who were apostles before I was"* he is deliberately assuming the title apostle "to emphasis his equality with them, for his authoritative commission comes from the risen Lord".

He went to Jerusalem "to get personally acquainted with" them, not to get information from them or to make inquiry of them.[30] As he only stayed there for a fortnight he could not have got his gospel message from them. Afterwards he returned to Cilicia and had no further contact with any of the original apostles (v 18–24). Campbell[31] concludes that "Paul had emphasized that he did not receive his message from men before or at the time of his conversion. Now he affirmed that he was free from human influences afterward as well".

Paul's Message Approved (Ch 2:1–10)

Campbell[32] comments that while Chapter 2 continues Paul's defence of his apostolic authority and the gospel he preached, he focuses "not on the source of his message but on its content". First of all he seeks to show how 'his gospel was precisely the same as that of the other apostles".[33] "He maintains that he had begun his missionary work before meeting the authorities in the church at Jerusalem".[34] "Fourteen years later" (which most scholars take to mean fourteen years after his conversion) Paul met the apostles. He went to Jerusalem because God told him to and not due to any request by the apostles. With him he took Titus, a Gentile Christian, which is of some significance given that Jerusalem was the Judaisers' stronghold (v 1–2). As Titus was not circumcised, his presence forced the Christian leadership to take a stand concerning the necessity of circumcision for Gentile converts to Christianity.

However, some of the Judaisers managed to gain access to this meeting between Paul and the other apostles (v 3–5). Even so, Titus was not forced to be circumcised and Paul's gospel "was not contradicted or even modified in any way".[35] The other apostles "acknowledged his successful work among Gentiles and glorified God because of it".[36] In other words, Paul's view, that Gentiles do not need to keep the Law of Moses or submit to circumcision, was approved by the original apostles. They also encouraged him to continue such work in the future (v 6–10). Guthrie[37] concludes that "his apostleship was unquestioned".

Paul rebukes Peter (Ch 2:11–21)

The incident in Antioch shows how many Jewish Christians saw themselves as simply a renewal movement within Judaism and regarded newly converted Gentiles as proselytes who needed to be circumcised and to submit to the Jewish Law if they were to become fully certified as members of the covenant community. Fitzmyer[38] explains that such an attitude would affect the unity of the church itself.

Peter had paid a visit to Antioch and enjoyed 'table-fellowship' (eating) with the Gentile Christians there. Even though they were not circumcised or bound by the Law of Moses, Peter had no problem whatsoever in spending time with them, socialising, having meals and sharing in the Lord's Supper. However, it seems some Judaisers arrived at Antioch and their influence on Peter was such that he stopped having table-fellowship with the Gentile Christians. Fitzmyer[39] explains that such behaviour "gave the impression that only Jewish Christians … were the real Christians". Suddenly it was as if the Gentile Christians were no longer good enough for his company. Paul was outraged at such shameful behaviour and told Peter what he thought of him in front of the whole congregation. Paul's equality to the other apostles is evident in this verbal attack on Peter (v 15–16). Guthrie[40] argues that "this was an active demonstration of his apostolic authority".

Freed[41] explains that "Paul's reprimand would be pointless if Peter had not at least partly shared his ideas, especially about food laws". When Peter and Paul had been Jews they had firmly believed that God would only accept them as righteous if they managed to keep the whole Law of Moses. As Christians they now rejected that belief and instead accepted that sinners can only be justified by faith in Jesus. This is known as 'justification by faith' and is one of the major themes of Galatians. If Peter was no longer associating himself with the Gentiles it would look as if he could no longer accept that they were saved because they did not keep the Law of Moses. Paul regards this as very serious because "to submit to the law again would be to become involved again with sin".[42] Furthermore, "if the law was still in force as a way of salvation and life, the messianic age had not yet dawned, and Jesus accordingly was not the Messiah".[43]

"It is perhaps curious that nobody seems to have recalled that Jesus ate 'with publicans and sinners', which can scarcely mean that he conformed to strict Jewish practice." [cf Mark 7:19][44]

 TASK

With reference to Galatians chs 1–2, discuss Paul's response to the accusation of the Judaisers that he was not a proper apostle.

A discussion may include the following, eg
- First to preach in Galatia
- Conversion and call
- Met risen Christ
- Message approved by other apostles

PAUL'S TEACHING ON LAW AND GRACE, JUSTIFICATION BY FAITH

Overview of Chapters 3–4

In Chs 3–4 Paul seeks to prove that his message of salvation by faith alone is still the only true gospel message. People cannot be saved by keeping the Law of Moses or submitting to circumcision. Paul uses two main methods in presenting his arguments:

- He appeals to the Galatians' own experience.
- He appeals to Old Testament Scripture.

The Galatians' Own Experience (Ch 3:1–5)

Paul challenges the Galatians with a series of rhetorical questions (a question to which no answer is expected; Paul is being sarcastic), which are obviously challenges against the Galatians and not polite inquiries. He reminds the Galatians of the experience they had when he first preached the gospel and they became Christians. "What they knew of Christ ought to have shown them that they had received the Holy Spirit, not because they had obeyed the Old Testament law, but because they had exercised faith in Jesus".[45]

This in itself should have been enough to prove he was right. The Holy Spirit was a sign that they had been accepted by God. "A return to 'the deeds of the law' would mean that the Spirit was received to no avail."[46] Guthrie[47] explains that Paul thought for the Galatians to 'retrogress' or return to the law could only be evidence of 'bewitched minds' (brainwashed).

For Paul, Christ is everything or nothing. Either God has inaugurated the new, eschatological age of the Spirit through Christ, or not. Either justification, or life in the Spirit, is received by faith, or not.[48] As Guthrie[49] explains, "the real issue was a choice between Christ and the law".

"Gal 3:1–18 is one of the most familiar and closely studied portions of Paul's letters."[50]

The Example of Abraham (Ch 3:6–9)

For further proof, Paul uses the Old Testament (Genesis 15:6) and appeals to the example of Abraham. In Jewish history Abraham was a very important man of God. Abraham was the first person who became righteous through faithfulness towards God.[51] The Jews has descended from Abraham and through him God had promised that the same blessing that he had given to Abraham would be given to all people. Therefore Abraham's true descendants were those who, like Abraham, trusted in God, and were saved by faith alone.

The Danger of Relying on the Law (Ch 3:10–14)

The importance of observance of the law for any Jew of Paul's day goes without saying.[52] Therefore it is understandable that "what made the Gentiles sinners in the estimation of the Jews was not only that they did not observe the law but also that they did not even possess it and consequently lacked the possibility of obtaining righteousness through it".[53]

The Galatians had started to believe the Judaisers that the only way to be saved was by keeping the Jewish law. However, the Judaisers' view that salvation was gained through keeping the Law of Moses was impossible. To break just one commandment (3:10; James 2:10–11) would lead to condemnation. Freed[54] comments that the law was ineffective in helping mankind attain righteousness in God's sight. Ryken[55] explains that since we cannot keep the law, the law cannot bless us. "Instead of bringing blessings, the law brings a curse on whoever breaks the law…".[56]

The scriptures taught, "clearly no-one is justified before God by the law, because, the righteous will live by faith" (Habakkuk 2:4). Therefore to say there was another way to be saved was to contradict the scriptures. Paul's most basic problem with the Law is that it is obsolete and therefore following it is no longer appropriate. However, the good news is that "Christ had removed this by becoming a curse for us".[57] Bruce[58] explains that for Jews anyone who was crucified was under a curse (1 Cor 1:23). Paul explains that this is the reason why God sent Jesus to die on the cross. Through Jesus' death people have been set free from the punishment they deserve because of their sins. Through his suffering, Jesus took the punishment for people's sins becoming a curse for them (3:13). All that people need to do is believe in Jesus. Therefore, the promise God made to Abraham that sinners can be saved even though they have not kept the law, can be fulfilled.

Freed[59] argues that when Paul talks about the works of the law he usually means works of the law in a specific and limited sense, mostly with reference to circumcision and dietary regulations, not the law as a whole, and not works in the sense of good deed. De Silva[60] agrees, commenting that Paul is not arguing against "good works" but "works of the law". He is opposing the continued observance of a code, an entire body of laws given to Israel as a mark of her distinctiveness and separation from the Gentiles.

What is the Purpose of the Law? (Ch 3:15–25)

God had promised Abraham that one of his descendants would save the world through faith. 430 years after this God gave the law through Moses to prepare his people for this Saviour. Guy[61] explains that "the Law of Moses came into being centuries after the time of Abraham, as a kind of afterthought". Therefore, it could not possibly alter a direct promise made to him by God.[62] So in Galatians Paul argues that the Law of Moses "was always secondary to faithfulness because Abraham believed

God before the law was ever given".[63] Morris[64] comments that this is "what endeared Abraham to many Jewish thinkers ... his virtues and his deeds. They understood him to have kept the law before it was written".

If the law is not needed to be saved, then the Galatians might wonder what the point of having a law was (3:19). Paul explains that the law was given "on account of sin" (3:19). In other words, the law showed them that they needed to be saved because it was impossible for them to be able to stop sinning. The law enabled them to work out what was right and what was wrong. With the threat of punishment hanging over them, people were more likely to do what was right.

The purpose of the law, however, was not to make the Jews feel bad about themselves. It was to make them realise that they needed a Saviour. Morris[65] explains that "a law can lay down what people ought to do, but it cannot give them the power to overcome the temptations to do evil". Therefore the function of the law was to point people to Christ.[66] Paul clarified that the Law was only a temporary measure designed to function until Christ came.[67] When this time came the people would be ready to turn to Christ in faith (3:19, 21, 24).

The promise had now been kept because the Saviour (Jesus) had come. So the purpose of the law had been served. There was no longer any need to try to keep it (3:25). Guthrie[68] argues that "the gist of Paul's argument is to show that ... Christianity according to the law is inferior to the doctrine of faith".

 TASK

The following quotations provide a summary of this argument. In pairs, explain what each quotation means in your own words:

- "For Paul, the law can be described as weak in respect of justification simply because it was not given by God for the purpose of justification, but rather as an interim provision pointing forward to the Christ, in whom justification would become a reality. To seek justification by the law, therefore, as the Galatians were mistakenly trying to do, is to attempt to direct the law towards an end for which it is essentially unsuited by the purpose of God ...".[69]
- "The gospel is the fulfillment of the promise made to Abraham that in him and his offspring all nations would be blessed (cf 3:8, 16). The law, which was given later, was a parenthetical dispensation introduced by God for a limited purpose; its validity continued only until the promise to Abraham was fulfilled in Christ, and even while it was valid it did not modify the terms of the promise"[70] (cf 3:17–25).

The True Descendants of Abraham (Ch 3:26–29)

Freed[71] explains that "Paul never gave up his belief that the Jews were God's special people. He simply broadened the concept to include all persons who through their faithfulness toward God are children of God in Christ Jesus". After accepting Christ, the Galatians had been baptised by Paul (3:27), which was an act to show that they belonged to Christ and 'were one with him' (3:26). "Putting on clothes is a metaphor for assuming inner moral or spiritual qualities or a different status in life."[72] Because there was now but one way of justification, all who belonged to Christ were equally regarded as God's children. Therefore there was no difference between Jews and Gentiles (3:28).[73] "All are one in Christ Jesus so that there is neither Jew nor Greek, slave nor free, male nor female."[74] All are counted as Abraham's descendants and are entitled to everything that God promised to Abraham (3:29).

 OTHER ASPECTS OF HUMAN EXPERIENCE

The place of women in Christianity

"There is neither Jew nor Greek, there is neither slave nor free, there is neither male nor female; for you are all one in Christ Jesus." Galatians 3:28

It has been said that no other verse in Galatians has attracted as much attention during the debate about the role of women in the church as Galatians 3:28. When Paul states that "there is neither … male nor female … in Christ," is he referring to the role of women in the home and in the church? Most scholars agree that the main point of this verse means that all believers are united in Christ. But does the verse go beyond that? Clearly salvation does not eliminate all of our human differences. As Christians we keep racial, social, and gender distinctions. So what does it mean that in Christ there is neither male nor female? Does Galatians 3:28 do away with gender specific roles? Can women now have equal roles to men, for example, in the church?

In groups, discuss the above points and assess what you think Paul means by Galatians 3:28.

God's Dealings with the Jews (Ch 4:1–7)

Paul provides further explanation by using an example from everyday life. In Roman society a son would receive his inheritance from his father when he came of age (a bit like reaching the age of eighteen in our society). Up until that time the son would have to answer to a guardian or tutor whom his father had put in charge of him. Such a tutor may have been "a slave charged to lead a boy to and from school and to watch over his studies and conduct".[75] Even though the son may be an heir to a fortune, in reality, until he came of age he would be no better than a slave.

Paul explains that this is what it was like for the Jews. The Jews were expected to keep the Law of Moses until such times that they would be free of it. Fitzmyer[76] explains that "the termination of such discipline came with Christ, 'the end of the law'". Now that Christ had come, the Jews could enjoy their inheritance, that is, their salvation. The guardian or tutor (ie, the law) is no longer needed. God was treating them like mature sons, the proof of which was in the gift of the Holy Spirit.

Paul's concern for the Galatians (Ch 4:8–20)

Freed[77] asks the obvious question: "'Now that Gentile believers know God and are known by him, how can they think of returning to pagan gods and pagan ways?" Witherington[78] stresses that if the Law was meant to function only until Christ came, "then it is a mistake, indeed a serious mistake to go back to keeping it, or in the case of Gentiles to begin to submit to it in any form or fashion". Witherington continues to explain that what bothers Paul the most is that keeping the Law implies that Christ's death did not accomplish what in fact he believes it did accomplish. To submit to the Mosaic Law is to "nullify the grace of God (Gal 2.21) and to deny that justification or righteousness, whether initial or final, comes through the death of Christ".

Paul states that he cannot understand why the Galatians want to revert back to keeping the Law of Moses, when they had recently enjoyed freedom from the law. Paul is concerned that his work among them will have been a waste of time.

Paul reminds the Galatians of his friendship towards them. They had treated him like an angel and had looked after him when he was sick. Fitzmyer[79] suggests this (4:14) may be "an allusion to some repulsive physical ailment?" However, now it seems that they were regarding him as their enemy, when really he had only had their welfare at heart (4:12–16). Paul was worried. He believed that the Judaisers were only pretending to be their friends. They wanted the Galatians to turn their backs on Paul and to accept their ways (4:17–20).

The True Sons of Abraham (Ch 4:21–31)

Paul closes this doctrinal section using the Old Testament scripture to explain the identity of the true sons of Abraham. The Judaisers had argued that the only way to be saved was to become a true descendant of Abraham, which could be achieved by being circumcised and keeping the Law of Moses. Paul, however, disagrees, using scripture to support his argument.

Abraham had two sons, Isaac and Ishmael. Isaac was the son of Abraham's wife, Sarah, a 'free woman'. Ishmael was the son of a slave woman, Hagar. Which of these sons was Abraham's true son and heir? Fitzmyer[80] suggests that "the women represent two covenants: Hagar represents the Sinai covenant, and Sarah represents the one made with Abraham". As the Sinai covenant is the giving of the law which happened after the promise made to Abraham then the Sinai covenant is the inferior one.

Drane[81] explains that these verses are "an allegory of the superior position of the good news of Christ over against the legalism of the Jewish law". God rejected Ishmael, the son of the slave woman, even though he was circumcised. Instead God accepted Isaac as he had been born by the power of the Holy Spirit. Paul compares this story with the situation in Galatia. The Galatians had been born again by the power of the Holy Spirit and were free, just like Isaac who was regarded as Abraham's true descendant. However, the Judaisers were in bondage (to the law), like Ishmael, the son of the slave woman.

 TASK

Critically assess the view that Paul's teaching on the Law is still important today.

A critical evaluation of the view might include, eg:
- The context has changed
- The specific challenge of the Judaisers
- Justification by faith
- Issues related to circumcision
- Contemporary 'laws' which alter or add to the gospel of faith

PAUL'S TEACHING ON LIFE IN THE SPIRIT AND CHRISTIAN FREEDOM

Overview of Chapters 5–6

Having explained what is meant by 'justification by faith' Paul now draws out some practical lessons for the Galatians to learn. He explains how they are to hold tight to the freedom that Jesus has given them. With that freedom they are to live a life that pleases God and not let their newly found freedom be an excuse for wrong or reckless living.

The Importance of Standing Firm (Ch 5:1–6)

In the previous chapter Paul has explained how the true descendants of Abraham are free. He continues the theme of freedom explaining that the reason Jesus died on the cross was that we might be free from the 'curse of the law' and from having to keep the law to win God's approval (5:1). Such freedom was a privilege and one that the Galatians should not give up by being circumcised. If they submitted to circumcision they would be obligated to keep all the other Jewish laws as well (5:3). If that was the case then Christ would have died for nothing (5:2, 4). Fitzmyer[82] explains that "the Galatians must choose one or the other: Christ and freedom, or the law and slavery ... but Paul warns: if you accept the 'sign' of a Jew, you oblige yourself to the whole way of life" (see also comment on Ch 3:10–14). Paul concludes that the only thing that matters to God is faith which shows itself through love (5:6).

Paul's Hope for the Galatians (Ch 5:7–12)

"Paul often compares Christian effort to that of a runner in a race."[83] Here he reminds the Galatians that they had made a good start in their Christian lives but the Judaisers have been getting in the way and they have been sidetracked from the true path (5:7). He compares the influence of the Judaisers to yeast in dough; while there was only a small number of Judaisers, there were enough of them to affect the whole Christian community (5:9). Paul is convinced, however, that God will judge these troublemakers (5:10, 12).

The Proper Use of Freedom (Ch 5:13–25)

By his death, Jesus had set the Galatians free from having to obey the Jewish law. However, Paul never said that the law has been abolished in every sense, or that its ethical demands are now irrelevant. Freed[84] argues that Paul "usually means works of the law in a specific and limited sense, mostly with reference to circumcision and dietary regulations, not the law as a whole, and not works in the sense of good deed". Murder is still murder, adultery is still adultery, and theft is still theft. Paul stresses that freedom or liberty "must not be confused with libertinism".[85] In other words, freedom from the Law did not mean licence to live as the Galatians pleased, for example, by gratifying their sinful desires (5:13a, 19).[86] The Christian is not the person who has become free to sin, but the person, who, by the grace of God, has become free *not to sin*.[87] They were to use the power of the Holy Spirit to live a life of loving service to others (5:13b, 16). The Holy Spirit would enable them to develop a Christ-like character (5:22). Freed[88] explains that "according to Paul, for converts who live as new creations, the differences between right and wrong is quite explicit ... Good conduct is the work of God and the fruit of the Spirit; wrong conduct is the works of the flesh". Bruce[89] agrees, commenting that to "walk by the Spirit" means "let your conduct be directed by the Spirit". Guthrie[90] explains that "spiritual freedom will lead to an attitude of sympathy for the burdened". This will result in mutually helping one another through gentleness, not pride, to refrain from wrongdoing.[91] The irony is that if the Galatians lived their lives in this way, they would in fact be actually keeping God's laws. Paul explains that the whole purpose of the law is summed up in the command "love your neighbour as yourself" (5:14).

The Law of Christ: Helping Others (Ch 5:26–6:5)

While the Galatians did not have to keep the Law of Moses, this did not mean that they were allowed to live as someone with no laws. They were in a way under a new law, the law of Christ (6:2b) which meant that just as Jesus had been humble and willing to bear the burdens of others, so should they be towards one another (6:1).

Sowing to the Spirit (Ch 6:6–10)

These verses are a reminder to the Galatians of the gift of the Holy Spirit that God had given to the Galatians when they first believed in Jesus. If they were willing to give their hearts over to the Holy Spirit, ie 'sow to please the Spirit', then the Spirit would produce in them a character that God would approve of, and would reward them with eternal life (ie reap a harvest; 6:7; 8b–10).

Conclusion (Ch 6:11–18)

It is clear that Paul is now physically writing the letter himself (6:11). Up until this point he had probably been dictating it to a secretary. The size of his handwriting may be an indication of Paul's poor eyesight, which has been hinted at elsewhere (4:15).

The Judaisers are afraid that if they preach the real message of the cross they will be persecuted for it by Jews or other Judaisers. They prefer to put on a good show to others by preaching circumcision.[92] However, even though they insist on circumcision and observance of the law they are unable to keep the law themselves. For Paul the only thing sinners can boast about in God's presence is what Jesus has done for them through his death on the cross. Circumcision means nothing; all that matters is a new creation.

Paul concludes his letter with words similar to a standard prayer in the Jewish synagogue liturgy: "Peace and mercy to all who follow this rule, even to the Israel of God" (Gal 6:16).[93] The core issue of Galatians thus boils down to a simple but profound choice – Christ or the Torah.'[94]

 TASKS

Comment on the claim that the focus of Galatians Chs 5–6 is a plea for the responsible use of freedom.

A critical evaluation of the claim could include, eg:
- Definition of Christian freedom
- The law
- Freedom not to sin
- Holy Spirit
- Responsibility to others

RELEVANCE OF GALATIANS TODAY

Longenecker[95] argues that Paul's letter to the Galatians, though directly relevant to the Galatian situation, speaks also to our situation today. Hunter[96] agrees, commenting that "The precise issues of Galatians – 'except you be circumcised you cannot be saved' – are long dead ones; but the message of the letter is not out of date."

For example, the question addressed in Galatians concerning circumcision can be asked in another way: 'What makes a person a Christian?' Paul's answer is perfectly clear, "For in Christ Jesus neither circumcision nor uncircumcision has any value. The only thing that counts is faith expressing itself through love." Christians in our society obviously don't argue over issues like circumcision, but Christians believe that the principle is still the same. Many ask how a person can get right with God. Consider the following suggestions:

- By going to church
- By belonging to a certain Christian denomination
- By being baptised
- By keeping the Ten Commandments
- By avoiding alcohol
- By only having Christian friends
- By not working on a Sunday
- By not smoking
- By giving to the needy
- By not using bad language

And so the list goes on. Paul's message is that people can never earn God's favour by obeying laws or conditions. He argues that a true Christian with the help of the Holy Spirit will live a moral and upright life without effort. It will just happen. Therefore, even today, to place any burden on a Christian by telling them to behave in a certain way is to deny them their freedom in Christ.

OTHER ASPECTS OF HUMAN EXPERIENCE

Use the diagram below for ideas to explore the relevance of Galatians to other aspects of human experience:

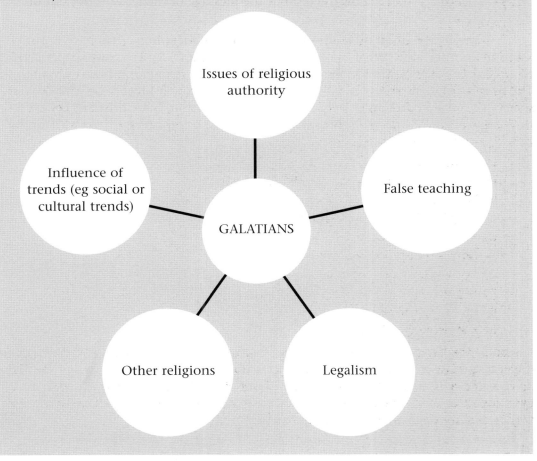

Endnotes

1 Stott, *op cit*, p12

2 Schürer, History, 3.150–76; Donaldson, Paul, 54–65

3 Walter B. Russell III, "Rhetorical Analysis of the Book of Galatians, Part 2," *Bibliotheca Sacra* 150:600 (October–December 1993):436.

4 Cwiekowski, FJ, *The Beginnings of the Church*, Dublin: Gill and Macmillan Ltd, 1988, p104

5 Drane, *op cit*, p289

6 Longenecker, RN, *Galatians*, Word Biblical Commentary Series, Dallas: Word Books, 1990, p1vii

7 Freed, *op cit*, p92

8 Boice, JM, Galatians, In Romans – Galatians, Vol. 10, *The Expositor's Bible Commentary*, ed. by Gaebelein, EE, and Douglas, Grand Rapids: Zondervan Publishing House, 1976, p409

9 Guy, *op cit*, p66

10 Freed, *op cit*, p90

11 *ibid*, p91

12 Fitzmyer, JA, The Letter to the Galatians, in *The New Jerome Biblical Commentary*, ed. Brown, RE; Fitzmyer J A, and Murphy, RE, London: Geoffrey Chapman, 1989, p781

13 Cwiekowski, *op cit*, p104

14 Drane, *op cit*, p290

15 Gorman, MJ, *Apostle of the Crucified Lord: a Theological Introduction to Paul and his Letters*, Grand Rapids: Eerdmans, 2004, p192

16 Fitzmyer, *op cit*, p781

17 Guthrie, D, *New Testament Theology*, Leicester: IVP, 1981, p486p486

18 Freed, *op cit*, pp91–92

19 Longenecker, *op cit*, p11

20 Fitzmyer, *op cit*, p782

21 Ryken, PG, *Galatians, Reformed Expository Commentary*, Phillipsburg; P & r Publishing, 2005, pp81–82

22 John MacArthur, *The MacArthur Bible Commentary* (Thomas Nelson, Inc., 2005), 1664. *ibid*, 1665, p41

23 Freed, *op cit*, p91

24 Stott, JRW, *The Message of Galatians, BST*, Leicester: IVP, 1968, p24

25 Freed, *op cit*, p93

26 Morris, L, *Galatians, Paul's Charter of Christian Freedom*, Leicester: IVP, 1996, p46

27 *ibid*, p53

28 Drane, *op cit*, p290

29 Fitzmyer, *op cit*, p782

30 O. Hofius, "Gal 1:18: *historesai Kephan*", *Zeitschrift für die Neutestamentliche Wissenschaft* 75 (1984):73–84. Cf. R. Schnackenburg, "Apostles before and during Paul's Time," in *Apostolic History and the Gospel*, p290, n. 1.

31 Campbell, DK, Galatians, in *The Bible Knowledge Commentary: An Exposition of the Scriptures* by Dallas Seminary Faculty, Walvoord, JF, and Zuck, RB, editors, Dallas: Chariot Victor Publications, 1983, p592

32 *ibid*, p593

33 Stott, *op cit*, p40

34 Freed, *op cit*, p92

35 Stott, *op cit*, p42

36 Freed, *op cit*, p92

37 Guthrie, *op cit*, p486

38 Fitzmyer, *op cit*, p784

39 *ibid*, p784

40 Guthrie, *op cit*, p486

41 Freed, *op cit*, p98

42 Fitzmyer, *op cit*, p785

43 Bruce, FF, The Epistle to the Galatians, New International Greek Testament Commentary Series, Exeter, Paternoster Press, 1982; reprint ed., Grand rapids: WB Eerdmans Publishing Co., 1983, p83

44 Morris, *op cit*, p77

45 Drane, *op cit*, p290

46 Fitzmyer, *op cit*, p785

47 Guthrie, *op cit*, p487

48 Gorman, *op cit*, p216

49 Guthrie, *op cit*, p486

50 Longenecker, *op cit*, p98

51 Freed, *op cit*, p101

52 Barclay, JMA, *Obeying the Truth, A Study of Paul's Ethics in Galatians*, Edinburgh: Clark, 1988, pp60–72

53 Fung, RYK, *The Epistle to the Galatians: New International Commentary on the New Testament Series*, Grand Rapids: Eerdmans Publishing Co., 1988, p113

54 *ibid*, p92

55 Ryken, *op cit*, p110

56 Freed, *op cit*, p101

57 Guthrie, *op cit*, p487

58 Bruce, *op cit*, pp237–38

59 Freed, *op cit*, p94

60 DeSilva, D, A*n Introduction to the New Testament: Contexts, Methods and Ministry Formation*, Leicester: IVP, p505

61 Guy, *op cit*, p68

62 Drane, *op cit*, p290

63 Freed, *op cit*, p92

64 Morris, *op cit*, p98

65 *ibid*, p115

66 *ibid*, p113

67 J. Daniel Hays, "Applying the Old Testament Law Today," *Bibliotheca Sacra* 158:629 (January–March 2001):21–35

68 Guthrie, *op cit*, p486

69 Bayes, *The Weakness of the Law, God's Law and the Christian in New Testament Perspective*, London: Paternoster Press, 2003, p138

70 Bruce, *op cit*, p219

71 Freed, *op cit*, p101

72 *ibid*, p102

73 Bruce, *op cit*, p124

74 Freed, *op cit*, p104

75 Fitzmyer, *op cit*, p787

76 *ibid*, p787

77 Freed, *op cit*, p103

78 Witherington, B, *Grace in Galatia: A commentary on Paul's letter to the Galatians*, Grand Rapids: WB Eerdmans Publishing, 1998, p354

79 Fitzmyer, *op cit*, p788

80 *ibid*, p788

81 Drane, *op cit*, p291

82 Fitzmyer, *op cit*, p789

83 Fitzmyer, *op cit*, p789

84 Freed, *op cit*, p94

85 Guthrie, *op cit*, p487

86 Guy, *op cit*, p69

87 Barclay, *op cit*, p50

88 Freed, *op cit*, p105

89 Bruce, *op cit*, p243

90 Guthrie, *op cit*, p487

91 Freed, *op cit*, p103

92 Fitzmyer, *op cit*, p789

93 Cwiekowski, *op cit*, p105

94 Hubbard, MV, *New creation in Paul's Letters and Thoughts*, SNTSMS 119, Cambridge: Cambridge University Press, 2002, pp199–200

95 Longenecker, *op cit*, p235

96 Hunter, *op cit*, p123

Paul's 1st Letter to the Corinthians

PURPOSE

YOU WILL RECALL from the AS course that Acts provides us with information about the founding of the church at Corinth (Acts 18). We learn no more until the Corinthian correspondence, a series of letters, some of which are lost. Therefore in order to try to work out what happened in Corinth after Paul left, we have to rely upon the information Paul provides as he writes.

Most scholars are agreed that the Corinthian correspondence is something like this:

1. Paul's first letter, which is either completely lost, or else a fragment of it is in 2 Corinthians (6:14–7:1).
2. The Corinthians' own letter to Paul, which is mentioned in 1 Corinthians 7:1, also now lost.
3. 1 Corinthians, written by Paul in answer to their letter, and part of the New Testament.
4. The 'severe' letter mentioned in 2 Corinthians 2:4 and 7:8, and probably preserved in 2 Corinthians 10–13.
5. The 'letter of reconciliation' which forms 2 Corinthians 1–9.

Above: A map showing the location of Corinth

Background to 1 Corinthians

After Paul left Corinth, things did not go well there. During Paul's three year stay at Ephesus, he heard disturbing news about the church at Corinth. He wrote to them immediately, warning them about the dangers of immorality. After this, "Chloe's people"[1] brought more reports to Paul, this time to tell him that the members of the church at Corinth were splitting into opposing parties. Not only that, but Paul's own authority as an apostle was being questioned. These reports were also confirmed by Stephanas and some others who carried a letter[2] from the Corinthian church to Paul, asking him for guidance over certain pressing issues. 1 Corinthians was probably Paul's reply. A number of the issues that Paul deals with in the letter give an idea of the purpose of 1 Corinthians.

1. To warn the Corinthians of the danger of divisions

Society in Corinth was varied in that people came from many different spiritual and intellectual backgrounds. Even so, while in Corinth with the young church, Paul was able to hold the congregation together. However, after he left the new Christians tried to work out their new faith for themselves, with the result that they began to come up with different answers and ideas.

They had divided into four groups, which reflected the different backgrounds they had come from. Some claimed that they owed their spiritual allegiance to Paul, others to Apollos, others to Peter, and others to Christ. Paul's followers, the 'libertines', encouraged their fellow Christians not to worry about immorality. Those who followed Peter, the 'legalists', asked whether Christians could eat food that had been previously offered to idols. Apollos' followers were convinced that they possessed a wisdom that was superior to anything Paul preached. Finally, the 'mystics', who claimed to follow Christ himself, insisted that they had reached a spiritual level that was superior to the other believers.

One of Paul's purposes in writing to the Corinthians was, therefore, to deal with the confusion that had arisen as a result of these divisions in the church. He knew that the answer could not be found in himself, or Peter, or Apollos, or even the kind of Christ that was being promoted. 1 Corinthians attempts to provide an answer.

Petty arguments were also a cause for division in Corinth. Some Christians were having arguments and then going to pagan courts to sort out their grievances. As well as being upset that arguments were happening at all, Paul was concerned that they were going outside the church for help.

2. To encourage the believers to avoid immorality

Paul was worried about maintaining morality in the church at Corinth. For example, it emerged that a man was having a sexual relationship with his step-mother. Paul had to warn the Corinthians about the seriousness of this sin. His main argument is that freedom in Christ does not mean freedom to be immoral.

3. To encourage order in worship

Paul wrote to stress the importance of respect and order in church worship services. For some of the believers at Corinth the agape meal, which took place alongside the Lord's Supper, had been turned into an excuse to have a party and get drunk. This was not appropriate behaviour for the celebration of the Lord's Supper.

Another problem was the Corinthians' desire for the more glamorous spiritual gifts, such as speaking in tongues. The ability to speak in tongues had led to chaos in services where people were all using their gift at the same time. Paul felt that this was definitely not the way to behave and wrote to advise the believers about how to bring more order into their worship services.

CHARACTERISTICS AND MAIN THEMES

A Personal Letter

Paul's first letter to the Corinthians is a very personal letter, probably because of the deep attachment Paul had to the Corinthians following his long stay with them (Acts 18). Foreman[3] comments that Paul had good reason to know the Corinthian church, its members and its problems. He had founded the church himself from nothing at all. The Corinthian letters were written to personal friends in a situation Paul knew very well. Paul felt a strong responsibility for their spiritual development. Prior[4] comments "because of his deep attachment to the Christians in Corinth, Paul was bound to put pen to paper when strange teachings began to divide the church."

A Pastoral Letter

"The letters to the Corinthians are long and reveal a continuing discussion, perhaps over a long period of time, between Paul and the church at Corinth."[5] 1 Corinthians stands out as being a pastoral letter and provides some very practical advice and guidance, particularly on moral issues and issues of public worship. Much of Paul's teaching is still relevant today. Another feature is that on occasion, Paul gives his own advice if he does not have a direct command from God (for example 7:25).

Theological Guidance

In 1 Corinthians Paul is interested in giving theological guidance, as well as practical advice on certain issues. Hafemann[6] comments that "it is striking that most of the commands throughout 1 Corinthians centre on some aspect of Church unity." This comes in the form of teaching on divisions (Chs 1–4); lawsuits (Ch 6); the true meaning of the Lord's Supper (Ch 11); and the unity of the Spirit (Chs 12–14).

The Corinthians are both "the temple of the Holy Spirit" (3:16–17; 14:24–25) and the "body of Christ" (6:17; 10:17; 11:29; 12:12–16, 27). While the kingdom of God has arrived, it is not yet here in all its fullness. Therefore, Paul stresses throughout this letter the importance of the Christians having control over their own moral lives.

Warnings

Warnings are another characteristic of 1 Corinthians. Paul warns the Corinthians to stand firm in their faith. He refers to "the present crisis" in Ch 7; he refers to those who oppose him and oppose his teaching; and he ends the letter with a plea to the Corinthians to "be alert, stand firm in your faith"'.

TASK

Complete the following table explaining the main themes covered in 1 Corinthians.

	Main Themes	List the issues
1 Corinthians 1–6	Chs 1–6 deal with the concerns Paul heard of independently from the Corinthian Church. He heard of these problems from "Chloe's family" (Ch 1:11). It is significant that Paul feels the need to address these issues first before considering the issues in their letter.	
1 Corinthians 7–14	Chs 7–14 deal with issues they wrote to Paul about, seeking advice.	
1 Corinthians 15	Ch 15 is Paul's response to skeptics who denied an important doctrine.	

ISSUES RAISED BY PAUL

Paul was concerned with the disturbing news that had come to him from Chloe's people concerning divisions, immorality and lawsuits. Moffat[7] explains that "the Church was in the world, as it had to be, but the world was in the church, as it ought not to be." In the first six chapters of 1 Corinthians Paul deals with this news before moving on to write an answer to the letter from the church at Corinth.

Unity (Chs 1–4)

Divisions in the Church (Ch 1:10–17)

Following Paul's greeting to the Church at Corinth and his usual thanks giving, Paul launches into the report received from Chloe's people. No information is given about Chloe, but she was probably a wealthy woman with servants. He warns them that if their quarrelling continues "outright division might be the result."[8]

Morris[9] explains that the condition of the Corinthian Church was far from what it should have been. Paul challenges the issue of disunity within the Christian community, which had arisen through preference being shown for different key figures or teachers. "Clearly the trouble was widespread, and cliques had appeared, each attaching itself to a favourite teacher."[10] These cliques or groups were refusing to have fellowship with each other and there was clear disagreement between them.

1. The Paul Party

Many of the Corinthians had become Christians through listening to Paul's preaching and as a result they were very attached to Paul. They clung on to every word he said as the ultimate truth and probably regarded other teachers as second best compared to Paul.

2. The Apollos Party

As you will remember from your AS study, Apollos came to Corinth during Paul's Third Missionary Journey (Acts 18:24–19:7). He was a very intelligent man and an excellent speaker, which explains why he, too, had a group of devoted followers. Prior[11] comments, that while Apollos probably did not stay that long in Corinth, he was there long enough for some to start comparing him favourably to Paul.

3. The Peter or Cephas Party

Peter had been a Christian longer than both Paul and Apollos. He had emerged as the leader of the twelve apostles, and in Acts we see that he seems to have been more at home with the Jewish Law than Paul. Barrett[12] argues that it seems to be generally accepted that "the Cephas-group represented Jewish Christianity in some form." The temptation to return to the law seems to have been strong among some of the Christians at Corinth. For example, in Chs 8–10, there is a debate about whether or not a Christian should eat food that has previously been offered to idols (Chs 8–10 are not part of the A2 course).

4. The Christ Party

This group of believers looked upon Christ as their only leader and they were probably opposed to any human leadership in the church. They regarded themselves as super-spiritual and their presence may have made other Christians in Corinth feel spiritually inferior.

Paul was not prepared to ignore the potential divisiveness that these groups might create. Making a strong appeal (1:10) he stresses that unity is essential to the church and develops his argument in three steps:

1. Is Christ Divided?

This is an example of a 'rhetorical' question because the Corinthians know that the answer is 'no'. Christ is no more divided than a person's body is divided. "Christ is one, and the Church, which is his body, must be one."[13]

2. Was Paul crucified for you?

Again the answer to this question is a resounding 'no'. Morris[14] explains that "the Corinthians, with their emphasis on wisdom, seem to have overlooked the truth that Christ's cross is absolutely central." Prior[15] argues that Paul is challenging the Corinthians to drop their personality cults and to fix their attention on "Jesus Christ and him crucified." It was Jesus who had died to save them; not Paul or Apollos or Peter.

3. Were you baptised in the name of Paul?

The obvious answer is again 'no'. They had obviously forgotten that they had been baptised into Jesus' name alone. Prior[16] explains that when a person was baptised in someone's name his life was regarded as being signed over to that person. Paul was simply thankful that he had carried out few baptisms in Corinth as he was adamant that Christ was central, and no individual man.

Divine and Secular Wisdom (Ch 1:18–31)

Paul continues his argument by focusing on something that the Corinthians had come to value: wisdom. Morris[17] describes this as "worldly wisdom that they so admired and that was so ineffective." It seems that by focusing on the importance of individual leaders in the church, the Corinthians were also placing more value on the wisdom of the world rather than on the wisdom of God. Prior[18] argues that to Paul "the wisdom of the world seemed to arise clearly out of man's rebellion against God." Paul not only rejected this wisdom but also the way it was proclaimed. For example, Barclay[19] explains that "the Greeks were intoxicated with fine words." Christians in Corinth were equally becoming impressed with how eloquently a leader could speak. Barrett[20] explains they were "glorying in men and wrongly evaluating their gifts." Paul valued changed lives, holiness, faith and love, not the ability to take part in vain discussion or eloquent persuasion.

Paul explains how God's wisdom seems to be beneath the sophisticated Corinthians with their worldly wisdom. The worldly-wise despised the message of the cross. The Jews regarded it as a stumbling block and the Greeks saw it as a scandal, because "cursed is everyone who hangs on a tree" (cf Gal 3:13–14). They believed it was unwise to believe that the Messiah could be crucified. Paul, however, insists that through Christ's crucifixion salvation is possible (v 18). Until the worldly-wise stop relying on their own insight they will never receive God's wisdom in Christ.

Paul illustrates God's power by reminding his readers that many of the people God had chosen were, from a worldly point of view, unimportant (v 26). Prior[21] explains that God is shunning the notion that those who matter most to him are "the wise, the well-bred, the articulate, the gifted, the wealthy, the wielders of power and influence." There is no room for pride in the Christian church. God's reason was that no one would have anything to boast about, except in the Lord (v 30).

How Paul Preached the Gospel (Ch 2:1–5)

Paul reminds his readers of his arrival at Corinth "in weakness and fear and with much trembling" (v 3). Bruce[22] explains this may have been due to "a sense of complete personal inadequacy in view of the task of evangelizing such a city as Corinth."

Paul reminds the Corinthians that when he first preached to them he did not use fine and eloquent words or philosophical arguments to try to persuade them. "It had been a plain, unvarnished setting forth of the simple gospel."[23] He simply told them about the crucifixion of Jesus, which he regarded as being at the heart of the gospel. They were convinced by what he said because "he was inspired by God, not because of his own human wisdom."[24] Prior[25] comments, that in his preaching, Paul relied completely on the power of the Spirit. Morris[26] also notes that Paul's intention had been to make the Corinthians independent of human wisdom.

The Ministry of the Spirit (Ch 2:6–13)

While Paul rejects human wisdom, he does not reject all wisdom. God's wisdom is superior to worldly wisdom. It is simply that Jesus has been crucified and has been revealed as the Son of God and the Saviour of the world. However, God's wisdom has only been revealed by the Holy Spirit[27] to those who love him. In other words "it is not the learned philosophers but the humble Christians to whom God's truth has been revealed."[28] The fact that the wisdom has been revealed prevents any feelings of superiority or pride among the believers.

Three Kinds of Men (Ch 2:14–3:4)

Paul speaks to three different kinds of men. At the lowest level is the "natural" or "unspiritual" man (2:14) who refuses to hear the gospel message. Next in line are those who are young in their Christian faith, "infants in Christ" (3:1). At the top of the scale are mature Christians. It is only to these Christians that God's wisdom can be truly revealed. The Christians at Corinth fall into the second category. They had received the Spirit, but they did not live as those who had received him.

Splitting into opposing groups to follow 'Paul' or 'Apollos' was not a spiritual activity.[29] Davies[30] explains that God's wisdom is not revealed to such people who are quarrelsome and jealous "because they have stunted their own growth by their foolishness and selfishness." Whereas Christians should be considerate of others, the Corinthians were asserting themselves and acting like the natural or unspiritual man.[31] God's wisdom is a spiritual wisdom that can only be taught by the Holy Spirit. "Maturity comes from growth and development."[32]

Example of Planting and Watering (Ch 3:5–8)

Apollos and Paul were Christ's servants, performing the tasks assigned to them. Paul uses the example of a plant. Paul planted and Apollos watered but neither of them made the plant grow. Prior[33] explains that both activities are vital and each depends on the other. However, only God enabled the plant to grow.[34] Both men need to work hard and in the end they will be rewarded. The point of these verses seems to be to play down the importance of individual leaders. Therefore the implication is that the Corinthian Christians should stop following different individuals but work together.

Example of Foundations and Buildings (Ch 3:9–17)

Paul asserts his own apostolic authority as the founder of the Church at Corinth. God enabled Paul to lay a strong foundation for a church at Corinth by proclaiming the gospel.[35] Paul himself was not the foundation stone as some thought (Paul party); rather Christ was the foundation of the church at Corinth. Paul warns that all those involved in the life of the church at Corinth were responsible for the quality of their own contribution; "warning those who are now teaching and influencing his converts that the worth of what they are doing will eventually be judged."[36]

Paul looks to the day when every Christian's work will be revealed for all to see. Prior[37] explains that it will not be a matter of how successful, or effective, or popular or commended they are by men. Will their work be shown to be what God has done through the Holy Spirit or what they have done in their own power and for their own benefit? Those who use "gold, silver and costly stones", that is quality materials, will be rewarded with profitable work. However, those who resort to using "wood, hay or straw" will achieve nothing.

A Personal Warning (Ch 3:16–17)

Thrall[38] argues that Paul probably has the different cliques in Corinth in mind in these verses. Intentional damage to the life of the church can be compared to desecrating a temple. Guilty people will be judged by God himself. Morris[39] agrees, "to engage in making divisions is ... to invite God to destroy the sinner."[40]

The foolishness of Worldly Wisdom (Ch 3:18–23)

Paul reflects upon the pretentiousness of those in Corinth who claim to have a wisdom superior to others. He reminds them of the inferiority of human wisdom. There is no place for pride in the church no matter how gifted, successful or eloquent a person might be. It is a mistake to "exaggerate the importance of one or another of the apostles and set him up on a pedestal."[41] All of the leaders, he argues, Paul, Apollos and Peter, belong to the church at Corinth. Furthermore, all the Corinthian believers belong to Christ, not just those of the 'Christ party' (1:12). They belonged to Christ, not to one of his servants. Even Christ belongs to God in the sense of being under his authority and protection (cf. 8:6; 11:3; 15:28).

Servants and Stewards (Ch 4:1–7)

"Being man-centred, the Corinthians were giving their allegiance to men, men of God, but only men".[42] Paul regards such men simply as Christ's servants and as such they are expected to be trustworthy. Paul stresses that they are not responsible to anyone but Christ for the quality of their work. Pointing to his own humble attitude regarding his own importance, Paul warns his converts "against the pride and spiritual arrogance which leads them not only to flout (ignore) an apostle of whom they disapprove but also to patronise the one whom they profess to support."[43] Paul comments that if a man deserves to be commended for his work, then the Lord will commend him.

The Christians in Corinth even saw the gifts of God as grounds for boasting.[44] It is ridiculous to take pride in one man over against another because all true ministry in the church is given by God.

The Trials endured by the Apostles (Ch 4:8–13)

Paul highlights the trials which the apostles have endured and their despised position in society. He condemns the pride and arrogant attitude of the Corinthians. The real consequences of being Christians are suffering and humiliation. This too should be the case for the Corinthians if their faith is genuine.

Fathers and Children (Ch 4:14–21)

"Paul writes as a father who is concerned for the welfare of his children."[45] He did not mean this in a dominant way, but rather that it was through him that they became Christians and he felt responsible for them. Many of the Christians in Corinth had become arrogant, dismissing Paul and his ministry and causing division in Corinth.

TASK

With reference to 1 Corinthians, critically discuss Paul's teaching on 'Unity in Christ'.

Your answer may include a critical discussion of some of the following, e.g.

- Reports from Chloe's people about the divisions in the Church at Corinth.
- Paul's own authority as an Apostle was being questioned by some in Corinth and the Church had written to Paul for advice on certain issues. 1 Corinthians is Paul's reply to these issues.
- Reasons for division: Corinth was characterised by people of many different spiritual and intellectual backgrounds. Such people had brought very different concepts and ideas into the Church. After Paul's departure, these new Christians began to divide.
- Divisions over Leadership (Chs 1–4).
- Paul's frustration over divisions regarding leadership in the Church. He encourages the Corinthians to "be completely united, with only one thought and one purpose."(Ch 1 v11)
- Four different groups. spiritual allegiance to Paul, Apollo, Cephas (Peter) and Christ. Paul knew that the answer to the Corinthians situation lay in Christ (Ch 1 v13). Paul wanted to show the Corinthians that neither he, nor Cephas, nor Apollos, nor the kind of Christ that was being followed could actually achieve any lasting result.
- The foolishness of being impressed by human wisdom.
- Law Suits: Further divisions are evident (Ch 6). Paul had heard of disputes arising between Christians and leading to the pagan courts. Paul suggests that the Church members should deal with issues within its membership since the pagan judges had no status within the Church (6:5).

Immorality (Chs 5–6)

Sexual Sin (Ch 5:1–5)

Paul turns his attention to the issue of sexual sin. While the Jews had very high standards regarding sexual morality, it was a different case in the rest of society, especially among the Greeks. It seems Paul has just heard a report of 'a particularly scandalous' incident of a sexual sin in the church at Corinth. A member of the congregation was having an affair with his stepmother. This was a form of incest that was not only condemned by the Law of Moses (Leviticus 18:8), but was prohibited by Roman law and even frowned upon by pagans. Not only had the church turned a blind eye but they did not seem bothered about it and were continuing with their superior attitude.

"Since the woman is not mentioned, she was probably not a Christian."[46] Paul insists that this man should be excommunicated because of his sin. His removal should take the form of a solemn act of excommunication at a special meeting of the church.[47] When Paul says "hand this man over to Satan, so that the sinful nature may be destroyed" (v 5) he may be implying something similar to the discipline of Ananias and Sapphira. Davies[48] argues that Paul was not being vindictive here but was calling for such harsh action for the sinner's own benefit. He explains that the man would realise the consequences of his actions, and would be more likely to repent and be restored to salvation.

Call to Clean Out All Evil (Ch 5:6–8)

Paul warns the Corinthians (v 6) that by allowing this situation to continue there was a danger that the sinner would have a bad influence on the rest of the congregation: "even if only one member of the church is involved his conduct will rapidly influence the rest, just as only a very small amount of yeast is necessary to leaven a large lump of dough."[49]

Paul continues with the example of baking. He compares the Corinthians to a new batch of dough with no yeast. However, to ensure their complete purity they must get rid of any old yeast that might still be there. Like yeast having an effect on dough, sin can spread until it affects the whole church. Now that they have become Christians and left behind their pagan ways, the Corinthians must not bring back sinful ways (the old yeast) into the church. Paul refers to Christ as the "Passover lamb" to remind the Corinthians that Christ's death was a sacrifice for them.

A Misunderstanding (Ch 5:9–13)

There seems to have been some confusion among the Corinthians concerning who they were allowed to associate with. Some thought it meant they were not allowed to mix with pagans. However, for many of the Christians, for example, slaves in pagan households or workmen, "they would lose their jobs if they took absolutely literally the injunction to have nothing to do with people who were leading immoral lives."[50] Paul explains that he meant they were to avoid professing Christians who were "sexually immoral or greedy, an idolater or a slanderer, a drunkard or a swindle" (Ch 5:11).

Sexual Immorality (Ch 6:12–20)

Some scholars argue that this passage refers to prostitution which would have been acceptable in secular society at that time. Paul, however, is shocked that Christians would think that they were allowed to be promiscuous or sexually immoral. Using the experience of the Corinthians, Paul outlines four reasons why Christians should not be sexually immoral:

1. It seems the Christians in Corinth were under the impression that being free from the law meant freedom to do whatever they liked. Paul agrees that a

Christian is free, but suggests that a genuine Christian will only act in a way that is beneficial to the Christian life. Freedom should build people up, not destroy.

2. The Corinthians thought that sexual intercourse was a natural function of the body, like eating or drinking. They completely separated sex from the spiritual life. "Since food and stomach alike will pass away, why attach religious importance to either – or, for that matter, to sexual relations?"[51] Paul argues that natural functions like eating or drinking will come to an end. However, he did not think that sex should be equated with such natural functions because sex 'involved' the body. By the word 'body' Paul included the whole personality, which he argued will continue after the body dies. "But sexual relations were on a completely different footing; they affected the personalities of the parties involved as food did not."[52] He refers to Christ's resurrection (v 14) and the eventual resurrection of Christians. God's care for the body would be shown by its resurrection. "If our bodies are to be raised, God must attach importance to actions performed in and through the body."[53] Therefore the Christian should not take part in immorality.

3. Paul stresses that Christians are united with Christ. Therefore it is outrageous to suggest that it is fine for Christians to also connect their personalities with prostitutes.

4. Finally, Paul makes the point that Christians' bodies, their whole personalities, are Temples of the Holy Spirit. Christians have given their bodies over to Christ. They now belong to Christ, not to them and as such should be treated with respect.

Lawsuits Among Believers (Ch 6:1–11)

Paul is stunned to learn that some Christians were taking other Christians to pagan courts to sue them. Paul felt so strongly about this that he suggests they should put up with injustice rather than go to pagans to sort out any disputes (v 7). Paul's words imply that surely there must be someone in the church who could sort things out (v 4). "They may not be qualified for the more serious responsibilities of church government, but they are perfectly competent to judge the trivial disputes [which] arise within the fellowship."[54] Paul regards those who cheat and do wrong as unrighteous (v 8) and reminds the Corinthians that such people will not inherit the kingdom of God.

ISSUES RAISED BY THE CORINTHIANS

"In replying to the Corinthian letter (Ch 7:1) Paul deals with a wide variety of questions, but the treatment is not haphazard."[55] He deals first with problems of social status (7:1–40), then with those arising from contact with the pagan environment (8:1–11:1 not on the A2 course), and finally with those relating to worship services (11:2–14:4). His tone and treatment are modified according to the nature of the problem.

Marriage (Ch 7:1–40)

The transition from Chapter 6 to Chapter 7 shows how Paul had to deal with two extremes. In Ch 6 he was dealing with the 'libertines' who believed that everything was allowed and had immoral views and potentially damaging views regarding sex. In Chapter 7 we see Paul dealing with the 'ascetics', who spoke against every kind of sexual relationship, even that within marriage.

Advice to the Married (Ch 7:1–7)

The sexual freedom which was part of the Corinthian way of life, and from which even the church in Corinth was not immune, made some members of the church feel that sex should be avoided altogether.[56] Murphy-O'Connor[57] explains that certain Corinthians even "idealistically believed that married couples should abstain from sexual relations." They summed up their view in the statement 'It is good for a man not to marry'. Bruce[58] explains that some of these Corinthians confidently expected Paul to agree with this. They knew of his preference for the celibate life, and thought that he would applaud this preference in his converts.

It is true that Paul seems to regard the ability to remain single as a gift from God. However, he stresses that if a Christian does not have that gift then it is better to marry. "Monogamy, he says, not celibacy, is the norm for Christians."[59] So unless a person had a special vocation for celibacy, then any attempt to try to remain celibate was against nature and would expose them to the very kind of sexual temptation which they detested.

Paul continued, stressing that within marriage a couple should fulfil each others' sexual needs. It is not fair to deprive the Christian man or wife of sex, except if both have agreed to abstain so that they can devote themselves to prayer. Paul adds that the couple should only agree to this for a time in case Satan tempts them to go looking elsewhere for sex. Paul is aware that as far as sex is concerned some people may struggle with a lack of self-control. "After the agreed period of abstinence they should resume normal relations: to adopt any other course would be to court disaster."[60]

Advice to the Unmarried (Ch 7:8–9)

Again Paul recommends the single life. However, if a person feels they cannot commit themselves to a life without sex then it is best that he or she looks for a marriage partner.

Murphy-O'Connor[61] explains: "The single have a choice, which must be based on practical consideration. Flaming frustrated passion is a hindrance to Christian living".

Divorce forbidden (Ch 7:10–11)

This advice on divorce is Paul's, not Christ's. He says Christians should simply not get divorced at all: "reconciliation, not estrangement, is the course for Christians."[62] If it does happen then remarriage should not take place as long as the divorced partner is still alive.

Mixed Marriages (Ch 7:12–16)

In Paul's time it was very common to find a Christian married to a pagan. Some Christians might have wondered if cohabitation with a pagan would pollute the faith of the Christian. Paul argues, however, that if the pagan partner is willing to stay in the marriage then the Christian should not ask for a divorce, because there was the possibility "that the pagan partner might be won for the gospel through the other's witness: such a marriage had missionary potentialities."[63] So to divorce a pagan partner is to deny them the chance of being saved. Paul also argues that continued cohabitation with a Christian would 'sanctify' the pagan and the children of such a union would share in that 'sanctification'. What do you think he means by this? It may mean that the pagan husband now belongs to God through the faith of his Christian wife and vice versa. Their children also belong to God. This highlights the importance of the Christian family for Paul.

Calling and Status (Ch 7:17–24)

Paul is stressing in these verses that a Christian should not try to change their status in life when he or she becomes a Christian. For example, if someone was a slave they should not go out of their way to become free, although if freedom is offered they should take it. It is important to realise that Paul is not supporting the system of slavery. He is simply using this as an illustration to say be content with what you have. Murphy-O'Connor[64] explains that "no change, therefore, will raise one in God's estimation."

Virgins (Ch 7:25–38)

It should be noted that this passage is dominated by the fact that Paul thought that the end of the world was going to happen within his own life time. So he is giving advice with that in mind. Therefore, he advises single people to remain single and married people not to look for a divorce. He is asking Christians to take their minds off worldly matters and to concentrate on Jesus' return. He points out that living in such times a person is at an advantage if he or she is not married. A married man, for example, has the responsibility of looking after his family. The same applies to a married woman. However, the unmarried can devote themselves to God.

Verses 36–38 are quite difficult to understand. It seems that at Paul's time there was a practice in existence where a man would marry a "spiritual bride".[65] Such an arrangement involved getting married but agreeing to abstain from sex altogether, the idea being that it was an act of self-control.

Other scholars[66] view these verses differently, arguing that they probably refer to the practice of 'betrothal'. Should a virgin who was engaged to be married stay as she was, ie not get married? After all, it was common belief that the end of the world was going to happen very soon. Paul does not pass any judgment one way or the other.

Widows (Ch 7:39–40)

Paul explains that the situation regarding remarriage is slightly different for a widow. She is not forbidden to remarry, although her new husband must also be a Christian.

 TASK

With reference to 1 Corinthians, critically discuss Paul's understanding of marriage and the single life.

Your answer may include a critical discussion of some of the following, e.g.

- Paul is replying to a letter he received from them seeking advice on issues relating to marriage.
- Paul makes it clear he favours the state of celibacy: "A man does well not to marry" (7:1); a man can give his undivided devotion to God without the distraction of a family.
- the influence of ascetics in Corinth, a group who denied themselves physical pleasures, including sexual relations. Paul disagrees, promoting marriage as a means of avoiding sexual immorality.
- Paul accepts that a couple may wish to refrain from sexual activity for a while in order to devote themselves to prayer; this should only be a temporary arrangement and is not a command from him.
- God's intention was that divorce should not occur; accepts that it does and so discourages remarriage; there should always be the hope of reconciliation.
- Advice to those Christians who have become converted whilst married and whose partner is therefore not a Christian; the Christian partner's faith will have a 'holy influence' over their non-Christian partner and any children.
- Paul regards both marriage and singleness as gifts from God.
- Paul's advice to those who believed that because they were now a Christian they had to radically change their circumstances in relation to marriage.

Worship and Lord's Supper (Ch 11:1–26)

The Veiling of women (Ch 11:1–16)

While Paul was pleased that the Corinthians had remembered to practise the teachings he had passed onto them, he was concerned, however, about another matter. It seems that a group of women were participating in the church services with their heads uncovered (11:5). In other words they were not wearing a veil which was the custom for women when they were in public. Freed[67] explains that although women were allowed to pray and prophesy in public worship, Paul's Jewish upbringing made it compulsory that they be veiled when doing so. These women may have felt that they were entitled to act like this because in Christ distinctions between male and female had been abolished (11:11–12; cf Galatians 3:28). Not only that, but since they had received the same Spirit of prophecy (11:5) as the men, they regarded themselves as equal to them. So prophesying bare headed was an expression of such perceived equality.

The problem with the behaviour of these women was related to wider society in Corinth. Their action could be interpreted by outsiders as an attempt to undermine the conventions or traditions of society, which would present the church in a negative light and bring unwelcome criticism upon it. Davies[68] explains that "it is probably true, although not stated, that for a woman not to wear a cover for her head indicated that her reputation was dubious." Guy[69] agrees, commenting that "a woman without a veil on her head would arouse suspicion on her moral character."

The reason for this is that "women's hair was a prime object of male lust in the ancient Mediterranean world; societies which employed head coverings thus viewed uncovered married women as unfaithful to their husbands, that is, seeking another man (virgins and prostitutes, conversely, were expected not to cover their heads since they were looking for men). Women who covered their heads could thus view uncovered women as a threat".[70]

Paul deals with this issue in three ways:

1. He stresses the divine pattern of relationships. Aside from the fact that in Christ there is no difference between male and female, Paul points to the fact that God is the 'head' of Christ; Christ is the 'head' of man; and man is the 'head' of women. This does not mean that one is superior over the other, but that one chooses to submit to the other. Prior[71] comments for example, "as Christ chose to submit himself to his Father, so the wife should choose to submit herself to her husband." The normal meaning of the word 'head' is origin or source. Man was created directly by God whereas woman was made from man. Man was created to reflect God's glory (11:7), whereas woman was created for man, to reflect his glory (11:7 and 9).

   Paul argues, therefore, that this order of relationships should be reflected in church worship. For a woman to abandon her head dress or veil, the symbol of her status as a woman in society, was regarded as a refusal to respect the position God had given man in creation. Not only would such action invite criticism from pagan society, but it would offend the angels who watched over the church.

2. Paul appeals to the need for respect. There should be no distractions in Christian worship.[72] It was not considered to be acceptable behaviour for a woman to "flout these standards and appear in public with her head covered."[73] Christian women were to cover their heads to ensure that there was freedom of worship for all present.

Bruce[74] further stresses that "needless breaches of convention were to be discouraged." In other words, Christians should not get people's backs up unnecessarily. They were already standing out as being different by following Christ. There was no point in them attracting negative attention. By not wearing a veil and letting her hair hang loose she would be behaving like an adulteress.[75]

Some scholars argue that Paul's words are promoting a positive reason for the wearing of the veil. He stresses that people were created to bring glory to God (11:7–10). Bruce[76] explains that in Christ a woman has received equal status with man: "she might pray or prophesy at meetings of the church, and her veil was a sign of this new authority."

Other scholars, however, feel that the wearing of the veil could be interpreted that a woman must have a sign of the authority which her husband exercises over her. Davies[77] points to the practice at Jewish weddings where the bride keeps her head uncovered, to represent the freedom which she still possesses; however, from the moment of marriage she wears a veil to show that her freedom has lessened. The action of wearing the veil is to show respect for her husband. Morris[78] explains that long hair is a glory to a woman; as well as securing her own place of dignity and authority, at the same time "she recognises her subordination."[79]

3. Paul's third argument is an appeal to nature (11:14–15). In the world at the time it was natural for a man to have shorter hair than a woman. "Generally speaking, men have reflected the distinctions made in nature by using shorter hair styles than those of women."[80] Some people wonder then why art portrays Christ and the disciples as having long hair. For example, look at DaVinci's painting of the Last Supper. However, it must have been the case in Corinth or else Paul would not have used such an argument.

Abuses during the Lord's Supper (Ch 11:17–22)

This passage focuses on abuses that were taking place during the celebration of the

Lord's Supper. Foreman[81] describes it as "a shocking and almost incredible picture of a church meeting which, Paul says, actually made the worshippers worse and not better."

Paul had heard reports that divisions were developing in the congregation at Corinth due to behaviour during the Lord's Supper. In churches today the Lord's Supper or communion (Eucharist) usually takes place as part of a normal worship service. However, in Paul's day, the celebration of the Lord's Supper was divided into two parts. The first part, which only survived for a certain length of time in the early church, was called the "love feast" or "agape meal" (Jude v 12; 2 Peter 2:13). The idea was that believers coming to worship brought food and drink along with them, which would be pooled together and shared out equally among everyone present. After this meal the second part of the celebration, the actual Lord's Supper, would take place. However, in Corinth, "when celebrating the Lord's supper some wealthy members of the church brought their own food and went off into a corner by themselves, eating and drinking in a carousing manner and ignoring those who were too poor to bring food."[82]

Murphy-O'Connor[83] explains "only the wealthier members of the community could afford to arrive early and were concerned exclusively with the gratification of their own desires. Poorer members of the community might have worked all day without eating." Davies[84] describes how some of the wealthy believers would have eaten and drunk so much that by the time it came to celebrating the Lord's Supper 'they were not in a fit state to do so.'

The result was discrimination and disorder,[85] which led to social divisions in the church. Paul could not praise them for their actions. Bruce[86] explains "selfish conduct was an outrage on the sacred occasion; those who participated in such an unworthy spirit, far from deriving any grace from their participation, were eating and drinking judgment upon themselves." Paul regards the Lord's Supper as a solemn occasion, initiated by Jesus himself in remembrance of him, and it is to be observed accordingly.[87]

The True meaning of the Lord's Supper (Ch 11:23–26)

"In order to bring the point most vividly and properly home to his people, Paul reminds them of what happened on the original occasion of the Lord's Supper."[88] Foreman[89] comments that this is "among the most cherished and familiar passages of the entire Bible." Paul gives the earliest account which we have of the institution of the communal meal.[90]

Paul's main point was made "by citing the tradition which he had received concerning the meal and which he had previously passed on to the church by word of mouth."[91] Paul reminds his readers that this teaching had been given to him from the Lord (11:23), perhaps through a vision. Whatever way it was received, Marshall[92] believes it to have been 'an accepted and authoritative tradition'.

Therefore anyone wanting to celebrate the Lord's Supper should observe it in the way that God expected.

The words of this tradition are known as 'the words of the institution.' Some scholars suggest they may in fact have been taken from the actual service used at Corinth. It provides a description of the Last Supper, which most scholars accept was the Passover meal, which was celebrated once a year by Jews to remember the deliverance of their ancestors out of Egypt. For example, during the Passover meal it was normal for thanks to be given for the food (11:24), and Jesus, acting as host, had done this. The term 'breaking of bread', which is used today by some denominations for the Lord's Supper, may originate from the words of verse 24: "and when he had given thanks, he broke it". The bread was then shared among the believers. When Jesus took bread (and wine) and distributed them to his disciples, he added that they were his "body" and "blood". The disciples were also told to repeat the practice in memory of Christ. Marshall[93] suggests that "the meal was thus intended to be a memorial of his death, through which it would be proclaimed."

OTHER ASPECTS OF HUMAN EXPERIENCE

The Meaning of communion

The words, "This is my body, which is for you", have caused much debate among scholars and theologians over the centuries as to whether Paul's teaching indicates that the Lord himself is present at the supper. Some scholars tend to find a presence of the Lord in the bread and the cup on the basis of "This is my body". This is known as 'transubstantiation' and is a belief held by the Roman Catholic Church. Protestant denominations reject this theory, arguing that the phrase means 'this is a symbol of my body'.

TASKS

1. Find out why there are different views on the words of 1 Corinthians 11:24: "and when he had given thanks, he broke it and said, This is my body, which is for you; do this in remembrance of me."

2. Using two columns, explain arguments for and against each view.

3. What is your opinion? Give reasons for your answer.

(Ch 11:27–34)

Paul's anger over the treatment of the poorer members of the congregation at Corinth was therefore justified. Jesus had given freely of himself through his death on the cross; it followed that the believers should follow his example of self-giving. "Paul warns against eating the bread and drinking the cup of the Lord in an unworthy manner."[94] Murphy-O'Connor[95] believes that "Paul has in mind the lack of loving concern for one another displayed by the Corinthians ... If participants in the eucharist meal are not united in love, they class themselves among those who murdered Jesus." Paul therefore demands the members of the church to think carefully before taking part in communion, to ensure they were not sinning against the body and blood of Christ. Unworthy conduct would bring judgement upon them.

Verse 30 suggests that such judgement could actually involve illness or even death. Morris[96] explains that "spiritual ills may have physical consequences". Foreman[97] however, argues that it is best not to take these words literally. An alternative suggestion is to interpret the verse spiritually: "some of the Corinthians are weak in soul and ill in spirit; they have taken communion in a spirit of selfish meanness, and so they have not only profaned what God has given them, they have also denied the very spirit and meaning of it all."[98]

The right action for the Corinthians, therefore, is to judge themselves before contemplating taking part in the Lord's Supper. Also, Paul stresses the need to treat each other courteously and graciously. "Church members should welcome one another when they came together for their meal... the rich should welcome the poor".[99] The rich should eat in the privacy of their own homes if they wanted to have a big meal and so avoid bringing social divisions into the church.

SPIRITUAL GIFTS (CHs 12–14)

In this section Paul deals with the division and disorder that was happening in the Church at Corinth because of the believers' obsession with the more spectacular gifts such as 'speaking in tongues' or 'glossolalia' (refer to chapter 2 of this book for a discussion on glossolalia).

Most of the Christians in Corinth had come from a pagan background, where spiritual experiences were not unusual. In their Greek mystery religions, they were well used to being moved by a supernatural force into trances. Therefore it is perhaps not surprising that when they came to the church their interest in the supernatural continued. Many of them regarded a Christian who had been blessed with the gift of tongues to be a particularly spiritual person. The Corinthians seem to have asked Paul about this (12:1) although we do not know what exactly they wanted to know.

Discerning Spiritual Utterances (Ch 12:1–3)

Paul reminds the Corinthians that no one can be a Christian without the power of the Holy Spirit. For each individual Christian, the result of the indwelling of the Spirit was evidence of a particular gift, such as the power to heal or to prophesy. Verse 3 is difficult to understand. Thrall[100] suggests that while some members of the church were in a state of supernatural inspiration, they were in the habit of shouting blasphemous phrases such as 'Jesus be cursed'.

Spiritual Gifts (Ch 12:4–11)

It seems that spiritual gifts were the cause of jealousy and envy among the congregation. "The Corinthians wanted to know which were the most important charismata, to find out, if possible, if the one they had was more important than the one that other people had."[101] Bruce[102] explains that "in the eyes of some Corinthian Christians, the most important manifestations of the indwelling of the Spirit were spectacular phenomena like speaking in tongues." Those who possessed these more supernatural gifts were being viewed by the church members as being more important than those with less striking gifts. People were starting to question their own faith if they had not been given what they thought were the greater gifts.

Speaking in tongues or 'glossolalia' was considered to be "the gift above all other gifts; if you could make that kind of noise you were obviously one of the saints."[103] So the question on everyone's lips was why do all Christians not have the gift of glossolalia, which is the most obvious sign of his presence?

Paul answered this in four ways:

1. Being preoccupied with one particular sign of the Spirit is wrong. The Spirit's presence can be seen in the variety of gifts that he gives.

2. All spiritual gifts come directly from God. The Corinthians had created division, encouraging believers to be proud if they possessed certain gifts. This led to some Christians thinking they were better than others. Paul said this was wrong. He pointed out that while there may be very different gifts, they all came from the same Holy Spirit.

3. God was the one who decided who would receive particular gifts. It was nothing to do with the Corinthians themselves. The Greek word for gifts, 'charismata' means 'gifts of grace', and that perfectly describes how the gifts were given.

4. The purpose of the gifts was for the benefit of the whole Christian community and not for personal advancement.

Gifts of the Holy Spirit

1 Corinthians 12:8–10 and 28 provides a list of the gifts of the Holy Spirit. Paul gives other lists in his letters to the Romans (12:6–8) and to the Ephesians (4:11–12). These lists vary, with the gift of prophecy common to all.

Wisdom/Knowledge	The difference between wisdom and knowledge is unclear
Faith	All Christians have faith; faith here means a special kind of faith, "the kind of faith that, when everybody else is doubting, remains staunch."[104]
Healing	
Miraculous powers	
Prophecy	Inspired speech. Prophets in the Old Testament often predicted the future, so too did those with this gift in the New Testament
Ability to distinguish between spirits	
Ability to speak in different kinds of tongues	Glossolalia, a spiritual or heavenly unintelligible language, which is different from the speaking in foreign languages in Acts Ch 2
Ability to interpret tongues	This is the gift that makes sense of the gift of tongues. It makes the meaning of a message given in tongues known to the believers.

One Body, Many Parts (Ch 12:12–26)

Paul explains his point using the human body as an illustration. He explains that God made the body with many parts, each part having its own functions to perform. The body needs all parts to work so no part is regarded as unnecessary, or less important, than another part.

Similarly, Paul argues, the church can be regarded as the body of Christ (12:12) with members representing the different parts. Just as the body does not have one body part, so too, the church is made up of people with a variety of gifts and abilities (12:28). All are necessary so no Christian should be made to feel inferior because he or she does not have the more spectacular gifts (12:15–17). Foreman[105] explains that each member of the body is useful to all the rest but in turn needs the rest. "If one organ suffers, they all suffer together. If one flourishes, they all rejoice together."[106]

The Exercise of Spiritual Gifts (Ch 12:27–31)

Paul describes the different gifts that are evident in the body of Christ (the church). "Many people have taken this to be a list in order of priority."[107] Some had the gift of apostleship; others the gift of prophecy; others teaching and so on (12:28). Clearly not everyone had the same gift. Paul's point is not that one is more important than the other, but that we aren't all apostles, all prophets; we aren't all teachers, or miracle workers.

As the Corinthians were keen to receive spiritual gifts, Paul encourages them to seek the "higher gifts", that is, gifts that would build others up in their faith. His final words introduce us to the focus of Ch 13; Paul explains that he will show the Corinthians the best way of all, that of "love".

Love (Ch 13:1–13)

1 Corinthians 13 is one of the most famous chapters of the New Testament. Harnack[108] describes it as "the greatest, strongest, deepest thing Paul has ever wrote". Davies[109] comments that "anyone who attempts to comment on this chapter of the Bible comes away feeling that he has only left the mark of soiled and clumsy hands on a thing of beauty and holiness." It is a chapter that does not call for explanation so much as illustration.[110] You may have heard it recited at a wedding you have attended, as it is a popular choice for newly weds at their marriage ceremony. The theme of the passage is 'love' and Paul includes it as part of his teaching about spiritual gifts. Bruce argues that it is an essential part of Paul's whole argument.[111]

Love is essential (Ch 13:1–3)

Paul's teaching here implies that for the Christian, love "is not a human achievement but a divine gift."[112] He knows that the Corinthians are very keen on gifts but is also aware that their enthusiasm for such gifts is to draw attention to themselves rather than edify the church as a whole. His opening words of Chapter 13 show his concern that the Corinthians are not inspired by love and that therefore their actions achieve nothing.

What love is (Ch 13:4–7)

Paul's words explain that love is not a feeling but a deliberate action which is expressed in how Christians treat others. The recent behaviour of the Corinthians stands in clear contrast to Paul's description of the outworking of such love.

TASK

Read the descriptions given below about what love is and what love is not. Complete the table using examples of:

    a. how the list might relate to the situation of the Corinthians concerning spiritual gifts

    b. where these characteristics of love are needed in the church today

What Love Is	
Patient	
Kind	
Rejoices with the truth	
Always protects	
Always trusts	
Always hopes	
Always perseveres	
Never fails	

What Love Is Not	
Does not envy	
Does not boast	
Is not proud	
Is not self-seeking	
Is not easily angered	
Keeps no record of wrongs	

Clearly there is nothing that love cannot face; there is no limit to its faith, its hope, and its endurance.[113] Paul explains that the Corinthians should be running for love as they would run for a prize. The preoccupation they had for spiritual gifts was childish (13:11), especially because gifts are only temporary and one day will no longer exist (13:8–9). Paul stresses that only faith, hope and love are permanent and of these three the greatest is love (13:13).

OTHER ASPECTS OF HUMAN EXPERIENCE

Love

Some people regard true Christian love as going further than the love of one person for another. That love should mean that Christian communities should respect other Christian communities – be willing to learn from them, pray for them and seek the best for them.

In light of these comments, find out what you can about inter-church and inter-faith contacts and explain how Paul's principle of love can be seen in their work.

Gifts of Prophecy and Tongues (Ch 14:1–33)

In this chapter Paul appears to be playing down the importance of the gift of speaking in tongues. He comments that it is a useful gift to those who possess it, but not of much use to the rest of the church. Paul regards prophecy as a much more important gift. Thrall[114] explains that prophecy corresponds quite closely to our idea of preaching. A prophet is inspired by the Holy Spirit to deliver a message to the church which should encourage believers or even convince unbelievers of the truth of the gospel.

Gifts of Prophecy and Tongues (Ch 14:1–12)

Paul compares speaking in tongues to a musical instrument that "makes unrelated and meaningless sounds instead of playing a proper melody."[115] Paul suggests that those with the gift of tongues should realise that their gift is merely an individual religious experience that would be best practised in private. Prophecy stands poles apart from tongues. It can be described as a direct line of communication between God and his followers.

Tongues Must Be Interpreted (Ch 14:13–19)

Paul's criticism of tongues indicates that the Corinthians attached undue importance to this gift. "The mysterious babble of unintelligible sounds was seen as the clearest sign of possession by the Spirit and so offered enhanced social prestige."[116] However, Murphy-O'Connor[117] points out that although audible, glossolalia is intelligible only to God, the author of the gift.[118] Speaking in tongues is only useful, Paul argues, if there is someone who can interpret what is being said. "Tongues can make a contribution to the community provided they are accompanied by the exercise of the mind, which makes them intelligible."[119] Furthermore, every church member should be able to feel part of the worship service. Speaking in tongues without interpretation prevents this.

273

Bruce concludes that "only when an interpreter was available would glossolalia be helpful to an assembled congregation; otherwise its value was confined to private devotion."[120]

A Sign for Unbelievers (Ch 14:20–25)

Bruce[121] explains that "prophecy is a sign for believers in the sense that it produces believers; the unbeliever or outsider who would be put off by an outburst of tongues will be impressed if, on entering a church meeting, he hears all the members speaking words in a language he knows, which pierce direct to his heart and conscience, expose his inmost secrets, and convict him of sin." In other words a Gentile visitor to the church might think someone who is speaking in tongues is completely mad, especially if more than one person is speaking in tongues at the same time. "Prophetic utterance, on the other hand, may move a non-Christian visitor to repentance and belief in God."[122]

Orderly Worship (Ch 14:26–33)

It was foolish for too many members of the church to concentrate on the exercise of speaking in tongues "when so many more gifts, some of them obscure and unspectacular but none the less valuable, were needed for the common good."[123] However, for those who were determined to speak in tongues, Paul advises that at least it should be in an orderly manner. It seems that up until now Corinthian members of the church were free to contribute to the church service as the spirit moved them. But this freedom was causing chaos and confusion. Paul suggested therefore, that only two speakers or at most three should take part, and that each should have their own turn. Afterwards each should be interpreted. If there is no one available to interpret then speaking in tongues, it should be kept for private devotion. All things were to be done to build the people up in their faith.

Paul also argued that prophecy should be carried out in an orderly manner. Only two or three prophets should speak and there should be time to digest what is being said. If someone sitting in the congregation receives a message from God then whoever is speaking at the front should graciously step aside and allow them to speak.

The Role of Women (Ch 14:33–36)

These verses are difficult to follow when they are compared with Ch 11:5, where Paul says "and every woman who prays or prophesies with her head uncovered dishonours her head". The implication here is that it is fine for a woman to pray or prophesy in public worship as long as her head is covered. However, Ch 14:34–35 seems to suggest that women should not speak at all! Some scholars think that Paul is simply warning about needless chatter in the worship service. Thrall,[124] for example, believes "Paul is referring not to a woman's exercise of the gift of prophecy, which he did not forbid, but to the practice of women joining in congregational discussion of what a prophet or a teacher had said." Their lack of self-discipline was "causing confusion and disorder in the worship of the church."[125] Bruce simply sees Paul "forbidding them to interrupt proceedings by asking questions."[126] Whatever way you wish to interpret these verses it is perhaps wise to follow Morris' advice, to "take due caution in applying his principle to our own very different situation."[127]

Summing Up (Ch 14:37–40)

Paul claims to have the Lord's authority for what he has written. Again he encourages the gift of prophecy, although it is important to note that while he is not keen on the gift of speaking in tongues, he does not forbid it.

 PRACTICE ESSAY TITLES

1. **Critically discuss Paul's teaching in 1 Corinthians on the use of Spiritual Gifts.**

   A critical discussion may include some of the following, for example:
   - Importance of these chapters, which provide an insight into Church worship in the first century.
   - Disorder arising in the Corinthian Church, causing divisions due to the preoccupation with certain gifts.
   - The pagan background of the Corinthian Christians; supernatural experiences were the norm; valued such experiences as the sign of true spirituality.
   - Paul makes it clear that the possession of a gift is not the true sign of a 'genuine believer' – instead it is the proclamation of the Lordship of Christ.
   - Christians were setting one believer against another depending on the possession of this or that gift. Paul denounces this disunity and points out that the preoccupation with supernatural gifts is to restrict the spirit's power and activity.
   - The spirits power is shown in diversity – there are many gifts. It is God who decides who receives what gift. To question why a believer does not have a gift is therefore to question God.
   - Paul outlines the variety of gifts; wisdom, knowledge, faith, healing, miracles, speaking God's message, interpreting between gifts of the spirit and gifts not of the spirit, tongues, interpretation of tongues.
   - The purpose of these gifts is to benefit the whole Christian community, not for individual personal advancement.
   - The analogy of the human body to show how all the gifts used together can benefit the Church and work as God intended.

- Paul concentrates on the two gifts of prophecy and speaking in tongues, and clearly favours prophecy because it can be understood and because it edifies. Paul points out that tongues are useless unless accompanied by the gift of interpretation.
- The Christian life is not merely an emotional exercise – there is a place for enthusiasm but one should also use ones intellect; the example of singing and prayer; both must be done intelligently with the use of the mind.
- Paul's main principle is that Church worship should be orderly.
- He gives practical advice to curb the use of tongues when he suggests that only two or three people should speak in tongues in a service and only if there is an interpreter.

2. **Critically evaluate the view that this letter offers guidance for Christians in the modern world.**

   A critical evaluation of the view may include some of the following, eg:
   - In his first century letter Paul is writing to a particular Church in a specific situation and context. Some issues to which Paul refers are cultural and of his time (head covering) and therefore not immediately relevant to today.
   - He is replying to queries they have raised with him on a number of issues. Despite this there are principles which should apply to the Church today as much as the Corinthian Church; important teachings and principles which transcend time and culture, and speak to us today.
   - Morality: Paul emphasises the need to guard against sexual immorality. The Christian Church today must not tolerate any immorality from within its membership but must take appropriate action. Refer to attitudes to many sexual partners/homosexuality/Aids. The church must not give in or weaken towards more liberal attitudes but must guard against sexual immorality. Give examples.
   - Sanctity of marriage: Paul upholds the sanctity of marriage in this letter; defends the rightful use of the act of sexual intercourse within marriage; and emphasises the dependency of man and wife. Relevant for today's Church, where marriage break ups are on the increase; adultery is common; 'living together' is much more acceptable in today's society. The Church must not feel under pressure to give in to pressure from society to lower its standards. Refer to attitudes to marriage today (divorces are common/gay marriage/attitude to monogamy). Church must promote the sacredness of marriage in light of these attitudes.
   - Respect for the body: Paul emphasises that our bodies belong to God and are temples of the Holy Spirit. Relevance for the issues of drugs, abortion, eating disorders.
   - Church worship: Paul's advice that everything must be done in a proper and orderly way, especially concerning the more spectacular spiritual gifts. Such gifts are still in use in charismatic churches today, so advice is relevant. Charismatic/Pentecostal

churches today can take heed from Paul's teaching regarding gifts. Need to recognise that the over-exaggerated use of the gifts can weaken worship or set believers against each other.

- The principle can be applied to all worship. Give examples.
- Divisions: there are frequently divisions and frictions which affect churches and congregations today, making worship and fellowship difficult. Churches reminded of our unity in Christ and under the one, unifying spirit.

Endnotes

[1] Davies, RE, *Studies in 1 Corinthians*, London: The Epworth Press, 1962; p17 tells us that Chloe was a leading lady in the church at Corinth.

[2] Morris, L, *1 Corinthians*, Revised Edition, Leicester: IVP, 1996, p25

[3] Foreman, KJ, Romans, *Corinthians, Layman's Bible Commentaries*, London: SCM Press Tld, 1961, p6262

[4] Prior, D, *The Message of 1 Corinthians, BST*, Leicester: IVP, 1993, p17

[5] Freed, *op cit*, p64

[6] Hafemann, SJ, Letters to the Corinthians, in *Dictionary of Paul and His Letters*, ed. Hawthorne, GF, Martin RP and Reid, DG, Leicester: IVP, 1993, p178

[7] Moffat, J, *The First Epistle of Paul to the Corinthians*, London: Hodder & Stoughton, 1943, pxv

[8] Bruce, FF, *The New Century Bible Commentary*, I and II Corinthians, London: WM B Eerdmans Publishing Co., Grand Rapids, 1992, p32

[9] Morris, *op cit*, p39

[10] *ibid*, p40

[11] Prior, *op cit*, p32

[12] Barrett, CK, *A Commentary on the First Epistle to the Corinthians*, London: A & C Black, 1968, p44

[13] Morris, *op cit*, p41

[14] *ibid*, p41

[15] Prior, *op cit*, p36

[16] *ibid*, p37

[17] Morris, *op cit*, p43

[18] Prior, *op cit*, p40

[19] Barclay, W, *The Letters to the Corinthians, The Daily Study Bible*, Edinburgh: The Saint Andrew Press, 1954, p22

[20] Barrett, *op cit*, p59

[21] Prior, *op cit*, p46

[22] Bruce, *op cit*, p37

[23] Morris, *op cit*, p50

[24] Thrall, ME, *I & II Corinthians, The Cambridge Bible Commentary*, Cambridge: the Cambridge Univrsity Press, 1986, p23

[25] Prior, *op cit*, p49

[26] Morris, *op cit*, p52

[27] 'The work of the Holy Spirit is stressed repeatedly in chapter 2.' Prior, p49.

[28] *ibid*, p56

[29] Bruce, *op cit*, p42

[30] Davies, *op cit*, p25

[31] Morris, *op cit*, p62

[32] *ibid*, p61

[33] Prior, *op cit*, p57

[34] Morris, *op cit*, p63

[35] Thrall, *op cit*, p31

[36] *ibid*, p32

[37] Prior, *op cit*, p59

[38] Thrall, *op cit*, pp32–33

[39] Morris, *op cit*, p67

[40] The Corinthian church was a temple that God's Spirit indwelt. Paul was not speaking here of individual believers being temples of God, although he later refers to individual Christians as such (6:19).

[41] Thrall, *op cit*, p33

[42] Prior, *op cit*, p62

[43] Thrall, *op cit*, p35

[44] Prior, *op cit*, p64

[45] Thrall, *op cit*, p37

[46] Murphy-O'Connor, J, *The First Letter to the Corinthians in The New Jerome Biblical Commentary*, ed. by Brown, RE, Fitzmyer, JA and Murphy, RE, London: Geoffrey Chapman, p803

[47] Bruce, *op cit*, p54

[48] Davies, *op cit*, p50

[49] Thrall, *op cit*, p41

[50] *ibid*, pp41–42

[51] Bruce, *op cit*, p63

[52] *ibid*, p63

[53] Murphy-O'Connor, *op cit*, p804

[54] Bruce, *op cit*, p60

[55] Murphy-O'Connor, *op cit*, p804

[56] Bruce, FF, *Paul, Apostle of the Free Spirit*, Exeter: The Paternoster Press, 1977, p266

57 Murphy-O'Connor, *op cit*, p804

58 Bruce, *op cit*, p267

59 *ibid*, p267

60 *ibid*, p267

61 Murphy-O'Connor, *op cit*, p804

62 Bruce, *op cit*, p268

63 *ibid*, p268

64 Murphy-O'Connor, *op cit*, p805

65 Davies, *op cit*, p57

66 For example, Bruce, *op cit*, p76

67 Freed, *op cit*, p79

68 Davies, *op cit*, p76

69 Guy, *op cit*, p104

70 Keener, CS, Man and Woman, in *Dictionary of Paul and his Letters*, ed. by Hawthorne, GF, Martin, RP, and Reid DG, Leicester: IVP, 1993, p585

71 Prior, *op cit*, p181

72 *ibid*, p181

73 Bruce, *op cit*, p107

74 *ibid*, p107

75 Prior, *op cit*, p181

76 Bruce, *op cit*, p106

77 Davies, *op cit*, p76

78 Morris, *op cit*, p154

79 Note that Paul in this passage is speaking about veils and not hats.

80 Morris, *op cit*, p154

81 Foreman, *op cit*, p95

82 Freed, *op cit*, p79

83 Murphy-O'Connor, *op cit*, p809

84 Davies, *op cit*, p78

85 Guy, *op cit*, p105

86 Bruce, *op cit*, p265

87 Freed, *op cit*, p79

88 Davies, *op cit*, p78

89 Foreman, *op cit*, p76

90 Bruce, *op cit*, p265

91 Marshall, IH, Lord's Supper, in *Dictionary of Paul and his Letters*, ed. by Hawthorne, GF, Martin, RP, and Reid DG, Leicester: IVP, 1993, p572

92 *ibid*, p572

93 *ibid*, p572

94 Foreman, *op cit*, p96

95 Murphy-O'Connor, *op cit*, p810

96 Morris, *op cit*, p161

97 Foreman, *op cit*, p97

98 *ibid*, p97

99 Marshall, *op cit*, p572

100 Thrall, *op cit*, p86

101 Davies, *op cit*, p30

102 Bruce, *op cit*, p272

103 Davies, *op cit*, p32

104 Davies, *op cit*, p31

105 Foreman, *op cit*, p100

106 Davies, *op cit*, p33

107 *ibid*, p34

108 Harnack, A, cited in Morris, *op cit*, p176

109 Foreman, *op cit*, p101

110 *ibid*, p101

111 Bruce, *op cit*, p117

112 Davies, *op cit*, p35

113 Davies, *op cit*, p36

114 Thrall, *op cit*, p97

115 *ibid*, p99

116 Murphy-O'Connor, *op cit*, p811

117 *ibid*, p811

118 and so is different from the foreign languages of Acts 2:2–11.

119 *ibid*, p811

120 Bruce, *op cit*, p272

121 *ibid*, p133

122 Thrall, *op cit*, p100

123 Bruce, *op cit*, p273

124 Thrall, *op cit*, p102

125 Prior, *op cit*, p252

126 Bruce, *op cit*, p135

127 Morris, *op cit*, p197

Paul in Acts and Letters

INTRODUCTION

In this chapter we will be looking at how the apostle Paul is portrayed in the book of Acts compared to his own writings. In particular we will be focusing on the personality of Paul and his teaching on the Resurrection.

THE PERSONALITY OF PAUL: THE PAUL OF ACTS AND THE PAUL OF THE LETTERS

"There are two main sources for our knowledge of Paul – his own writings and the Acts of the apostles."[1] These two sources appear to be completely independent of each other because "the apostle portrayed in Acts is very different to the one who emerges from his letters."[2] Acts tells us the story of Paul's conversion, missionary journeys and journey to Rome; whereas "he is in fact one of the great letter writers of world literature."[3] Most scholars agree that the writer of Acts makes no use of Paul's letters in composing Acts, even though his letters would have been in existence. Packer[4] explains that "... the differences between Acts and Paul's letters could indicate that Acts was written much later."

However, the differences between Acts and Paul's letters are so great in places that there has been some doubt over the portrayal of Paul in Acts. Some scholars even oppose the "view that the author of Acts was a close companion of Paul."[5] Hanson[6] comments that it has been suggested that nobody who knew Paul at all well, who knew his convictions and his teaching, could draw the picture of Paul that Acts draws.

Other scholars, for example, Bruce,[7] argue that although these two main sources for our knowledge about Paul appear to be independent of each other, there are impressive parallels between their respective portrayals of Paul. In this chapter we will be looking at both sides of the argument.

You might ask why scholars accept the portrayal of Paul in his own letters over that of his portrayal in Acts. The reason for this is, of course, that Paul's letters are actual first-hand eyewitness accounts of his own life and views. Acts, on the other hand, is at best a third or fourth hand account by an author writing, almost half a century after the events, with his own purposes in writing in mind.

What is a discrepancy?

A discrepancy can be described as an 'inconsistency', a 'difference' or a 'disagreement'. For our purpose it means a difference between facts and observations in Acts and Paul's letters. Before moving on to look at the personality of Paul, it might be useful to look at some general discrepancies between Acts and Paul's letters to help you understand the concept.

For example, Acts and Paul's letters differ over how many visits Paul made to Jerusalem following his conversion. Acts mentioned five visits to Jerusalem by Paul while the letters only assume three such visits.

 TASK

Compare Acts 9, 11, 15, 18:22, 21 with Galatians 1:18, 2:1 and the (planned) visit to Jerusalem in Romans 15:25.

According to Acts Paul had already been to Jerusalem twice (Acts 9, 11) before the Jerusalem Council (Acts 15). However, according to his letter to the Galatians, Paul had only been to Jerusalem once (Galatians 1:18) before the Council (Galatians 2:1). This sort of discrepancy has caused much speculation and debate among scholars.

Another example concerns the differences between Acts 15 and Galatians 2. In Galatians 2:1–3, Paul speaks of a second visit to Jerusalem, which focused on the issue of circumcision. Many scholars believe that visit is a description of the Council of Jerusalem, which is described in Acts 15, arguing that there are striking similarities between the two accounts. Other scholars disagree with this because they feel there are too many discrepancies between the accounts. In fact, Stein[8] records that there are at least eight different ways in which scholars have sought to relate the two sets of accounts:

1. Galatians 2 = Acts 15
2. Galatians 2 = Acts 11
3. Galatians 2 = Acts 11 = Acts 15 (Luke may have reported the same event twice)
4. Galatians 2 = Acts 18
5. Galatians 2 = Acts 15:1–4
6. Galatians 2 = Acts 11 + Acts 15 (Luke may have misinterpreted what happened in the visit of Galatians 2 and reported what happened on this occasion as occurring at two separate occasions)
7. Galatians 2 is not reported in Acts
8. Galatians 2 = Acts 9

Of these views the three that are the most probable are: 1, 2, and 6.

Of course you will not need to know this detail for your A2 examination. These theories are merely listed here to illustrate that there are discrepancies between Acts and Paul's letters. The focus of our study is how Paul's personality is portrayed in Acts compared with 1 Corinthians and Galatians. At times, mention may be made to some of Paul's other letters to explain a certain point more fully.

Paul's self-image

Bruce[9] describes Paul as Luke's hero. He emerges as a strong leader who dominates most of the narrative in Acts. Luke records Paul's successful missionary journeys, his charisma, his ability to keep going when trouble emerges, and his consistent determination to reach Rome. However, "if he was a hero to Luke, Paul was no hero in his own eyes." His letters show continual attack from his opponents regarding his apostolic authority; at times he did assert his authority (Galatians 1–2) but it has been suggested that he found it easier to do this by letter from a distance than in word spoken face to face.[10]

Paul the missionary

We have complementary information concerning aspects of Paul's missionary activities in both his letters and Acts. For example, in both sources Paul supports himself by his own work so as not to be a financial burden to his friends and converts.[11] And in both sources Paul is portrayed as taking the gospel to the Jews first (Acts 13:14, 14:1, 17:1, 17:10, 17:17, 18:4, 18:19, 19:8; Romans 1:16). However, there are other more prominent aspects of Paul's missionary career where there are discrepancies between the two sources. These discrepancies are particularly evident when we look at Paul's gift of public speaking and his miracles.

Paul as an outstanding speaker

In Acts Paul is presented everywhere as an outstanding speaker. "Whether he speaks before Jews or Gentiles, governors or philosophers (Acts 17:22–31), he is never at a loss for the right word. He is a born orator."[12]

 TASK

Look at the following references and explain how they present Paul as being an outstanding speaker:
- Acts 24:1–21
- Acts 21:40–22:21

In the letters the impression given of Paul's ability to speak is the exact opposite to that given in Acts. For example, Paul describes his opponents' criticism of him in 2 Corinthians 10:10: "His letters are weighty and strong, but his bodily presence is weak, and his speech of no account."

However, the charge that Paul was a poor speaker was made by opponents who compared him to Apollos, who was an outstanding speaker. This does not necessarily mean that Paul was a poor speaker in his own right. Both Acts and the letters show Paul to be an educated 'man of the world', a loyal Jew, and someone that others have strong feelings about. Evidently in Galatians and 1 Corinthians Paul's strength is seen more in his skill as a letter writer than a speechmaker.

Paul as Miracle Worker

In Acts miracles are reported as part of Paul's missionary work. The miracles Luke attributes to Paul include:

- Healing of the blind man (Acts 13:6–12),
- Healing of the lame man (Acts 14:8–10)
- Raising of a young man from the dead (Acts 20:7–12).
- Even his handkerchief had miraculous powers (Acts 19:12)
- His miraculous powers which enabled him to survive stoning unharmed (Acts 14:19–20)
- His power to survive what should have been a lethal snakebite (Acts 28:3–6).

Paul himself makes little of his own miracles in his letters. Paul uses vague terms like "signs of the Apostle" (2 Corinthians 12:12), "demonstration of the Spirit and of power" (1 Corinthians 2:4) and 'the power of signs and wonders' (Romans 15:18 –19). Paul's tone in making these comments was generally defensive, in that they were made against some accusations of his opponents. In 2 Corinthians 12:12, it seems that

Paul's opponents are critical that he had performed few and unimpressive miracles.

However, in the letters, Paul is writing many years after his missionary work with the congregations in question. Therefore, there is no need to bring up the miracles he has performed, which, in any case, not even Acts says were performed in every place Paul visited.

Paul as a Loyal and Practising Jew

In Acts, although Paul is presented as being the missionary to the Gentiles, he is also portrayed as a loyal and practising Jew. Vielhauer[13] summarises this portrayal of Paul with eight examples:

1. Paul's missionary activity in a new location often begins with preaching at the synagogues (Acts 13:14, 14:1, 17:1, 17:10, 17:17, 18:4, 18:19, 19:8)
2. He submits to the Jerusalem authorities (Acts 9:26, 15:2)
3. He has Timothy circumcised (Acts 16:3)
4. He preaches the apostolic decree (Acts 16:4)
5. He assumes a vow (Acts 18:18)
6. He makes trips to Jerusalem for Jewish religious festivals (Acts 18:21, 20:16)
7. He participates, on the advice of James, in a Nazarite vow (Acts 21:18–28)
8. He stresses his Pharisee credentials during his trial and asserts that he preaches merely the 'resurrection': something the Pharisees already believed (Acts 23:6–8, 26:2–5)[14]

Clearly in these examples, Luke presents a positive picture of Paul's attitude towards the Law and his continued adherence to it. Guy[15] agrees, pointing out that "in Acts he appears to be more conciliatory towards the Judaisers, who wished to make the Gentile converts conform to the Jewish Law, than he is in his letter to the Galatians where he is very stern in his denunciation of the false brethren." In some of Paul's other letters, too, he shows his disdain for those who followed the Law. For example, in Philippians 3:5–9 we see how he abandoned his former Pharisaic zeal for righteousness based on the Law and counted everything as "loss" and "refuse", finding salvation solely in faith in Christ.[16]

Paul and circumcision ("all things to all men")

Another area where the accounts in Acts seem to contradict Paul's own opinion is in the area of circumcision. Hanson[17] points out, for example, that Luke represents the question of circumcision as having been solved once and for all at the Apostolic Council described in Acts 15, when in fact Paul had to fight for his principles throughout the whole of his career. Fernando[18] agrees: "his letters show him in constant conflict with those who resisted the free admission of the Gentiles to the church, whereas in Acts the problem is largely settled in chapter 15 and not mentioned again."

Another example which illustrates the differences between Acts and letters concerns the circumcision of Timothy. In Acts 16:1–3, Paul has Timothy circumcised to avoid problems for his mission with the Jews in the region. "It is alleged that the Paul of the letters, who spoke so strongly against circumcision, could not have done this."[19] This action certainly does not tie in with what Paul says about circumcision in Galatians 2:1–6. Paul tells us that he took Titus, an uncircumcised Greek, to Jerusalem during the meeting on the very issue of circumcision for non-Jewish Christians; that he stood his ground before the apostles and that Titus was not circumcised.

However, the matter of Timothy's circumcision goes back to the marriage of Timothy's Jewish mother to his Greek father. Some Jews in this region married into dominant Gentile families, and though the practice was rare, it "still took place often enough."[20] It is generally accepted therefore that the circumcision of Timothy was a gesture of concession to the Jewish community. Timothy, whose father was Greek, would be considered an offence and an apostate Jew, therefore the circumcision was done to facilitate missionary work among the Jews.[21]

In his letters Paul strongly objects to those who demand circumcision as a sign of salvation. Although, Fernando also points out that "the Paul of Acts also considered the circumcision issue so important that he made the long trip to Jerusalem to battle the Judaisers".[22] It seems that "the apostle did not object to circumcision as a Jewish rite ... but when circumcision was presented as a means of salvation, he strongly opposed it."[23]

So he has no problem at all with those who practise circumcision, and the other Jewish laws, as a matter of ancestral tradition and culture.[24] And this is what the circumcision of Timothy was about, showing respect for traditions so as not to cause offence among those who still held them in high esteem. It could be argued that Paul only circumcised Timothy in order to win the Jews for Christ.

To further explain this some scholars refer to 1 Corinthians 9:19–23 which shows that by practising circumcision on occasion Paul is simply being "all things to all people". In 1 Corinthians 7:17–20, Paul explains that he does not expect a Jew or a Gentile to totally abandon their way of life in order to live as a Christian.

Clearly the letters present Paul as a very flexible person. Bruce[25] argues that this quality is also evident in Acts too: "In Acts, Paul is the most adaptable of all people. He is equally at home with Gentiles and religiously observant Jews." For example, Fernando[26] points to his decision to participate in a purification rite in the Jerusalem temple, pointing out that it is in keeping with his teaching in the letters about becoming a Jew in order to win the Jews (1 Cor 9:20).

Paul and his apostolic authority

In Acts, the office of 'apostle' is presented as one which could only be given to someone who was one of the twelve; and who had been with Jesus when he was alive. This is made very clear in Acts 1:21–25 in Peter's speech before they chose a replacement for Judas.

Later in Acts the criteria for apostleship is extended to include that of *"having eaten and drank with the risen Jesus"* (Acts 10:41). Even Paul accepts that this is confined only to those who came with the earthly Jesus from Galilee and experienced his resurrection (Acts 13:30–31). Most scholars agree that in Acts, Luke is generally consistent in not applying the title of 'apostle' to Paul.

Hanson[27] argues that in Acts, Luke "takes no account of Paul's passionately held conviction that he was an apostle, as much an apostle as Peter and James and John." For example, Acts 1:21ff and 10:39, do not include Paul in the group of original witnesses to the resurrection or among the disciples.

However, it must be pointed out that in Acts, no one is accusing Paul of making up his apostolic credentials. By the time Acts is written, the problem of his credentials, by Luke's perspective, has already been solved and Paul is clearly presented as Luke's hero. The situation is very different in Paul's letters, which are written in the heat of controversy concerning his apostolic authority. Paul addresses the problem of attacks on his authority specifically. He makes much of his status as an apostle in his letters, whereas Luke only calls him an 'apostle' twice, both times in chapter 14.
In his letters it is evident that Paul desperately wants himself to be called an apostle. In 1 Corinthians 9:1–3, for example, it reads:

"Am I not free? Am I not an apostle? Have I not seen the Lord? Even though I may not be an apostle to others, surely I am to you!"

In Galatians 2:8, Paul considers himself to be an equal apostle to Peter:

"For he who worked through Peter making him an apostle to the circumcised also worked through me in sending me to the Gentiles.'"

Guy argues that this account shows that the conflict between Paul and Peter was a bitter one, of which there is no suggestion at all in the Acts, where Peter is made to agree with Paul's point of view wholeheartedly (v 10).[28]

Paul's Relationship with the Apostles

There are three incidents in particular where Acts presents Paul as having great respect for the apostles:

1. In Acts 9:26–28, we are told that almost immediately after his conversion, Paul went to Jerusalem to meet with the apostles:

   "And when he came to Jerusalem, he attempted to join the disciples; and they were all afraid of him, since they did not believe he was a disciple. But Barnabas took him and brought him to the Apostles, and declared to them how he had seen the Lord on the road and that he had spoken to him, and how in Damascus he had preached boldly in the name of Jesus. And he was with them going in and out of Jerusalem, preaching

boldly in the name of the Lord".

2. In Paul's speech at Pisidian Antioch (Acts 13:29–32) he announces that:

"He [Jesus] appeared during many days to those who came up with him from Galilee to Jerusalem, who are his witnesses to the people."

By describing those who came up with Jesus from Galilee to Jerusalem as the main witnesses, it could be argued that the Paul of Acts is excluding himself from this exalted group.

3. In Acts 15:1–2, the church at Antioch decided to send Paul, Barnabas and some others to resolve the issue regarding circumcision. It could be argued that this shows the submission of the Christians at Antioch, including Paul, to the authority of the Jerusalem apostles.

However, in his letters, Paul is keen to assert his apostolic authority as independent from the Jerusalem apostles:

1. In Galatians 1:16–19, Paul says he did not go to Jerusalem immediately after his conversion, but went to Arabia. It was only after three years that he first went to Jerusalem as a Christian. When he was there he met only Peter and James. This contradicts what we are told in Acts 9:26–28, which shows Paul eagerly going to Jerusalem to meet the apostles and actually preaching with them.

2. 1 Corinthians 9:3 and Galatians 2:8 show that Paul considered himself equal to the apostles in Jerusalem and that his witness to the resurrection was equal to theirs. (Compare with Acts 13:29–32.)

3. In Galatians 2:6, when referring to the leaders in Jerusalem, Paul comments:

"And from those who were supposed to be acknowledged leaders (what they actually were makes no difference to me; God shows no partiality) – those leaders contributed nothing to me."' The tone of these verses almost suggests scorn for the Apostles on Paul's part. As far as Paul is concerned his gospel message is independent of that of the Jerusalem leaders.[29]

Paul's Theology

Vielhauer's paper 'On the Paulinism of Acts', exposes serious discrepancies between the theology of Paul as it is presented in Acts and in Paul's own letters. The following areas are the main issues of Paul's theology:

Natural Theology

Paul's only sermon to the Gentiles in Acts is the one at the Areopagus (Acts 17:22–31). He praises the Athenians for being so religious (17:22) and he tells them that mankind was created to seek God (17:27); that all humanity "live and move" and have their being in the divine; and that everyone is "God's offspring" (17:28).

In his letters, Paul also acknowledges that man has a natural knowledge of God (Romans 1:19). But rather than claiming that this makes man religious, as in Acts 17:22, this knowledge led to ungodliness and wickedness (Romans 1:18) which brings God's anger. Crowe[30] explains the discrepancy here with Acts. In Romans Paul writes of the widespread immorality of the pagans as God's punishment for their refusal to worship him. However, in Paul's speech at Athens he claims that God has "overlooked the times of ignorance" in the past and concedes that pagans have indeed "been worshipping the true God, even though they did not know him."

Therefore, on the one hand we have Paul in Acts saying that mankind can reach some relationship and knowledge of God by independent, natural means. On the other hand, the Paul of letters would never say such a thing. Man is separated from God and only through Christ could he be reconciled back to the divine.[31]

Paul and the Law

Unlike Paul's letters, Acts presents him as a Jewish Christian who was observant of Jewish law.[32] Acts 13:38–39 is the exception and some scholars argue that there is evidence in these verses of Paul's theology as found in his letters.

However, there are some contradictions with Paul's arguments concerning forgiveness and justification in his letters:

- The phrase "forgiveness of sins" is not to be found in the genuine Pauline letters.

- Paul of letters usually talks about sin in the singular, which he looks upon as a kind of power, for example:
  1. Romans 6:23 ("for the wages of sin is death")
  2. Romans 3:9 ("both Jews and Greeks are under the power of sin ...")
  3. 1 Corinthians 15:56 ("The sting of death is sin")

- Forgiveness is linked to Jesus being the Messiah, which is based on the resurrection. There is no mention in Acts that Jesus' death itself had any redemptive significance.[33]

Justification by Faith

Fernando[34] comments that "the strong emphasis on the atoning death of Christ and justification by faith that is found in the Paul of letters is said to be missing in the Paul of Acts." However, Robertson argues that there is some evidence of it in Paul's speech at Pisidian Antioch.[35] Fitzmyer[36] agrees, emphasising that "it is the only time in Acts, when Paul's teaching about justification by faith is mentioned, the topic that is prominent in his letters to the Galatians and Romans."

It must be pointed out that Fernando[37] concedes that while justification by faith in Christ and the message of the cross are not given as much emphasis in Paul's speeches as they receive in the letters, "these teachings are always implied" (13:38 –39; 20:17–38). Examples are:

- justification and the inability to be justified by the Law of Moses (v 39)
- death on a tree (v 29)
- sin (v 38),
- grace (v 43) – Paul was addressing the Galatians at this time

Stott[38] observes that these ideas provide the foundation stone to his letter to the Galatians, which he would write a few months later. You will recall from Chapter 8 of this book how Paul's views on justification and forgiveness apart from the Mosaic Law are well developed in his letter to the Galatians. He probably wrote Galatians shortly after he completed his first missionary journey to the same people he spoke to here at Pisidian Antioch. "So we do not need to assume, as some do, that the Paul of Acts could not have written letters like Galatians and Romans."

Christology

Acts is seriously lacking on any statements regarding Christology ('the person of Christ'). There is only really one occasion where it is touched upon. In Acts 13:13–43, Paul claims that Jesus' crucifixion was a result of a mistake committed by the people of Jerusalem (13:28) and a consequence of fulfilment of the scriptures (13:28 –29). There is no mention anywhere of the saving significance of the cross of Christ. However, in Paul's own letters we are told that the cross "is a judgment on all mankind and at the same time a reconciliation." (Romans 5:6–11; 2 Corinthians 5:14–21).

Eschatology

By the time Luke was writing Acts, the *'parousia'* or the end times were no longer expected to occur in the near future. This is reflected in the writing of Acts. For example, in Acts 1:6–8, Jesus tells the apostles it was not for them to speculate about this event and in Acts 17:30–31 Luke shows Paul giving a vague statement about the coming day of judgment: *"While God has overlooked the times of human ignorance, now he commands all people everywhere to repent, because he has fixed a day on which he will have the world judged in righteousness by a man whom he has appointed, and of this he has given assurance to all by raising him from the dead."*

However, in Paul's letters there is a clear expectation of the nearness of parousia. In 1 Corinthians 7:29, for example, Paul writes:

"What I mean, brothers, is that the time is short. From now on those who have wives should live as though they had none; those who mourn, as if they did not; those who are

happy, as though they are not; those who buy something, as if it is not theirs to keep; those who used the things of the world, as if not engrossed in time. For this world in its present form is passing away."

Paul the pastor/encourager

In Acts Paul can be regarded as a pastor in that he was deeply committed to the churches he founded, often staying on with the young Christians for a considerable length of time to provide support and presumably teaching. We do not, however, know much of the content of Paul's teaching from the book of Acts, and instead we are forced to rely heavily upon Paul's letters.

Constable[39] however, argues that "Paul's farewell address to the Ephesian elders is the nearest approximation to the Pauline letters in Acts.' Lewis[40] agrees, commenting that 'more than any other speech of Paul's in Luke's book it catches the true accents of its hero as he is revealed to us in the genuine letters." Witherington[41] points out that even the critics admit that the Paul whom Luke portrays sounds a great deal like Paul in his letters.

The reason why we see so much of the Paul of letters in this speech is because it is the only speech that Paul makes in Acts to fellow Christians. In his three missionary sermons (13:16–41; 14:15–17; 17:22–31) and five defences (Chs 22–26), Paul addressed non-Christian audiences. However, as this is the only Pauline speech delivered to Christians "it is not surprising to discover how rich it is in parallels to the Pauline letters."[42]

The general content of this speech recalls how in his letters Paul encouraged, warned, and exhorted his converts.[43] Stott[44] outlines the common themes between this speech and Paul's letters:

- the grace of God (24, 32),
- the kingdom of God (25),
- the purpose of God (27),
- the redeeming blood of Christ (28),
- repentance and faith (21),
- the church of God and its edification (28, 32). Note Marshal[45] comments that the church is here called the church of God, which is a phrase found exclusively in Paul's letters (eg 1 Cor.1:2)
- the inevitability of suffering (23–24),
- the danger of false teachers (29–30),
- the need for vigilance (28, 31),
- running the race (24)
- our final inheritance (32)

Fitzmyer[46] reminds us that "the echoes of Pauline teaching in the speech are not an indication, however, that Luke had read any of Paul's letters. He shows here that he was not wholly unfamiliar with Pauline phraseology." However, Fernando[47] argues that "the language of this speech is more like Paul's than Luke's." Keener[48] suggests that "because presumably Luke had little access to Paul's letters (they were not collected from the various churches until long after Paul's death), he must have learned Paul's style from direct contact with him."

Paul's speech to the Elders at Ephesus provides a strong point against those who allege that Acts cannot be historically reliable because of alleged differences between the Paul of Acts and of the letters.

Conclusion

Some critics seem unable to differentiate between the style and purpose of Acts versus the letters. Fernando[49] comments that "the purposes and occasions of Acts and the letters are different." Clearly Acts is different from the letters regarding the personality of Paul and the things he was up against. Freed[50] points out that "in Acts Paul is no longer faced with the same kinds of problems and dangers as in his letters." It must be remembered that "the aims which Luke had in mind and the circumstances in which he wrote were very different from the conditions which called forth the letters of Paul, who was not writing his autobiography but dealing with a specific situation in a particular church or locality."[51] Fernando[52] describes Paul in the letters "as a theologian responding to needs in the churches." In Acts, however, we see him as a missionary and a founder of Christian communities.

Another point, of course, is the fact that the author of Acts, who was probably writing after Paul's death, did not have the same sense of urgency regarding issues that were important to Paul, for example, regarding apostolic authority. Luke presents Paul as founding churches, looking after his converts there with care, and regarding himself as responsible for their spiritual welfare (Acts 20:17 –35).

Fernando[53] suggests that "for a complete picture of who Paul was, we must look at both his letters and the historical description of his life in Acts." Acts can be regarded as the source for Paul's life and the letters as the source for his teaching. In defence of Acts, it should be pointed out that it is an attempt to cover the history of the early church in such a short space. Things are bound to be left out. Just because they are not said does not mean they are not known. Polhill[54] makes a very valid point when he comments that we "would never guess Paul's emphasis on justification as found in Galatians from reading 1 Corinthians." Similarly, Luke should not be accused of being unreliable because he leaves something out that others think he should have included.

TASK

Critically discuss the portrayal of Paul in Acts and his letters.

A critical discussion may include the following, for example:

- Paul as a missionary
- Paul's views on circumcision
- Paul and the law
- Paul's theology
- Paul as a pastor

PAUL ON THE RESURRECTION

The resurrection is probably the most important doctrine within the Christian faith. In first reading Acts, "it is immediately clear that the early church was characteristically and specifically the Church of the Risen Christ."[55] Barclay[56] comments that it is true that in Paul's letters the emphasis shifts a little, and Paul focuses on the atoning nature of the death of Jesus. But at the end of the day it can be argued that for Paul the resurrection was central to the Christian faith.

Evidence from Acts

The earliest evidence for the resurrection goes back to the time immediately after the resurrection event is alleged to have taken place, and is contained in the early speeches in Acts.[57] Scholars have discovered that the language used regarding Jesus in these speeches is quite different from the letters of Paul, which were written long before the book of Acts. The central focus of the speeches in Acts is the death and resurrection of Jesus. A consistent pattern emerges in the speeches containing the following elements:

- Jesus has fulfilled the Old Testament prophecies
- Jesus died and was raised to life
- Jesus had been exalted to heaven
- Jesus had given Christians the gift of the Holy Spirit
- Jesus will return to earth in glory
- It is up to people to repent

Drane[58] argues that if we removed the resurrection from this pattern then most of it would no longer make sense: "The whole existence of the early church was based on the belief that Jesus was no longer dead, but was alive."

Hewitt[59] comments, however, that "the power of the revelation of the Risen Christ is nowhere seen better than in the experience of Paul on the Damascus Road." Paul regards his vision as no different to the resurrection appearances witnessed by the Twelve. Through it Paul can assert that he, too, is an apostle. The resurrection is of utmost importance to Paul and can be described as being "the foundation stone of his teaching."

 TASK

Paul's teaching on the resurrection in Acts forms part of the many speeches he made, many of which you will have studied in detail in this book.

Using your notes and a copy of Acts, complete the table below outlining the teaching of Paul concerning the resurrection as found in Acts:

Paul's teaching on the Resurrection in Acts[60]		
Pisidian Antioch	13:30ff	
Thessalonica	17:1–3	
Athens	17:31	
Before Jews in Jerusalem	22:1–21	
Sanhedrin in Jerusalem	23:1–9	
Before Felix	24:21	
Before Festus	25:19	
Before Agrippa	26:23	
Rome	28:23	

Evidence from 1 Corinthians 15

When Paul had visited Corinth he had preached "Jesus and him crucified". Some believers may have felt that he stressed the meaning of the cross more than the resurrection. However, as we shall see in this chapter, Paul is adamant that the two events, the crucifixion and the resurrection, are inseparable.

The reason why Paul includes this section of teaching on the resurrection in his first letter to the Corinthians is explained in 15:12. Paul has heard that there are people in Corinth who deny the resurrection, "not the resurrection of Jesus Christ in particular, but the whole idea of resurrection."[61] As the idea of resurrection is central to the

Christian faith it is not surprising that he spends 58 verses explaining his views in detail to the church at Corinth.

The Resurrection of Christ (Ch 15:1–11)

Paul goes over the basic facts of the gospel that he had taught the Corinthians from the beginning. He reminds them that the gospel had been passed on to them by word of mouth. By this gospel they had been saved; however, Paul is worried about the fragile state of the Corinthians' faith. Therefore he repeats the gospel facts to them:

- Christ died for our sins. Prior comments that "there is no true proclamation of the gospel which does not explain, in New Testament terms, the link between human sin and the death of Christ".
- The death and resurrection of Christ were 'in accordance with the Scriptures.'
- Christ appeared to James and all the apostles; but last of all he appeared to Paul himself. Prior[61a] believes that this is the most significant phrase in this account. Paul is implying that his encounter with the risen Christ is of equal validity and identical to that of the apostles. It is interesting that after Christ had appeared to Paul there were no more appearances.

Paul stresses that while he counts himself as an apostle, it is only through God's grace that he has become the man that he is.

The centrality of the resurrection of Jesus (Ch 15:12–19)

Paul asserts that if the lives and faith of the Corinthians revolve around the gospel that he preached to them, then nobody could reject the belief in the resurrection of the dead. If there is no such thing as the resurrection, then that means that Jesus did not triumph over death; it means, in effect, that Jesus is still dead (v 13). Paul's whole ministry had been based on belief in the resurrection. If there was no such thing then Paul's preaching had been a waste of time (v 14). More importantly, because the Corinthians' faith was based on Paul's preaching, it would mean that their faith was useless. As Prior[62] says, "Take out the resurrection of Jesus and there is nothing left on which to rest faith."

Paul develops his argument by explaining that God's reputation is destroyed if there is no resurrection (v 15). Prior[63] argues that "the only convincing reason for linking God to the person and work of Jesus is the fact of the resurrection. Only God has the power over death: if Jesus rose from the dead, God raised him." The seriousness for the Corinthians themselves is that this means they are still in their sins (v 17). Death is therefore the end and everyone will perish. Thrall[64] explains that this also means "that the members of the church who have died already are utterly lost." Paul concludes this section by proclaiming that if there is no life after death then Christians should be pitied because "anyone is better off than the Christian."[65]

The Consequences of the Resurrection of the Dead (Ch 15:20–34)

Its consequences for the future (Ch 15:20–28)

From v 20 onwards, Paul explains why the resurrection of Christ involves the resurrection of believers. He asserts that Christ has been raised from the dead and "he is the firstfruits of an immense harvest, consisting of all those who are in Christ (v 22) and who belong to Christ (v 23)."[66] Paul contrasts Adam with Jesus. According to Genesis 3, Adam disobeyed God and so God sentenced him to death. Foreman[67] explains that as descendents of the first Adam, mankind is destined for death because the death sentence was also applicable to Adam's descendants, i.e., the whole human race. "Christ resembles Adam because what happened to him potentially affects the whole human race ... in Christ all will be brought to life as a result of his resurrection."[68] As descendants of the 'last Adam' (Christ) Christians are creatures destined for life. Therefore this means that all those who are now in Christ, ie Christians, will also be raised from the dead.

Paul goes on to talk about the 'Parousia', the end times (v 24–28). Christ is reigning and gradually bringing his enemies under his control. His second coming will mark the final destruction of everything raged against God. At that time, everything will be under God's control. Davies[69] reminds us that Paul believed the Second Coming of Christ would take place in his own lifetime; "so he is describing the general resurrection in terms of the Second Coming in the near future."

Its consequences for the present (Ch 15:29–34)

The practice of being baptised on behalf of the dead was common in Corinth. People whose relatives had died before the time of Christ or who had died without believing in Christ, were anxious about them and sometimes were baptised on their behalf. The idea was that the benefits of baptism would be transferred to the dead.[70] Paul is not necessarily giving his approval to this practice but he uses it to illustrate a point. If there is no such thing as the resurrection, then Paul questions the point of this practice at all (v 29).

Paul refers to his own suffering for the sake of the gospel (v 30–32). He had faced many kinds of dangers but had persevered in the knowledge that his suffering was worthwhile. If there is no resurrection then Paul questions why he would subject himself to such a dangerous lifestyle. He argues that if this life is all there is, then eating and drinking and having a good time is about the most that people can do with it.

Paul's final comments on the consequences of denying the resurrection are of a practical nature. He warns the Corinthians that if they give up their faith in the resurrection then they will be vulnerable to being led astray. Some Christians had fallen back into paganism (v 34) and needed to hear Paul's strong rebuke.

The Resurrection Body (Ch 15:35–49)

The idea of resurrection had been scorned in Corinth by those who questioned what sort of a body people would have when they rose (v 35). Paul's outrage at these people is evident (v 36). He sees such people as fools and gives them an example from the harvest to try to explain to them the nature of the resurrection (v 36–39).

Paul tries to answer their question using an illustration from nature. The Corinthians sow a seed (v 36) and it grows into a plant. The seed sown in the ground corresponds to their human life, and the plant that grows corresponds to their resurrection existence.[71] Growth only follows if the grain first dies. Nobody can tell from looking at a seed what the plant will look like. So it is with the resurrection body. Paul uses this illustration to describe how the body that is raised in resurrection is so much more glorious than the body that was buried (v 37). Paul explains that God is in control of the whole process (v 38). All flesh is not the same (v 39–40). The flesh of men, animals, birds and fish are all different, which expresses the variety there is in the world that God has created. The implication is that there is therefore not only one kind of human body. The resurrection body (spiritual body) is as different from the living human body (natural body) as the plant that grows from the seed (v 42–44).

Paul concludes this section by referring to the contrast between Jesus and Adam. All people share the characteristics of Adam. Jesus, the last Adam, became a life-giving spirit and revealed his true origin when he was raised from the dead. Everyone who belongs to Jesus bears his image, both in the sense of being made like him and in the sense of sharing in his resurrection body.

The Victory Over Death (Ch 15:50–58)

Paul explains to the Corinthians that earthly bodies cannot inherit the spiritual and immortal but must be changed (v 50–51). This change, however, will be very quick, "in the twinkling of an eye" (v 52). The use of "trumpet" is a link to the Old Testament, where trumpets were used at times of triumph. Paul describes how the sounding of the trumpet will be a signal for the dead to rise.

Verses 54–55 are a fulfilment of prophecies by Isaiah and Hosea (Is.25:8; Hosea 13:14).

Death, sin and the law have all been destroyed by the resurrection of Jesus (v 56–57). Paul pleads with the Corinthians to be firm in their faith to ensure their effort is not in vain. If the resurrection is denied then their faith is empty; but if the resurrection is certain, then there is hope and purpose to the Christian life.

OTHER ASPECTS OF HUMAN EXPERIENCE

David Jenkin's view on the resurrection

The cross and the resurrection stand as the key events at the heart of the Christian faith. However, David Jenkins, the former bishop of Durham (England) prompted an outcry in the Church of England in the 1980s over his suggestion that the resurrection was 'real', but not an historical fact. Christ's resurrection was real, in the sense that the disciples experienced the 'livingness' of Jesus. Nevertheless, says the bishop, the resurrection of Jesus was not a bodily resurrection.

- Research what you can about the views of Jenkins and explain how you think Paul would answer him.
- Find out if any other Christians have denied the doctrine of the resurrection.

 TASKS

1. Critically discuss Paul's teaching on the resurrection

    A critical discussion may include the following, for example:
    - Examples of Paul's teaching from his speeches in Acts
    - Context of 1 Corinthians 15; reasons for the writing of this chapter
    - A reminder of Paul's message about Jesus' resurrection
    - The centrality of Jesus' resurrection
    - Consequences for the future and the present
    - The resurrection body

2. Comment on the claim that Paul's teaching on the resurrection is of no real value to Christians today

    A discussion of the claim may include, for example:
    - Paul's speeches are evangelistic and are not used for teaching Christians
    - Christians should be aware of and be able to defend their beliefs
    - Some Christians deny that there was a bodily resurrection; Paul's teaching in 1 Cor 15 would be very relevant in a discussion with such a person
    - Christians may be more concerned with modern issues, eg moral and political issues

Endnotes

1 Bruce, FF, Paul in Acts and Letters, in *Dictionary of Paul and his Letters*, ed. by Hawthorne, GF, Martin, RP, and Reid, DG, Leicester: IVP, 1993, p679

2 Fernando, *op cit*, p27

3 Bruce, *op cit*, 679

4 Packer, *op cit*, p13

5 Fernando, *op cit*, p27

6 Hanson, *op cit*, p24

7 Bruce, *op cit*, p680

8 Stein, RH, Jerusalem, in *Dictionary of Paul and his Letters*, ed. by Hawthorne, GF, Martin, RP, and Reid, DG, Leicester: IVP, 1993, p465

9 Bruce, *op cit*, p681

10 *ibid*, p681

11 Bruce, *op cit*, p681

12 Haenchen, *op cit*, p114

13 Vilhauer, Philipp, *On the Paulinism of Acts*, in Studies in Luke – Acts, ed. by Keck, LE, and Martyn, JL, Philadelphia: Fortress Press, 1980, p40

14 Guy also comments that "in his speeches in his defence in Acts 22–24 he appears to be much more of an orthodox Jew. He claimed that his message about Jesus and the resurrection was but the logical development of Judaism; he declared that he was not unorthodox in his beliefs but still a Pharisee." pp15–16

15 Guy, p15–16

16 Bornkamm, G, *Paul*, London: E.T., 1971, p xviii

17 Hanson, *op cit*, pp24–25

18 Fernando, *op cit*, p27

19 Fernando, *op cit*, p432

20 Haenchen, E, *The Acts of the Apostles*, Oxford: Basil Blackwell, 1971, p478n

21 Munck, J, *The Acts of the Apostles*, New York: Doubleday, 1967, p155

22 Fernando, *op cit*, p432

23 *ibid*, p27

24 Witherington, B, *The Acts of the Apostles: A Socio-Rhetorical Commentary*: Grand Rapids: Eerdmans, 1998, p474

25 Bruce, *op cit*, p681

26 Fernando, *op cit*, p27

27 Hanson, *op cit*, p24

28 Guy, *op cit*, p16

29 Haenchen, *op cit*, pp332–336

30 Crowe, *op cit*, p136

31 Vilhauer, *op cit*, pp34–37

32 It should be noted generally, though, that Luke's Paul also violates conventions of the Jewish law regularly (staying in the houses of Gentiles quite often), so that the gap is not as wide as critics suggest.

33 Mason, S, *Josephus and the New Testament*, Peabody: Hendrickson Publishers, 2003, pp195–196

Vilhauer, *op cit*, p41–42

34 Fernando, *op cit*, p27

35 Robertson, AT, *Word Pictures in the New Testament*, 6 Vols, Nashville: Broadman Press, 1931, 3:187

36 Fitzmyer, *op cit*, p508

37 Fernando, *op cit*, pp27–28

38 Stott, *op cit*, pp225–26

39 Longenecker, *op cit*, pp511–512

40 Lewis, *op cit*, p24

41 Witherington, *op cit*, p610

42 Bruce, *op cit*, p387

43 Constable, TL, Noted on Acts, www.soniclight.com, 2007, pp264–265

44 Stott, *op cit*, p324

45 Marshall, *op cit*, p334

46 Fitzmyer, *op cit*, p675

47 Fernando, *op cit*, p532

48 Keener, CS, *The IVP Bible Background Commentary: Exposition of Acts of the Apotles*, Grand rapids: Baker, 1990, p383

49 Fernando, *op cit*, p27

50 Freed, p24

51 Guy, *op cit*, p16

52 Fernando, *op cit*, p27

53 *ibid*, p28

54 Pohill, JB, *Acts, The New American Commentary*, Vol. 26, Nashville: Broadman, 1992, p26

55 Barclay, *op cit*, p109

56 *ibid*, p109

57 Drane, *op cit*, p99

58 *ibid*, p99

59 Hewitt, *op cit*, p225

60 Hewitt, *op cit*, pp225–227

61 Davies, *op cit*, p85

61a Prior, *op cit*, p261

62 Prior, *op cit*, p263

63 *ibid*, p264

64 Thrall, *op cit*, p107

65 Morris, *op cit*, p212

66 Prior, *op cit*, p266

67 Foreman, *op cit*, p107

68 Thrall, *op cit*, p108

69 Davies, *op cit*, p87

70 Foreman, *op cit*, p108

71 Thrall, *op cit*, p112

Glossary

Abrupt ending of Acts – the fact that the book of Acts appears to end in the middle of the story

Anti-Marcionite prologue – a preface to the third Gospel

Antonia – a military barracks built by Herod the Great in Jerusalem

Apology – a justification or defence of beliefs

Areopagus – the word 'Areopagus' simply comes from the hill on which this council would often meet

Aramaic – language of the Old Testament

Ascension – the return of Jesus to heaven after his resurrection

Baptism – the sacramental act of cleansing in water that admits a person as a full member of the Church

Blasphemy – irreverence towards God; false claims to be God

Colony – a territory under the political control of a state

Controversy – a dispute or argument

Conversion – in Acts it refers to becoming a believer in Christ

Court of the Gentiles – the outer court of the Temple in Jerusalem

Court of women – beyond the Court of the Gentiles; women were not allowed any further into the Temple

Day of Atonement – the most solemn and important of Jewish holidays, which centres on repentance, fasting and prayer

Deacon – derived from the Greek word *diakonos*, which is translated as servant. Deacons helped with the charitable work of the early church

Dead Sea scrolls – around 1000 documents, including texts from the Hebrew Bible, discovered between 1947 and 1979 in eleven caves in and around the Wadi Qumran in the West Bank

Elder – a person who holds an office of responsibility in the church

Eunuch – a castrated man

Evangelism – the Christian practice of trying to make converts

External evidence – evidence found outside the New Testament, usually in connection with the date or authorship of Acts

Exorcism – the practice of casting out demons or evil spirits

The Fall of Jerusalem – a decisive event in the First Jewish-Roman War. The city and its Temple were completely destroyed

Forerunner – someone who lays the groundwork for another

Gentile – someone who is not a Jew

Glossolalia – commonly called 'speaking in tongues'; unintelligible utterances

God-fearer – someone who respected the Jewish religion, worshipped the same God and held high morals. They were still regarded as pagans by the Jews in Palestine. However, there seems to have been a more liberal attitude held by Dispersion Jews

Hebrews – Jews. It describes someone who is totally Jewish in all aspects of life; someone who observed the Law of Moses and lived according to Jewish traditions

Hellenists – Jews who came out of the Dispersion. They were much more accepting of Greek ideas

Heretic – a person who expresses an opinion considered to be heresy

Historical reliability – the notion of how trustworthy a source can be

Idol – false god

Idolatry – worshipping false gods

Internal evidence – evidence found inside the New Testament, usually in connection with the date or authorship of Acts

Jew – a member of Judaism

Justification by faith – the idea that faith alone is needed to be justified before God

kergyma – early Christian preaching

Laying on of hands – a symbolic and formal method of invoking the Holy Spirit

Law of Moses – law given by God to Moses in the Old Testament

Liberation theology – the theology of using sociology and economics to understand poverty, focuses on Jesus as the liberator of the oppressed

Lourdes – a place of pilgrimage in France, renowned as a place of healing

Mass – worship service in the Catholic Church

Messiah – the redeemer

Miracle – an act of wonder which cannot be explained logically, eg a healing

Montanism – a Christian movement of the mid second century, named after its founder

Montanus – focused on the Holy Spirit, prophecy and spiritual gifts. Was favourable towards women in leadership

Muratorian fragment/canon – a compilation of New Testament collated around AD170

Nazarite vow – a vow described in Numbers 6:1–21

The sect of the Nazarenes – the term given to the early Christians

Neronian persecution – the period of persecution carried out by the Roman Emperor Nero

Oral traditions – laws and traditions passed on by word of mouth

Paradox – an apparently true statement that leads to a contradiction

Penance – repentance of sins/sacrament of reconciliation

Pharisees – comes from the Hebrew word meaning 'separated'; refers to a Jewish religious party at the time of Jesus

Predestination – the belief that before creation God determined the fate of mankind

Primitive church – the very first church

Proconsul – governor of a Roman province

Prologue – an introduction to a piece of work

Prophecy – a religious prediction

Proselyte – a Gentile who had fully accepted the Jewish religion by being circumcised

Purpose – the reason suggested for the writing of a book

Relic – an object or a personal item of religious significance, carefully preserved with an air of veneration

Religio licita – a lawful religion

Repentance – expressing sorrow for sin

Romans – the people who occupied Palestine at the time of Jesus

Sadducees – members of a Jewish sect at the time of Christ

Sanhedrin – the Jewish Council

Schismatic – a person who splits away from the faith

Second Coming – the belief that Jesus will return again to the earth

To shake off dust – a custom for Jews to shake off the dust of a pagan town from their feet when they returned to their own land, as a symbol of cleansing themselves from the impurity of sinners who did not worship God

Simony – the crime of paying for offices or positions in the hierarchy of the church, named after Simon Magus

The Seven – the deacons chosen in the early church

Sorcery – magic or witchcraft

Synagogue – a Jewish place of worship, which played a major role in Jewish life serving as a meeting place, schoolhouse, library and court. It was a centre of religious education and learning and the place where all Jews came to worship.

Tabernacle – a moveable place of worship carried by the Israelites in the desert

Team ministry – a group of Christians working together to spread the gospel

Two volume work – the term given to the work of Luke-Acts

Universalism – the idea that Christianity is open to everyone, Jews and Gentiles

Vision – a spiritual experience or message believed to have come from God

'We' passages – passages in Acts that are written in the first person, like a diary

Index